DECODINGAIRTRAVEL

A GUIDE TO SAVING ON AIRFARE AND FLYING IN LUXURY

NICHOLAS KRALEV

ISBN: 146101543X
ISBN-13: 9781461015437

Editors: Darrell Delamaide and Markus Nottelmann
Consultant: Gary Leff
Cover design by Reposition Inc.
Interior design by CreateSpace
Back cover photo by Mary F. Calvert

First edition: June 2011

To my parents, Yana and Simeon

Contents

Foreword

How to Be a Happy Traveler

Air travel can be inexpensive, seamless, comfortable, enjoyable and even luxurious – all at the same time.

I realize there is a good chance you think I'm crazy. You are probably more inclined to describe your travel experience as expensive, frustrating and miserable. I can't argue with that – it's today's reality for most people. But it doesn't have to be so, and this book's goal is to help you change that reality and improve your travel life.

No more overpaying for airline tickets, being stuck in a bad seat or having a trip ruined by others. Whether you like to travel or have to travel, the knowledge and insights you will gain from these pages will give you the power to control your journey – from the moment you get the idea for a trip until you return home. You will no longer be taken for a ride or mistreated by airline employees, because you will know how the complex air travel system works. More importantly, you will be able to work that system to your advantage.

How?, you might ask, and you would probably like a better answer than "Read the book." I'm happy to provide a preview.

Let's begin with saving money, which is the objective of Part I. The key to securing the lowest possible ticket price is building your own fare – making your own "sausage," so to speak – and not relying on automated booking engines. To do that, you need to access raw real-time airline data, such as published airline tariffs and flight inventory, and carefully match those components to produce the best fare. I have called that process the Kralev Method. There are lots of codes, and the process resembles a science, but it's worth learning if you don't like to be overcharged. You will appreciate it when you learn about the tricks airlines use to artificially inflate prices.

The next step in improving your travel life is creating a seamless journey, and that is the broad topic of Part II. Its goal is to help you best prepare for a trip by resolving any potential problems in advance, and to avoid the hassle and frustration of the airport experience. You will learn how to predict flight delays and cancellations hours before departure, and how to get rebooked on a different flight most efficiently, without waiting in long lines. I will also take you inside some of the most luxurious aircraft cabins and airport lounges, and share my dining, entertainment and sleeping routines during long flights. In addition, we will discuss customer-relations issues and receiving compensation from airlines when things go wrong.

Finally, Part III aims to help you enjoy the comfort and luxury of First and Business Class at coach prices by mastering the frequent-flier game, which has become almost as complex as the entire air travel system. You will learn how to choose the best frequent-flier program for you, how to achieve and maintain elite airline status, how to design the most effective upgrade strategies, how to maximize the miles you earn, and how to book the best airline award tickets. I will also offer a comparative analysis of the three global airline alliances – the Star Alliance, Oneworld and SkyTeam.

To illustrate how it all comes together, here are my 10 steps to a happy travel life:

1. Learn the basics of the air travel science – fare codes, tariffs, flight inventory, fare rules and permitted routing.

2. Build your own ticket price by matching published fares and flight inventory, as suggested by the Kralev Method.
3. If you don't like what an airline agent tells you on the phone, hang up and call again – three agents are likely to give you three different answers to the same question.
4. Beware of "code-share" flights, which are marketed and sold by one airline but operated by another, and distinguish "direct" flights from nonstops – many "direct" flights are actually regular connecting flights, with nothing in common but their number.
5. For the lowest U.S. domestic fares, book tickets on Tuesday, Wednesday or Thursday, and fly on Tuesday, Wednesday or Saturday when possible.
6. Get a seat assignment as soon as you make a reservation, and check the seat map periodically for a better seat.
7. Watch out for advance airline schedule changes to your itinerary, don't accept changes you don't like, and take the initiative in finding a better flight.
8. Complete as many tasks as possible, including check-in, online before leaving for the airport.
9. Stay loyal to a global alliance, which could have more than two dozen member-carriers, and secure top-tier elite status in at least one program before spreading yourself over several programs.
10. To minimize spending and maximize earned mileage, buy domestic tickets, which have very low taxes, and use miles for international tickets.

As you read this book, you will notice that some airlines and alliances are mentioned more often than others. I tried to include diverse examples involving a variety of U.S. and foreign carriers – still, the content is naturally influenced by my own experiences, and real-life cases and situations are much more valuable than abstract concepts when making a point.

Although I tried to cover all major parts of today's air travel system that affect consumers, my intention was not to mention every single piece of it or everything that could happen to you during a trip. After all, this is not meant to be an encyclopedia, but a practical and useful – and hopefully entertaining – read.

You may wonder how I learned all these things and what makes me an expert on air travel. I've never worked for an airline, and everything I know I've learned from experience, though I owe some credit to FlyerTalk.com, the largest online travel community. That's why this book is written from a customer perspective, and each sentence is meant to save you money or improve your travel life – even those with codes in them. I've flown almost 2 million miles and visited more than 80 countries, mostly in my previous positions as a correspondent for the Financial Times and The Washington Times.

When I started at the Washington Times in 2001, I had a very small travel budget, which had allowed my predecessor to make only three or four foreign trips a year. I was supposed to cover diplomacy and international affairs, and I didn't think that sitting in Washington almost the entire time was a good idea. I couldn't get more money, and my only option was to stretch the budget I had. So I decided to learn everything I could about airfares – and the air travel system in general – and within a year, I doubled the number of trips I took on that same budget.

But then I had another problem: I didn't want to sit in coach. Flying to three continents in a week was no fun in the back of the plane. Obviously, I couldn't afford expensive premium tickets, so I had to figure out how to sit in Business or First Class while paying for Economy. The solution was in mastering the frequent-flier game. I quickly achieved top-tier elite status and began learning all I could about airline alliances, miles, upgrades, award tickets and other benefits.

I have maintained that status for 10 years, and I haven't sat in coach on a domestic or intercontinental flight since 2002 – unless Economy was the only cabin on the plane, of course. I have flown in First and Business Class on the world's best airlines.

I have had gourmet meals and champagne I could hardly afford on the ground. I have been whisked to my planes on the tarmac in a Mercedes or Porsche.

I'm not talking about flying with the U.S. secretary of state, which I did for a decade. In fact, I traveled with four of them – Hillary Clinton, Condoleezza Rice, Colin Powell and Madeleine Albright. There is no question that jumping in a motorcade as soon as you land in a foreign country and not having to deal with customs and passport control is great, as is actually getting to know the secretary of state.

But commercial flying has advantages I wasn't ready to give up – it's cheaper, more comfortable and luxurious (in Business and First Class), offers much better food and entertainment, and gets you lots of miles. So at times I'd go on the secretary's plane, but at the end of the trip I'd return home on a commercial flight.

As many of you have no doubt discovered, visiting other countries and learning about their cultures, traditions and people is a life-changing experience. It broadens our horizons and helps us appreciate what we have. For years, it has pained me to hear people say that they hate traveling, because it's too expensive and too much of a hassle.

In an attempt to encourage both Americans and citizens of other countries to see other parts of the world, I've tried to explain that flying can be affordable, comfortable and fun. Those words are always followed by disbelief and one very short question: How?

This book aspires to answer that question. I truly hope it succeeds in making your life on the fly better, and in changing the widespread negative perceptions about air travel. If it leaves you hungry for more knowledge, you are welcome to take advantage of the training, consulting and other education opportunities offered by my new company, Kralev International LLC. You can get a discount equal to the full amount you paid for this book. Feel free to get in touch through KralevInternational.com or NicholasKralev.com.

Things in the airline industry can change very rapidly, so check out DecodingAirTravel.com for any updates to the information provided in the book, as well as video tutorials, pocket guides, mobile apps and other related materials.

Happy reading!

PART I

BUILDING YOUR OWN AIRFARE

Chapter 1

The Science of Air Travel

Buying a plane ticket has become an almost blind purchase for many travelers, who don't know what exactly they are getting for their hundreds or thousands of dollars. Our ability to quickly snag a ticket from one of the many travel- booking websites has given us the false sense that air travel today is a piece of cake.

But how many of us really know what a ticket entitles us to and how much extra we need to pay for various other services? Do we fully understand if and when we can return or change that ticket? Do we know which airline actually operates our flight? Are we often surprised to discover that the fare we bought doesn't earn frequent-flier miles or is ineligible for an upgrade – after the ticket has been issued? Do we understand what a "code-share" flight means, and how booking such a flight could affect the money we pay and the hassle we experience during travel? Do we know the difference between a "nonstop" and a "direct" flight?

For the majority of travelers around the world, the answers to most of these questions would be negative. Who is to blame for that?

Clearly, the airlines share a big part of the responsibility. They have made the system so complex in recent years – in an effort to make more money – that customers are utterly confused and frustrated. So much so that, for many, travel has become a burden. We can't blame the airlines for trying to maximize revenue, but should they try to educate travelers, and if so, how? More importantly, do they want travelers to be educated?

The question about customer responsibility usually stirs more controversy, with many travelers assigning the blame for the current reality entirely to the airlines. I believe that, if we want to pay less for plane tickets, avoid hassle and increase comfort, we should educate ourselves.

Whatever one thinks about customer responsibility, the air travel system is what it is, and there is little we can do to change it. Short of that, it just makes sense to learn as much as we can about that system – its intricacies, advantages, shortcomings and loopholes – and use it to our benefit.

We all want our travel experiences to be smooth, pleasant and even exciting – and knowledge is the best key I've found to achieving that goal.

What's in an airline ticket?

The most important part of an airline reservation is the ticket number. If you don't have a ticket number – a 13-digit number attached to the receipt – you won't be flying, because the airline system cannot issue a boarding pass. Showing up at the airport with a printout of an itinerary that was never ticketed won't do the trick. It's always wise to carry a copy of the receipt during a trip.

Unfortunately, many airlines make it really hard for customers to find the ticket number, especially if you book online. Make sure to call them and ask for a proper receipt with the ticket number. That could be crucial if your itinerary includes flights on other airlines. Unless they receive a ticket number from the issuing carrier, which is an automated process, they will cancel your seat.

As you probably know, a ticket entitles a passenger to transportation from one city to another on a certain date and in a certain class of service. On most airlines, it also covers one or two carry-on items, and on most international flights it includes at least one free checked bag.

What's not included? Services that once came with a ticket purchase, such as checked luggage, food and drinks, pillows and blankets, are no longer free. In the United States, non-alcoholic beverages are the only complimentary thing coach passengers get, and that's not an industry standard. Many carriers in various countries charge for water and soft drinks, including Ireland's Ryanair and Scandinavian Airlines. Ryanair has also imposed a check-in fee, which of course cannot be avoided.

On intercontinental flights, most airlines offer free meals and at least one checked bag, but on shorter flights you are likely to be charged baggage fees. It may also cost more to select a seat assignment in advance. You may not have access to every available seat on the plane – certain seats may require extra fees. We will discuss airline fees in more detail in Chapter 8 and will learn how to avoid them in Chapter 12.

There is also a chance that you may not arrive at your destination at the time specified in your originally ticketed itinerary because of advance schedule changes or last-minute flight disruptions. Plus, most airlines oversell their flights, so you may be denied boarding, in which case you are entitled to compensation. We will discuss that topic in Chapter 9. Finally, there is no guarantee your luggage will make it to your final destination at the same time you do – if it does at all.

This book's goal is not to scare you, but to depict a realistic picture of today's airline industry and help you overcome the barriers that airlines have erected so your travel can be smooth and hassle-free. You don't have to worry about many of the fees described above if you have top elite airline status, and it is one of the book's goals to help you achieve and maintain such status, and to reap its benefits.

Why bother with airline codes?

If you've already peeked at the next several pages, you probably wonder why you should go through the trouble of learning and understanding all those codes we are about to begin deciphering.

As I said in the foreword, I chose to learn all that theory several years ago because I needed to save money, and mastering what is essentially a science was the best guarantee of achieving that result. I just didn't trust the airlines' computer systems – or any other booking sources – to give me the absolute lowest available fares every time. Now that I know much of that science, I trust them even less. I'm sure you will feel the same way when you see some of the examples of how I've managed to beat the airline systems and save as much as thousands of dollars on a ticket.

I'm the first to recognize that there are occasions when going straight to a popular booking source – an airline website or a third-party online travel agency like Expedia – works just fine. If you need to fly nonstop from Boston to Chicago on a specific date, there isn't much space for creativity. That changes, however, as soon as you add connections or try to book a more complex trip – that's when having access to raw data, before it's processed by a booking engine, and knowing how to use those codes can make a big difference.

As with any machines, computers don't always give us what we want – in this case, our ideal itineraries – so human intervention becomes necessary. Using the codes and matching published fares with available flight inventory can save you significant amounts of money.

Accessing raw airline data, understanding and analyzing codes, and matching published fares with available flight inventory is the essence of what I call the Kralev Method. I'll explain it in detail in Chapter 5, but let me just say that it's designed to save you lots of money. It can give you the power to control the booking process from the very beginning, rather than rely on someone else's computer system. Think of automated airline booking as processed food – the raw kind is much healthier.

Let's get started.

How is the fare "sausage" made?

What determines the price of a plane ticket? A combination of airline data published and updated by each carrier through the Airline Tariff Publishing Company (ATPCO) or its only and much smaller competitor, SITA, which publishes some fares in Europe, Africa and Asia. ATPCO is owned by 16 of the world's largest carriers and the Federal Express Corp. The airline data has two main components: fares and availability, or tariffs and inventory, in airline lingo. I refer to them as *pillars* because of their supreme importance to the Kralev Method.

Both pillars are built on a foundation of fare codes, for which the airlines use letters of the alphabet. Each carrier uses different codes, though most of them follow some similar rules – for example, full fare is usually signified by F in First Class, C or J in Business, and Y in coach. Service classes are not the same as booking classes. First, Business and Economy are service classes, and they correspond to the cabins on a plane, while there are many more booking classes than just three.

Let's look at the booking-class codes used by the three largest U.S. network carriers. The codes are shown in Figure 1 in a descending order, beginning with the highest, or most expensive. These are only revenue booking classes, meaning that they are sold for money. There are separate booking codes used for upgrades and award tickets, and they will be among the subjects in Chapters 13 and 14.

As you can see, some codes mean different things on different airlines. Both United and American use S for coach, but on Delta S books in Business Class. The Delta column in the table may be a bit confusing, since Delta doesn't operate three-cabin aircraft.

Class of service	United Airlines (Star Alliance)	American Airlines (Oneworld)	Delta Airlines (SkyTeam)
First	F A	F A P	F A P
Business	J C D Z	J D R I	J C D S I
Economy	Y B M E U H Q V W S T L K G	Y B H K M L W G V S N Q O	Y B M H Q K L U T

Figure 1: Booking classes used by the world's three largest airlines. The global alliances to which they belong appear in brackets.

As frequent fliers in the United States know, most U.S. carriers call the only premium cabin on domestic flights First Class, while on international flight it's labeled as Business Class. The only two U.S. airlines with international First Class – or three cabins – are American and United.

The order in which the different codes appear may not be the same on all flights operated by a given carrier. For example, the Economy lineup for American in the table above applies only to U.S. domestic flights. On international flights, K class precedes H, and W class doesn't exist at all. On the other hand, R is published as a revenue booking class only on international flights, but it's used to indicate upgrades on domestic flights. Delta uses C class only on code-share international flights, which are marketed as its own but are operated by other airlines. We will discuss code-share flights in Chapter 6.

The booking classes in Figure 1 begin with full-fare codes, which are followed by discounted fares. On United, for instance, V class is higher than W but lower than Q. I often meet passengers who claim to be on a full-fare ticket, judging by the high price they paid, but when I look at it, I see H or Q booking class. The only truly full-fare coach code is Y, though some airlines also include B – and even M at times – in the same category, meaning they are fully refundable and changeable for free. A few international B fares do incur penalties, and a few M fares don't, but those are exceptions. All other fares carry penalties for changes and cancellations.

A ticket's actual monetary value plays no role in determining whether it's a full fare – it's all about the booking class. An H class ticket may be only $100 lower than B class and $500 higher than W class, but it's still considered discounted. Not all booking classes are created equal, of course. Depending on the airline, certain codes may not be eligible for upgrades, and different codes may earn different mileage in your frequent-flier account. Also, if you are on a waiting list for a flight or an upgrade, the higher your booking class is, the better your chances for clearing the list. Most importantly, as I said earlier, knowing how to work with those codes can save you a lot of money.

A word about G booking class on United: Until January 2011, that was a so-called travel industry discount fare, and it wasn't considered a published fare. It was ineligible for mileage accrual or upgrades. Now all that has changed, and G is a regular published fare – in effect, it's the new K, or the lowest in the 14-code coach lineup.

When we look at flight inventory later, the codes will already be arranged in the same descending order as in Figure 1. You don't really need to remember them all, though by the time you finish this book, you probably will have memorized a few.

In addition to this chapter, the first pillar of airline data – the fare tariff – will be the subject of Chapters 2 and 3. I've given U.S. domestic fares and international fares their own chapters because of the significant differences between them. Chapter 4 is dedicated to the second pillar, flight inventory.

Accessing raw airline data

Before we move to airline tariffs, let's talk about how to gain access to raw airline data. Most travelers have no idea how to do that – through no fault of their own. Until recently, that privilege was restricted to airline employees and travel agents with a subscription to a Global Distribution System (GDS), such as Travelport, Amadeus and Sabre. For the most part, each GDS gets its airline data from ATPCO or SITA.

The transparency brought about by the Internet has changed that. Since 2004, websites like ExpertFlyer.com and applications like the KVS Availability Tool (KVStool.com) have provided consumers with direct access to airline data. However, very few travelers use them, mainly because they don't understand the data. Almost no airline sites display availability in each booking class, though some do show the codes once an itinerary is built.

Naturally, the data transparency has caused controversy, with some airlines less happy about it than others. One of the thorny issues is how those independent sites get the data they display. While ExpertFlyer says it pays for it, the KVS tool doesn't. In private conversations, some airline officials have complained to me that KVS does screen-scraping – collecting data from their websites and other sources for free, which some call stealing.

Not surprisingly, the KVS tool's founder, who asked that I use only his first name, Victor, disagrees with the airlines. He denies he engages in screen-scraping, though he admits that his data-gathering method "may have some attributes of screen-scraping," just like other sites do. He described the tool as a "web browser application," which works similarly to any Internet browser – by providing a channel for a "conversation" to take place directly between a user and an airline website.

Gary Leff, who writes a travel blog called "View From the Wing," said the KVS tool "gives you a convenient, quick and easy way to access free data. It's hard for me to see how you can steal something that's already free." Leff said he uses both ExpertFlyer and the KVS tool. "ExpertFlyer will automate some searches for you and e-mail you when availability changes, which is hugely useful," while the KVS tool "has greater coverage" of award availability in the three global airline alliances, he said.

Critics of the KVS tool question its reliability, because it has lost some of its data sources and may lose others, as they find ways to protect themselves. But the tool's founder said that "losing and gaining sources is a natural part of the process," and he is not worried about his product's future.

Both ExpertFlyer and the KVS tool use a variety of sources, but there is a difference in how they approach each search request. The KVS tool leaves it to the customer to choose the data source. Knowing which source is best in each case can be rather daunting for most people, though for advanced users having a choice can be very helpful. ExpertFlyer, on the other hand, makes the choice for you. "Our benefit is that we pick the right source, based on the request, to get the best data," the company's president, Chris Lopinto, told me. For unlimited searches, ExpertFlyer charges $99 a year, while a KVS membership costs $75 a year.

ITAsoftware.com is a free and very useful site, which made news in 2010, when Google made a bid to buy it. It doesn't show booking codes and fare bases until after an itinerary is built, but there is a way to search by booking class. It also provides a detailed breakdown of both base fares and taxes. For advanced users, it offers various options to design their own itineraries, such as specifying connecting cities. We will talk more about ITAsoftware, which like ExpertFlyer and the KVS tool is not a booking site, when discussing international taxes in Chapter 3.

In my seminars, I've been using ExpertFlyer – not to promote it, but because it's the most practical choice in that particular setting, where most people have never seen raw airline data. I'll also use it for the purposes of this book, unless otherwise noted, to show you actual data, help you make sense of it and apply that knowledge to your own life as a traveler.

What is an airline tariff?

The first pillar of airline data, the airline tariff, consists of all published fares between any two cities served by the publishing carrier or its partners, including their fare bases, allowed routings and a series of rules, such as advance-purchase requirements, permitted days of the week, and blackout dates.

Typically, the prices published in a tariff represent only the "base fares" on a certain route, meaning there are other components that need to be added – taxes, fees and surcharges – in order to arrive at the ticket's total value. Those add-ons are fairly modest on U.S. domestic tickets – about $10 per flight segment, or about $20 for a nonstop round trip. International taxes and fuel surcharges, however, average between $400 and $500, as we will see in Chapter 3. It's worth noting that some airlines may include fuel surcharges in the published base fares, though that is not a consistent practice even for those carriers.

Let's start with an average U.S. domestic tariff. Figure 2 represents the United tariff between Washington (WAS) and New Orleans (MSY) as of October 10, 2010. Airline data changes all the time, so I will specify when the data I cite throughout the book was accurate. An important note: U.S. domestic fares are the same in either direction, unlike international fares, which can be very different depending on your point of origin, as we will see in Chapter 3.

Let's look at the first row in the table – the fare with a basis of TAK10MS. What does this mean? Most passengers only need to know that their flight will be booked in T class.

But if you want a more sophisticated understanding, that fare basis can tell you at least two other things. First, the number 10 indicates a 10-day advance-purchase requirement – in other words, you must issue your ticket at least 10 days before departure to qualify for this fare. Second, the presence of a third letter before the number – in this case, K – means that the fare is valid only on certain days of the week. Such a restriction usually doesn't exist for fare bases with only two letters before the number, as is the case with SA10MS in the table's third row. That rule doesn't necessarily apply to all airlines. American, for example, places the letter indicating the valid travel days after the first number in the fare-basis code.

Fare basis	Code	Type	Fare
TAK10MS	T	one way	$149.00
SAG10MS	S	one way	$159.00
SA10MS	S	one way	$184.00
LE21SFN	L	round trip	$209.00
TE213FN	T	round trip	$248.00
TE14SFN	T	round trip	$249.00
SE213FN	S	round trip	$304.00
SE143FN	S	round trip	$340.00
HA7FN	H	one way	$397.00
WE143FN	W	round trip	$412.00
VE213FN	W	round trip	$460.00
UA0FY	U	one way	$500.00
VE143FN	V	round trip	$524.00
EA0FY	E	one way	$600.00
QE213FN	Q	round trip	$602.00
QE143FN	Q	round trip	$656.00
HE73FN	H	round trip	$694.00
HE03FN	H	round trip	$840.00
MA0FY	M	one way	$960.00
BUA	B	one way	$1,032.00
HUAUP	A	one way	$1,090.00
YUA	Y	one way	$1,132.00
BUAUP	A	one way	$1,136.00
Y	Y	one way	$1,221.00
FUA	F	one way	$1,228.00
F	F	one way	$1,765.00

Figure 2: United Airlines fare tariff between Washington and New Orleans as of October 20, 2010.

If this wasn't enough detail and you are wondering about the letters MS after 10, let's just say that they have to do with other rules, such as blackout dates, additional surcharges, expiration dates and allowed routings.

Valid travel days and dates

Being able to decipher the fare basis saves time, but you can also read the spelled-out fare rules, which are usually just another click away. When you make a reservation, look for a link to the fare rules as soon as you build an itinerary – those links are rarely obvious, so pay close attention.

The rules page has several sections. For example, the "day/time" section for TAK10MS says this: "For -K type fares permitted Tue/Wed/Sat." So if you want to travel on a Friday, you won't qualify for TAK10MS and must book the SA10MS fare, whose rules don't even have such a section, because there are no day restrictions. Exactly which days of the week are eligible for a particular fare depends on that third letter before the number in the fare-basis code.

Some bases contain a fourth letter before the number, signifying an even more draconian restriction: You must travel not only on certain days but also during specific times on those days. In October 2010, United published a fare between Washington and Los Angeles with a basis of LAUT7GS and the following condition: "Permitted 7:00 a.m. to 9:30 a.m. Tue/Wed or 2:30 p.m. to 5:00 p.m. Tue/Wed or 7:00 p.m. to 10:30 p.m. Tue/Wed."

Another section of the fare rules covers travel dates. For our Washington-New Orleans TAK10MS fare, it says: "Travel on this fare component must commence by midnight on 26JAN 11." For the LAUT7GS Washington-LA fare it says, "Valid for travel commencing on each trip on/after 11OCT 10. Travel on this fare component must commence by midnight on 15DEC 10."

Some fares have no date restrictions and are valid until the "end of schedule" (EOS), or until the latest date in the future that is open for sale – usually about 330 days out, depending on the airline.

On U.S. domestic fares, travel "must commence by midnight" doesn't just mean that your outbound flight has to be taken by the deadline – you must begin your return trip by then, too. You can arrive the next day, as long as your departure is scheduled for before midnight, as is the case with a red eye. Even if you are making a connection, you only have to begin your return journey by midnight and can connect the next morning. International fares usually require that only the outbound flight be taken before the deadline.

Blackout dates and surcharges

Blackout dates are another important part of the fare rules. Some fares don't have any, but our Washington-New Orleans fare has quite a few – not only around Thanksgiving, Christmas and New Year's Eve, but also in March and April 2011. Here is what that section looks like:

> TRAVEL IS NOT PERMITTED 23NOV 10 THROUGH 24NOV 10 OR ON 27NOV 10 OR ON 25DEC 10 OR 31DEC 10 THROUGH 01JAN 11 OR ON 04JAN 11
> AND
> TRAVEL IS NOT PERMITTED 28NOV 10 THROUGH 29NOV 10 OR 17DEC 10 THROUGH 24DEC 10 OR 26DEC 10 THROUGH 30DEC 10 OR 02JAN 11 THROUGH 03JAN 11 OR 10MAR 11 THROUGH 14MAR 11 OR 17MAR 11 THROUGH 21MAR 11 OR 24MAR 11 THROUGH 28MAR 11 OR ON 31MAR 11 OR 01APR 11 THROUGH 04APR 11 OR 14APR 11 THROUGH 16APR 11 OR 17APR 11 THROUGH 18APR 11 OR 21APR 11 THROUGH 23APR 11 OR ON 25APR 11 OR 28APR 11 THROUGH 29APR 11 OR ON 01MAY 11.

Blackout dates are usually followed by surcharges. The Washington-New Orleans TAK10MS fare doesn't have any, but the LE21SFN fare in the fourth row of Figure 2 has a long list. Here are just two: "A surcharge of $18.60 [per] fare component will be added to the applicable fare for travel on 19 NOV 10," and "a surcharge of $27.91 [per] fare component will be added to the applicable fare for travel from 28 NOV 10 through 29 NOV 10."

All U.S. carriers imposed such surcharges on almost every day in the summer of 2010, and it appears they will do the same in 2011. Airlines also resort to those surcharges when the price of oil jumps significantly.

Penalties for voluntary changes

The penalties are usually among the longest sections in the fare rules. Full fares, of course, allow free changes and cancellations. The rest of the U.S. domestic fares are nonrefundable and currently carry penalties of up to $150, though they are lower on smaller carriers – for example, JetBlue charges $100 and Alaska Airlines $75. In April 2011, Frontier reduced its fee from $100 to $50. There is no change fee on Southwest Airlines, though you need to pay any fare differences. The most common penalty on U.S.-originating international tickets is currently $250, though those fees vary much more than on domestic tickets, as we will see in Chapter 3.

Contrary to popular belief, if you cancel a nonrefundable ticket, you won't lose the ticket's entire value, but only the penalty amount. We will look closely at the rules of changing and canceling nonrefundable tickets in Chapter 7.

Domestic First and Business Class fares are often nonrefundable and incur change fees, which is also the case with international fares, as we will see in Chapter 3.

One-way and round-trip fares

As we saw in the Washington-New Orleans United tariff in Figure 2, some fares are published as one ways and others as round trips. The one-way fares are certainly more flexible, because you can buy them as such or combine them as a round trip, and you don't have to worry about minimum-stay requirements, such as a Saturday night. Truly one-way domestic fares have become more common in recent years, thanks to low-cost carriers, and especially Southwest Airlines. We still see fares advertised as "$99 each way based on a required round-trip purchase," but they are no longer the norm. We will look more closely at deliberately misleading advertisements in Chapter 6.

So when does it make sense to buy a one-way ticket? Typically, a round trip is a better idea, because it's less confusing, keeps your entire itinerary in the same place and incurs only one penalty in case of a change or cancellation. But here are some possible reasons to choose a one-way ticket:

- You know your outbound date but not the return, and waiting to buy a round-trip ticket will increase the fare;
- The cheapest outbound flight is on one airline but the cheapest return is on another, and they can't be ticketed together;
- Two one-way tickets are cheaper than a round trip – it's very rare, but it happens, usually due to taxes and surcharges.

Chapter 1 Lessons Learned

1. Buying an airline ticket shouldn't be a blind purchase.

2. The most important part of an airline reservation is the ticket number.

3. A ticket entitles a passenger to transportation from one city to another on a certain date and in a certain class of service.

4. The ticket price may not include such previously free services and items as checked luggage, food and drinks, pillows and blankets, seat assignment and others.

5. Learning airline codes and other basics of the air travel science can save hundreds of dollars on one ticket.

6. The airline data has two main components (pillars): fares and availability, or tariffs and inventory, in airline lingo. Both pillars are built on a foundation of fare codes, for which the airlines use letters of the alphabet.

7. First, Business and Economy are service classes, and they correspond to the cabins on a plane, while there are many more booking classes than just three.

8. The only truly full-fare coach code is Y, though some airlines also include B – and even M at times – in the same category, meaning they are fully refundable and changeable for free.

9. An airline tariff consists of all published base fares between any two cities served by the publishing carrier or its partners, including their fare bases, allowed routings and a series of rules, such as advance-purchase requirements, permitted days of the week, and blackout dates.

10. The price of a ticket is determined by a combination of airline data published and updated by each carrier through the Airline Tariff Publishing Company (ATPCO) or its only and much smaller competitor, SITA.

11. Travel agencies access airline data through Global Distribution Systems (GDS), such as Travelport, Amadeus and Sabre, which get the data from ATPCO or SITA.

12. Consumers can access airline data through websites like ExpertFlyer. com, KVStool.com and ITASoftware.com.

Chapter 2

U.S. Domestic Fares

Airlines update their data 24 hours a day, but ATPCO sends that data out to its GDS clients in feeds several times a day. The North American feeds are published at 10 a.m., 1 p.m. and 8 p.m. Eastern time (ET) on weekdays, and at 5 p.m. ET on weekends and holidays. This means that, at those times, a certain fare can be put on the market, changed or pulled off the market. It also means that a fare can be filed in the afternoon and removed that same evening. Beginning October 1, 2011, ATPCO will add a fourth filing feed on weekdays, at 4 p.m. ET, said Jay Brawley, director of customer marketing.

These official filing feeds don't exclude the possibility that a fare may be changed or removed at other times on a booking source directly controlled by the airline, such as its website. In addition, the data changes in those feeds can take an hour or longer to update in various booking systems.

How do you know that a low fare to a city you need to visit has been published? You certainly don't have to wait for the airlines to announce a sale – in fact, "sale" prices are often far from a bargain. Thanks to the transparency provided by the Internet, you can actually keep an eye on fares, through websites like FareCompare.com and AirfareWatchdog.com. You can also subscribe to their e-mail alerts for fares between any two cities.

In January 2008, I was at the World Economic Forum in Davos, Switzerland, with Secretary of State Condoleezza Rice. Just before she began her speech, I received an e-mail alert from FareCompare about a $99 one-way base fare between Washington and San Francisco. As it happened, I needed to book a trip to San Francisco, but I couldn't act immediately, since I had to write and file a story for my newspaper. By the time I was free to look into booking a ticket, the fare was gone.

Not that there was anything I could have done in this case, but the experience taught me a valuable lesson: If you get word about a really good fare, book it as soon as you can. Most domestic fares usually stay on the market at least a couple of days, but there is never a guarantee, and some vanish within hours – the airlines can do whatever they want.

Cheapest days to book and to fly

Whenever I'm invited to talk about travel on radio or TV, I'm asked for five or six specific tips on making flying more affordable. One of the questions usually has to do with the cheapest travel days. Although I prefer to avoid generalizations – I often compare airfares to English grammar, because of the many exceptions to the rules they both have – I typically say that Tuesday, Wednesday and Saturday are the cheapest days to fly.

As we saw in the various fare rules above, every fare is published with permitted days of the week. Some fares are valid only on Tuesday and Wednesday. Others are allowed on Tuesday, Wednesday and Saturday. Yet others are good on any day except Friday and Sunday. And of course, there may be no restrictions at all. So it's fair to generalize, but that doesn't mean that you can't find a decent fare that might work on Monday or Thursday – or any day, for that matter. The best approach is to do your homework thoroughly.

What about booking days? Does it make a difference whether you buy a ticket on Wednesday or Friday? It could, as U.S. carriers typically publish their lowest domestic fares on Tuesday and remove them on Thursday. For some reason, they think that we all book tickets on weekends. Again, there are exceptions, and some very low fares stay unchanged on the market for a couple of weeks.

So if you can, book tickets between Tuesday and Thursday, and fly on Tuesday, Wednesday or Saturday.

Why fare wars are a traveler's dream

On a Thursday night in August 2008, I received an e-mail alert from FareCompare about a $99 round-trip base fare between Washington and Salt Lake City on United. I'd been trying to go to the Sundance Film Festival in Utah for years, but fares in January rarely drop below $500, so I'd never made it.

I was surprised that United was filing a $99 fare on a Thursday night and thought the fare must have many restrictions – perhaps it was only allowed on weekdays, which wouldn't work for me, and it probably expired long before the following January. To my surprise, a quick look at the fare rules proved me wrong – there were no restrictions whatsoever. As long as I could find availability in L booking class, the ridiculously low fare was mine. I thought it might be too late if I waited until the next day, so I rolled up my sleeves and issued a ticket before I went to bed. The next morning, the fare was gone.

So what had prompted the unusual price? As it turned out, that same United fare was available from many other East coast cities. It was a fare war – United had targeted routes to and from a competitor's (Delta) airport hub (Salt Lake City).

Several times in 2010, American and United were at war over Hawaii. American filed round-trip base fares from United's hubs in Washington and Chicago for less than $400, and United struck back with the same fares out of American's hubs in Miami and Dallas. American often challenges United out of Washington, offering round-trip base fares to the West coast for less than $200. United, of course, does the same out of Miami. In January 2011, it was selling MIA to SFO for $128 plus tax.

Many travelers prefer nonstop flights, of course, so they tend to fly the most on the dominant carrier at their home airport. If you live in Atlanta, you probably end up on Delta most of the time. If you are in Dallas, chances are you are a frequent flier on American Airlines. If you are a Phoenix resident, you are likely a US Airways customer. However, you may be better off financially if you don't give your business to the obvious carrier. In recent months, both American and Delta have been offering very low fares to and from Washington, a United hub. United, in turn, has filed great fares out of Philadelphia and Charlotte, North Carolina (US Airways hubs).

UP fares – Economy or First Class?

Let's look back at the United Washington-New Orleans tariff in Figure 2 on Page 13. For all fare bases, the first letter is the same as the booking class (TAK10MS and T) – except for two. If you look closely at HUAUP and BUAUP, you will see that they book in A (discounted First) class. These are the so-called UP fares, which have a coach fare basis but book in the next higher service class – Business or First, depending on how many cabins the plane has.

The UP fares are very common in the North American market. Most carriers book them in A class, though some use P class, as is the case with American. On three-cabin aircraft, UP fares book into Z class on United and I class on American. They are often significantly lower than regular premium fares, and only some of them are refundable and changeable for free.

In effect, these fares provide an instant upgrade, but is that an official upgrade? In other words, if for some reason you need to get rebooked on a different flight, do you deserve a coach or a First Class seat? It depends on the airline. Delta will most likely rebook you in economy, but United will try to keep you in the premium cabin – after all, even if your fare basis is HUAUP, your booking class is not H but A, and it's the booking class that counts, not the fare basis.

Standby and same-day confirmed changes

What you might not know about standby is that it's no longer free on most U.S. carriers – unless you have top elite status – and costs up to $50. As usual, standby is allowed only on domestic flights, and only on the originally ticketed travel day.

An often better alternative is a same-day confirmed change, which can be as much as $75 but will guarantee you a seat on another flight. You can request it from home, though exactly when you can do that varies by airline. United permits it only within three hours of your new flight's departure, while American allows 12 hours. In addition, your new routing on United must be identical to the original one, but different connections are allowed on American, as long as the origin and destination stay the same.

Southwest doesn't allow standby or same-day confirmed changes at all, even for a fee. If you want to be on a different flight, it will be treated as a regular voluntary change and may incur any applicable fare difference, but at least there will be no change fee.

Stopovers and "legal connections"

Many travelers are confused about the technical meaning of "stopover" when it comes to airline tickets. If you are spending a couple of hours in Dallas on your way from San Diego to Miami, that's not considered a stopover – it's a layover or connecting time.

You have probably heard the term "legal connection." Airlines like to use the word "legal" quite a bit, though "permitted" may be a better choice – they won't sue you if you "commit" an "illegal" connection.

There is minimum and maximum allowed connecting time. The minimum time usually starts at 30 minutes, but it really depends on the particular airport. How big is that airport? Do you have to change terminals? Are you transferring from one airline to another? Are you going from a domestic to an international flight? If you arrive from abroad, you need time to go through immigration and customs before connecting to a domestic flight. Minimum connection times are usually factored in airline reservations systems, but sometimes passengers get booked on "illegal connections" anyway. So if you are worried about missing a flight, call your airline, and if it turns out that your transfer is under the minimum required time, ask to be rebooked on flights with a longer layover.

As for maximum connecting times, there is a big difference between domestic and international travel. On U.S. domestic itineraries, the limit is **four hours** – any layover longer than that is considered a stopover. On international itineraries, including any domestic connecting flights, the limit is **24 hours** – a great benefit that make your trip much cheaper, as we will see in Chapter 3.

What if you want to stay in Dallas for six hours for a business meeting before continuing to Miami? You can certainly do that on the same ticket, but the fare will be different. If you limit your connecting time to four hours, you will pay a "through fare" from San Diego to Miami, which is as low as $139 base one way on American as I write this. But if you exceed the four-hour time limit, you will pay a "split fare" – at least $199 base one way from San Diego to Dallas and at least $169 base one way from Dallas to Miami. So that stopover will cost you double the "through fare."

Is there a way around that rule? As usual, yes, though it can be risky. When you arrive in Dallas, you can request a "same-day confirmed change" – not standby – either at a kiosk or a customer-service counter. If you don't have elite status, you will have to pay a fee, but that would be much cheaper than buying a "split fare." The risk is that the later flight you want may not have available seats.

What about staying in Dallas overnight on a "through" fare? That's not as easy as it was years ago, but sometimes it's possible if there are no other reasonable options. Even if there are other options, an airline supervisor may still be able to book you on the last flight for the day coming in and the first flight out the next morning, but that also depends on the circumstances and your elite status.

Transfers and "legal routing"

Where can you find the "legal routing"? As difficult as it may be to spot the fare rules on airline websites, at least they are there in most cases. The legal routing usually isn't, and sites like ExpertFlyer are among the few that carry that data.

Here is the routing American publishes on the San Diego-Miami route:

```
SAN-LAX/SFO-MIA
SAN-CHI/STL/DFW-MIA
SAN-SJC-MIA
```

The two most important things about these airport codes are their order and, oddly enough, the punctuation. There is a big difference between - and /. The hyphen means that both airports on either side of the hyphen are eligible for transit, while only one of the airports separated by a slash can be used. For example, as indicated in the first line of the routing above, you can make only one connection between San Diego (SAN) and Miami (MIA), and you have to choose between Los Angeles (LAX) and San Francisco (SFO) – you can't fly through both of them. Or you can choose Dallas (DFW) or Chicago (CHI) or St. Louis (STL). Only a single connection is allowed on this route.

Now let's look at American's legal routing on its lowest published fares from DFW to MIA:

TRAVEL MUST BE NONSTOP

Why is that? Because both Dallas and Miami are American hubs, with plenty of daily flights. One curious fact: If you read the transfers section of the fare rules, you will see that it allows four transfers each way. That text is a leftover from a different time that most airlines haven't bothered to delete from the templates they use. In any case, the published routing is what counts here, and in general the more restrictive rule determines what is allowed.

What about airlines that don't fly between Dallas and Miami nonstop? Naturally, they do allow connections. Here is Delta's routing, which permits up to two transfers:

DFW-MSP/DTT/CVG/MEM/ATL-MIA
DFW-ATL/CVG/MEM-ORL/FLL/TPA-MIA
DFW-CVG/MEM-ATL-MIA
DFW-ATL-MEM-MIA
DFW-MEM-CVG-MIA

In the first line, the choice for a transfer city is between Minneapolis (MSP), Detroit (DTT), Cincinnati (CVG), Memphis (MEM) or Atlanta (ATL). In the rest of the routing options, your first connections could be in Atlanta, Cincinnati or Memphis, and your second connection could be in Orlando (ORL), Fort Lauderdale (FLL) or Tampa (TPA).

Now let's look at United's routing. Below is what was allowed until late 2010 – it was rather liberal, because the carrier had no hubs anywhere close to either Dallas or Miami.

```
DFW-CHI-ATL/CLE/DTT/DAY/CMH/IND/RDU-NYC/
WAS-JAX-TPA-MIA
DFW-CHI-ATL/CLE/DTT/DAY/CMH/IND/RDU/CLE/DTT/DAY/
CMH/IND/RDU-NYC/WAS/WAS-ORL-MIA
DFW-CHI-BUF-ROC-NYC/WAS-JAX-TPA-MIA
DFW-CHI-BUF-ROC-NYC/WAS/WAS-ORL-MIA
DFW-CHI-ABE/HAR/ROA/SDF/RIC/CAK/CRW/ORF-NYC/
WAS-JAX-TPA-MIA
DFW-CHI-ABE/HAR/ROA/SDF/RIC/CAK/CRW/ORF/HAR/
ROA/SDF/RIC/CAK/CRW/
ORF-NYC/WAS/WAS-ORL-MIA
```

If you wanted to rack up frequent-flier miles, United gave you a great opportunity by allowing you to connect in both Chicago (CHI) and Washington (WAS) – it sounds ridiculous to do that on the way from Dallas to Miami, but it was possible. Moreover, from Dallas you could go up to Chicago, down to Atlanta, back up to Washington and then to Miami.

However, that all changed in early 2011, because Houston (HOU) effectively became a United hub, even though its merger with Continental wasn't quite completed. Here is the newly published routing:

```
DFW-DEN/HOU-CLT-MIA
DFW-DEN/HOU-FLL/FMY/MIA/ORL/PBI/TPA-MIA
DFW-DEN/HOU-MIA
```

As you can see, connecting in Chicago, Washington and several other northern cities is no longer permitted. Flying through

Denver (DEN) will give you more miles. United doesn't operate nonstop flights between Denver and Miami all year round, but you can transfer in both Denver and Charlotte (CLT), as there is a hyphen between them.

United was the last major carrier to tighten the transfer rules in 2010, and most of them now allow only single or double connections, and only in hubs. Travel between two hubs – for example, Washington and Los Angeles – often must be nonstop to qualify for low fares.

Why does that matter? Because having more connecting options can save you money. If you need to go from Washington to LA on United, the lowest booking classes now require nonstop travel. Who said nonstop flights were more expensive? In the past, if you wanted L class and it wasn't available on the nonstops, you could connect on flights that did have L availability. That's no longer allowed, so your only option is to buy up to a higher fare.

Some of the codes in the United routing signify cities instead of specific airports. For example, CHI includes O'Hare (ORD) and Midway (MDW), WAS covers Reagan National (DCA) and Dulles (IAD), but not Baltimore (BWI), and NYC means LaGuardia (LGA) and Kennedy (JFK), but not Newark (EWR).

Chapter 2 Lessons Learned

1. ATPCO publishes North American fare feeds at 10 a.m., 1 p.m. and 8 p.m. ET on weekdays, and at 5 p.m. ET on weekends and holidays. Beginning October 1, 2011, it will add a fourth filing feed on weekdays, at 4 p.m. ET.

2. A discounted domestic fare can be filed and removed in a matter of hours.

3. Taxes, fees and surcharges on U.S. domestic tickets are much lower than on international tickets, beginning at about $10 per flight segment.

4. Consumers can monitor when low fares are filed and subscribe to e-mail alerts on websites like FareCompare and AirfareWatchdog.

5. Although this is a big generalization, for the lowest fares, travelers should book tickets between Tuesday and Thursday, and fly on Tuesday, Wednesday or Saturday.

6. A fare war takes place when one airline "attacks" a competing carrier's airport hub by filing very lows fares out of that city.

7. UP fares have a coach fare basis but book in the next higher service class – Business or First, depending on how many cabins the plane has.

8. A same-day confirmed change guarantees a seat on another flight, as opposed to standby, and can cost as much as $75.

9. Change and cancellation penalties on domestic tickets run as high as $150.

10. The minimum connecting time between flights usually starts at 30 minutes and depends on the particular airport.

11. The maximum connecting time on U.S. domestic itineraries is four hours – any layover longer than that is considered a stopover. A connection ensures a "through fare," while a stopover results in a "split fare," unless the stopover is permitted by the fare rules.

Chapter 3

International Fares

The International Air Transport Association (IATA) has divided the world into three zones ("traffic conferences") for the purposes of commercial aviation. Zone 1 includes the Americas, Zone 2 Europe, Africa and the Middle East, and Zone 3 Asia, Australia and the Southwest Pacific. You can see multiple references to these zones in international fare rules.

ATPCO sends out feeds with international fares every hour, except for several hours on Saturday night, the company's Jay Brawley said. Discounted international fares typically stay on the market longer than discounted U.S. domestic fares – sometimes for weeks. As mentioned earlier, fares between two international cities can be very different depending on the direction. For example, as of November 15, 2010, Delta's lowest round-trip coach base fare from Hong Kong to Salt Lake City was $630. However, from Salt Lake City to Hong Kong the lowest fare was $970. American was also offering a lower fare out of Hong Kong ($773) than out of Salt Lake City ($940).

The difference can be much more significant in Business and First Class. For example, as I write this, the lowest Lufthansa Business Class round-trip base fare from New York to Kuwait City is $7,582, while from Kuwait City to New York it's $4,364.

International fares out of the United States to different cities in the same country are often similar – for example, Dubai and Abi Dhabi, both in the United Arab Emirates – except for large countries like China, Brazil and Russia.

Among the important but not widely known features of the international fare universe are the round-the-world and other so-called "circle" fares, which will be discussed in Chapter 11.

International taxes, fees and surcharges

As we saw in Chapter 1, U.S. domestic taxes are about $20-$40 for an average round trip. In contrast, international taxes and surcharges can add between $200 and $500 to a coach ticket on average, depending on specific countries and distances. That amount may be even higher if your itinerary includes London. As of January 2011, a British Airways ticket from Washington to Johannesburg via London included $753 in taxes. For comparison, the taxes on a Lufthansa ticket from Washington to Johannesburg via Munich were $487.

Some countries, such as Britain and France, impose even higher fees on First and Business Class tickets, though that doesn't usually affect transfer passengers. Also in January 2011, the UK Air Passengers Duty doubled to $185 in Business Class from $92 in coach from London to Washington. The French Air Passenger Solidarity Tax jumped from $5 to $53 from Paris to Washington.

The biggest part of a ticket's taxes is usually the fuel (YQ) surcharge, which vary by route and airline and fluctuate along with major changes in the price of oil. In January 2011, United's YQ charge for a round trip from Washington to Singapore was $392, while Japan's All Nippon Airways charged only $222 on the same route. On tickets originating in Singapore, the All Nippon amount remained the same, but United's changed to $280. That's because the YQ charge, like the base fare, is often different depending on the respective market.

In addition, some airlines increase the fuel surcharges on First and Business Class tickets. The above-cited $753 in British Airways coach taxes included a $572 YQ charge, which jumped to $800 in Business. United charged $320 for fuel from Washington to Johannesburg in coach, but $510 in Business. However, on the Washington-Singapore route, the YQ charge remained the same regardless of the class of service.

With oil prices on the rise again in early 2011, fuel surcharges may be even higher by the time you read this. In fact, let me illustrate how much some airlines raised their YQ surcharges in just two months. Below is a detailed breakdown of the British Airways taxes, fees and surcharges for a round trip from Washington to Johannesburg via London in coach as of January 25, 2011. The data is courtesy of ITASoftware.com, which I mentioned in Chapter 1. You will notice that British Airways has an add-on YQ charge.

BA YQ surcharge (YQ) $548.00
BA YQ surcharge (YQ) $24.00
United Kingdom Passenger Service Charge (UB) $71.00
US International Departure Tax (US) $16.30
US September 11th Security Fee (AY) $2.50
US Passenger Facility Charge (XF) $4.50
USDA APHIS Fee (XA) $5.00
US Immigration Fee (XY) $7.00
US Customs Fee (YC) $5.50
US International Arrival Tax (US) $16.30
South Africa Passenger Service Charge (ZA) $29.90
South Africa Air Passenger Tax (WC) $22.70
South Africa Passenger Safety Charge (EV) $1.70

Here is that same breakdown as of March 25, 2011. The fuel surcharge is $118 higher. The UK Passenger Service Charge also went up by $4.

BA YQ surcharge (YQ) $666.00
BA YQ surcharge (YQ) $24.00
United Kingdom Passenger Service Charge (UB) $75.00
US International Departure Tax (US) $16.30
US September 11th Security Fee (AY) $2.50
US Passenger Facility Charge (XF) $4.50
USDA APHIS Fee (XA) $5.00
US Immigration Fee (XY) $7.00
US Customs Fee (YC) $5.50
US International Arrival Tax (US) $16.30
South Africa Passenger Service Charge (ZA) $28.50
South Africa Air Passenger Tax (WC) $21.60
South Africa Passenger Safety Charge (EV) $1.70

Depending on your airline or booking source, you may see some taxes displayed separately, while others may be combined with the base fare in a single figure to make things simpler for customers. Taxes are usually priced in U.S. dollars, even if the base fare is published in another currency.

International airline tariffs

International airline tariffs typically include much longer lists of different fares than domestic ones. Let's take a look at Delta's tariff from Salt Lake City (SLC) to Hong Kong (HKG) as of November 24, 2010, in Figure 3.

You might wonder why there are so many Business Class fares on this Delta tariff, and how much each of them is different from the rest. Some rules, such as advance purchase and travel days, certainly vary, but several of these fares have very similar features – even those with the same booking class. You might also wonder who would pay $18,000 for a plane ticket,

Fare Basis	Code	Type	Fare
TSLHOL	T	round trip	$970.00
USLHOL	U	round trip	$1,170.00
KLXP04	K	round trip	$1,172.00
KLXPVJ4	K	round trip	$1,172.00
KLWP04	K	round trip	$1,252.00
KLWPVJ4	K	round trip	$1,252.00
QLXP03	Q	round trip	$1,372.00
QLWP03	Q	round trip	$1,452.00
HLXP02	H	round trip	$1,572.00
HLWP02	H	round trip	$1,652.00
MAPO	M	one way	$1,661.00
Y9	Y	one way	$2,740.00
Y	Y	one way	$2,741.00
MAPRT	M	round trip	$2,804.00
BEERT9	B	round trip	$3,803.00
BEERT	B	round trip	$3,804.00
Y1US9	Y	round trip	$4,603.00
Y1US	Y	round trip	$4,604.00
MLAPAS	M	round trip	$4,809.00
SXLEIS50	S	round trip	$5,524.00
BLEAS	B	round trip	$5,541.00
SWLEIS50	S	round trip	$6,124.00
DX	D	one way	$6,274.00
S6LEIS50	S	round trip	$6,524.00
D6	D	one way	$6,634.00
DW	D	one way	$6,634.00
SX7RT	S	round trip	$7,446.00
SW7RT	S	round trip	$8,046.00
Y9	Y	one way	$8,270.00
Y	Y	one way	$8,271.00
S67RT	S	round trip	$8,446.00
CX9	C	one way	$9,552.00
JX9	J	one way	$9,552.00
CX	C	one way	$9,553.00
JX	J	one way	$9,553.00
DXRT	D	round trip	$10,651.00
C9	C	one way	$10,739.00
CW9	C	one way	$10,739.00
J9	J	one way	$10,739.00

JW9	J	one way	$10,739.00
C	C	one way	$10,740.00
CW	C	one way	$10,740.00
J	J	one way	$10,740.00
JW	J	one way	$10,740.00
C9	C	one way	$11,047.00
J9	J	one way	$11,047.00
C	C	one way	$11,048.00
J	J	one way	$11,048.00
D6RT	D	round trip	$11,251.00
DWRT	D	round trip	$11,251.00
YR	Y	round trip	$13,142.00
CR9	C	round trip	$17,467.00
JR9	J	round trip	$17,467.00
CR	C	round trip	$17,468.00
JR	J	round trip	$17,468.00
CXRT9	C	round trip	$17,475.00
JXRT9	J	round trip	$17,475.00
CXRT	C	round trip	$17,476.00
JXRT	J	round trip	$17,476.00
CWRT9	C	round trip	$18,093.00
JR9	J	round trip	$18,093.00
JWRT9	J	round trip	$18,093.00
CWRT	C	round trip	$18,094.00
JWRT	J	round trip	$18,094.00
CR9	C	round trip	$18,493.00
CR	C	round trip	$18,494.00
JR	J	round trip	$18,494.00

Figure 3: Delta Airlines fare tariff from Salt Lake City to Hong Kong as of November 24, 2010.

even if it's in Business Class. In reality, very few people pay that price. There are obviously lower fares – starting with the S fare of $5,524 – though some are more restrictive. Most people who buy full Business Class fares have access to government or corporate discounts.

Unlike U.S. domestic fares, discounted international – especially long-haul – fares are published as required round trips most of the time. As you can see, the lowest one-way coach fare (MAPO of $1,661) is almost twice as expensive as the cheapest round trip (TSLHOL of $970). How does this make sense? It's supposed to make sense in terms of yield management, but to be honest, I haven't invested in learning more details because I don't think that would save me money or otherwise improve my travel life.

Valid travel dates and days

Discounted international fares usually have seasonality, as is the case with the TSLHOL fare on Delta's tariff from Salt Lake City to Hong Kong.

> OUTBOUND – PERMITTED 20 NOV 10 THROUGH 16 DEC 10 OR 21 DEC 10 THROUGH 26 DEC 10 OR 29 DEC 10 THROUGH 31 DEC 10 FOR EACH TRANSPACIFIC SECTOR. INBOUND – PERMITTED 01 DEC 10 THROUGH 16 DEC 10 OR 19 DEC 10 THROUGH 27 DEC 10 OR ON 31 DEC 10 OR 11 JAN 11 THROUGH 28 FEB 11 FOR EACH TRANSPACIFIC SECTOR.

If you look closely at the fare-basis codes in Figure 3, you will see that most of them include either X or W. The letter X means that the fare is allowed only on a weekday – usually Monday through Thursday, though some fares also consider Sunday a weekday. The letter W in the fare basis signifies a weekend fare. Sometimes, you will see S instead of X or W, which means that fare is valid only on Saturdays.

That said, the S in TSLHOL and USLHOL doesn't indicate a day of the week – in fact, these two fares have no day restrictions at all. You can learn all that, of course, by reading the full fare rules.

Valid flights and carriers

With all the alliances, code-sharing and other partnerships airlines have formed in recent years, the number of flights carrying
their own numbers has grown drastically. We will examine those
partnerships more closely in Chapter 6, but for tariff purposes
let's just say that many carriers limit the use of their discounted
fares to flights actually operated by themselves, which are also
known as "true flights."

Here is the "flight application" section of the rules of Delta's
TSLHOL fare from Figure 3:

> THE FARE COMPONENT **MUST NOT** BE ON ONE OR
> MORE OF THE FOLLOWING
> ANY DL FLIGHT OPERATED BY KE
> ANY DL FLIGHT OPERATED BY CI
> AND
> THE FARE COMPONENT **MUST NOT** INCLUDE TRAVEL
> VIA SEL
> AND
> IF THE FARE COMPONENT INCLUDES TRAVEL VIA EACH
> TRANSPACIFIC SECTOR THEN THAT TRAVEL **MUST NOT**
> BE ON ONE OR MORE OF THE FOLLOWING
> DL FLIGHT 280
> DL FLIGHT 281

The first condition is that you can't fly on Korean Air (KE)
or Taiwan's China Airlines (CI) if you want to use the TSLHOL
fare. The rule could have said instead that travel must be only
on Delta, which is the case with many other Delta fares. There
is an additional restriction here: You can't route via Seoul (SEL),
even on true Delta flights. SEL includes both Incheon (ICN) and
Gimpo (GMP) airports.

The third condition has to do with specific flights – DL280
and DL281, which operate between Atlanta (ATL) and Tokyo

Narita (NRT), are not valid on this fare. Given that this is the tariff from Salt Lake City to Hong Kong, having ATL on the itinerary wouldn't be the most logical or convenient thing anyway.

Transfers and "legal routing"

Most fares on the Delta tariff above allow "unlimited transfers on the fare component online on the primary carrier," which is of course Delta. Even though that may seem rather liberal, one look at the legal routing will show that's not quite the case. It's very different from what we've seen so far – it doesn't specify actual routings, but only says this:

MAXIMUM PERMITTED MILEAGE IS 8616

You can make as many transfers between Salt Lake City and Hong Kong as you like, provided you don't exceed 8,616 miles each way.

What does that mean in practice? Delta flies to Hong Kong nonstop only from Detroit (DTW) and Tokyo (NRT). If you choose the Detroit connection, the mileage will be about 9,330, which exceeds the limit. So your only option is Tokyo, and that will add another connection, because there are no nonstop flights from Salt Lake City to Tokyo. If you fly to Tokyo via Los Angeles (LAX), the distance will be about 7,880 miles, and via Minneapolis (MSP) about 8,780 miles. So it's clear that you have to transfer on the West coast.

The maximum permitted mileage (MPM) is different for every city, of course. If you look at the Atlanta-Hong Kong tariff, you will see that the limit is 10,068. Such routing rules are common for international fares, and many airlines apply them to award tickets as well.

What if you exceed the limit by 100 miles, and there is no way to get from one city to another on a particular airline or alliance for less mileage? Different airlines – and fares – have different rules. Some will let you go over the limit for an additional surcharge equal to a percentage of the base fare. Others don't offer that option, which results in a "broken" fare somewhere along the routing.

In 2009, I was looking at a fare from Stockholm (ARN) to one of the Hawaiian Islands. Whatever routing I tried, it was always over the limit by about 100 miles, and the computer kept "breaking" the fare. I spoke with an airline supervisor, who saw my point and overrode the obviously unrealistic requirement.

Many international fares don't have a mileage limit but regular routing requirements. Let's look at the routing combinations United publishes on the same Salt Lake City-Hong Kong route.

```
SLC-DEN-LAS-SFO/LAX/SEA-SFO/LAX/SEA/SAN-SFO/
LAX/SEA-HNL(UA/HA/WP)    LNY/ITO/KOA/LIH/OGG/JHM/
MKK (UA/HA/WP) HNL-HKG
SLC-DEN-LAS-SFO/LAX/SEA-SFO/LAX/SEA/SAN-SFO/
LAX/SEA-HNL(UA/HA/WP)    LNY/ITO/KOA/LIH/OGG/JHM/
MKK (UA/HA/WP) HNL-HAN (HX) HKG
SLC-DEN-LAS-SFO/LAX/SEA-SFO/LAX/SEA/SAN-SFO/
LAX/SEA-HNL(UA/HA/WP)    LNY/ITO/KOA/LIH/OGG/JHM/
MKK (UA/HA/WP) HNL-OSA/NGO-TYO-HKG
SLC-DEN-LAS-SFO/LAX/SEA-SFO/LAX/SEA/SAN-SFO/
LAX/SEA-HNL(UA/HA/WP)    LNY/ITO/KOA/LIH/OGG/JHM/
MKK (UA/HA/WP) HNL-BJS/SHA (KA) HKG
SLC-DEN-LAS-SFO/LAX/SEA-SFO/LAX/SEA/SAN-SFO/
LAX/SEA-HNL(UA/HA/WP)    LNY/ITO/KOA/LIH/OGG/JHM/
MKK (UA/HA/WP) HNL-OSA/NGO-TYO (UA/NH/CX/HX)
HKG
SLC-DEN-CHI-HKG
SLC-DEN-CHI-HAN (HX) HKG
SLC-DEN-CHI-OSA/NGO-TYO-HKG
SLC-DEN-CHI-BJS/SHA (KA) HKG
SLC-DEN-CHI-OSA/NGO-TYO (UA/NH/CX/HX) HKG
```

Don't be intimidated – I had to look up a couple of those airport codes myself, such as Kapalua (JHM) and Hoolehua (MKK) in Hawaii. I'd be surprised if anyone has ever connected in these places on Island Air (WP) on their way to Hong Kong, but the legal routing simply shows what's possible in theory, even if some of the allowed transfers don't work in practice.

If you recall the difference between - and /, you will notice in the very last line of the routing above that you can fly through both Tokyo (TYO) and Osaka (OSA) on your way from Salt Lake City to Hong Kong, but you have to choose between Osaka and Nagoya (NGO). OSA includes both Kansai (KIX) and Itami (ITM) airports. You can't make unlimited transfers – the legal routing simply shows what's possible. The transfers are limited additionally by the fare rules. Here is the United rule:

> 5 TRANSFERS PERMITTED IN EACH DIRECTION FREE
> 2 FREE IN THE UNITED STATES IN EACH DIRECTION
> 3 FREE IN AREA 3 IN EACH DIRECTION

In the United routings above, you can see two-letter airline codes between the airport codes in brackets, such as (UA/HA/WP) and (UA/NH/CX/HX). This means that, between the cities where the codes are placed, you can fly on United or any of the other carriers listed – Hawaiian Airlines (HA), Island Air (WP), All Nippon (NH), Cathay Pacific (CX) or Trans North Aviation (HX). Although flights on these airlines are allowed in theory, in practice some of the listed carriers don't operate the respective routes. For example, United currently doesn't fly between Tokyo and Hong Kong, or between certain Hawaiian Islands.

Stopovers and 'legal connections'

As I said in Chapter 2, on international itineraries, a stopover typically occurs when the time between connecting flights is

24 hours or more. This is probably one of the least known and consequently most underutilized benefits in the air travel system. I'm not suggesting that you force an overnight for no reason, but the ability to do so could save you a lot of money – and you could see places you normally wouldn't visit.

If you live in Salt Lake City and have never been to San Francisco, why not stop there for 23 hours on your way to Hong Kong? It would cost you only about $10 in additional airport taxes. Or if you were planning a separate trip to San Francisco for a business meeting around the time of the Asia trip, why not combine them and take advantage of the 24-hour rule?

Here is another scenario: Let's say you need to arrive in Asia on Monday, which means you have to leave the United States on Sunday. As we saw on the Delta tariff, the lowest published fare books in T class. Let's assume there is no T availability all the way from Salt Lake City to Hong Kong on Sunday, and you will be booked in the higher U class, which is $200 more expensive. However, if you flew from Salt Lake City and San Francisco on Saturday, and then on to Asia the next day, you will get T class all the way and would save $200. You will have to pay for accommodation in San Francisco, but you could certainly find a hotel for less than $200 – or maybe you know someone you can stay with.

By the way, you don't have to overnight specifically in San Francisco on your way to Asia – you can do it in any city between your origin and final destination included in the permitted routing of your fare. In this case, if you fly between Salt Lake City and Hong Kong on Delta, you can also choose Los Angeles, Seattle (SEA), Portland (PDX) or Tokyo.

Although most discounted international fares allow no stopovers, some do permit a free one – a real one, which could last months, if you like – on top of the 24-hour connections. On other fares, stopovers incur an additional charge. The fares from Salt Lake City to Hong Kong forbid a stopover on Delta, but not on United, whose rules say this:

> 2 STOPOVERS PERMITTED ON THE PRICING UNIT AT
> USD100.00 EACH ONLY AT THE GATEWAY
> NONE IN GUAM
> PERMITTED IN AREA 3

The "gateway" refers to the U.S. city from which you leave the United States en route to a foreign destination. In this case, that would most likely be San Francisco, from where United flies to Hong Kong nonstop. Even though you can connect in Denver, you can't remain there for more than 24 hours, because it's not your gateway. So if your first allowed stopover is in San Francisco, your second has to be in Asia (Area 3) – and it must be on the legal routing, of course. This is a great way to visit two Asian cities on the same trip, for only $100 more.

Changes and cancellations

International fares have more complex rules than domestic ones when it comes to changing or canceling a ticket. As I said in Chapter 1, the most common penalty for U.S.-originating coach tickets is currently $250. While all discounted domestic coach fares are nonrefundable, that's not the case on the international front. Some midrange international tickets can be refunded for a service charge, which can be equal to or bigger than the change fee.

Many international First and Business Class fares carry penalties, too. The heavily discounted Z and I fares in Business Class are often nonrefundable and incur a change fee of about $400. From the U.S. East coast to Europe, round-trip base fares of up to $5,000 have long fallen in that category. In recent years, however, airlines have imposed penalties even on fares as high as $10,000.

Let's take Washington-Paris and look at the two airlines operating nonstop flights between those cities, United and Air France. As I write this, they both offer round-trip Business Class base fares of about $8,000. Air France's books in D class and requires $400 for changes or cancellations. United's books in C class and slaps on a $500 penalty for cancellations and $250 for changes. On that same route, with a connection in London, British Airways charges up to $750 for changes or cancellations.

What about First Class? I'm glad you asked. How about we take a peek at Los Angeles-Sydney on United and Qantas, since the other two airlines with nonstop service on that route, Delta and V Australia, don't offer First Class service. United and Qantas both offer identical round-trip A fares of about $20,000. One might think that's enough money for an airplane seat to avoid penalties. However, one would be wrong. Both carriers charge $250 for cancellations and $200 for changes.

Just as international fares are very different depending on their origin and direction, so are their penalties. For Paris-Washington, the lowest coach fares on both United and Air France are nonrefundable and non-changeable, but for Washington-Paris, they can be changed for $250.

In Business Class for Washington-Bahrain, United has published a nonrefundable $4,800 round-trip Z fare that can be changed for $400. For Bahrain-Washington, it has a D fare of about $4,600 – refundable and changeable for free.

Another city from which Business and First Class fares are fairly low and liberal is Taipei. From there to Los Angeles, Continental has a one-way Z base fare of less than $1,300, with absolutely no restrictions. All Nippon offers a non-restrictive round-trip First Class fare – booked in full F class – for about $5,700 plus taxes.

One of the surprises when it comes to international penalties is their presence in the rules of B fares. As I said in Chapter 1, many airlines consider B to be a full-fare code. Still, some B fares cannot be changed or canceled for free – or even canceled at all.

Chapter 3 Lessons Learned

1.   ATPCO sends out feeds with international fares every hour, except for several hours on Saturday night.

2.   Discounted international fares typically stay on the market longer than discounted U.S. domestic fares – sometimes for weeks.

3.   Fares between two international cities can be very different depending on the direction.

4.   International taxes and surcharges can add between $200 and $500 to a coach ticket on average, depending on specific countries and distances.

5.   International airline tariffs typically include much longer lists of different fares than domestic ones.

6.   Discounted intercontinental fares are published as required round trips most of the time.

7.   Instead of specific published routing options, some international fares have maximum permitted mileage (MPM).

8.   On international itineraries, a stopover typically occurs when the time between connecting flights is 24 hours or more.

9.   Change and cancellation penalties on international tickets originating in the United States usually start at $250 and run up to $500, depending on the class of service and other factors.

Chapter 4

Flight Inventory

An airline tariff tells us what is possible if we comply with certain conditions, but having a published fare on the tariff doesn't necessarily mean that we can get that fare on the specific flights we want. For that, we need to consult the flight inventory – the second pillar of airline data – to see if the booking class we want is available.

By the same token, availability in a certain booking class is useless unless there is a fare on the tariff with that same code. A few years ago, I received an e-mail message from an economics professor at Colby College in Maine with a very common question. He was taking about a dozen students to Beijing on United and wanted to book the tickets in W class. Although there were W seats on his chosen flights, the computer was giving him V class, so he was confused. I looked at the United tariff at the time and found out that there was no W fare published at all – the lowest fare booked in V class.

U.S. domestic flight inventory

Seat availability changes constantly, based on airline computer models and depending on supply and demand. The domestic

tariff in Figure 2 on Page 25 was United's between Washington
and New Orleans, so let's look at the United inventory on its
three nonstop flights from Washington Dulles (IAD) on January
13, 2011 – as of 6 p.m. EST on December 11, 2010:

UA7414
IAD 12:15 p.m. – MSY 2:03 p.m.
Aircraft: CR7
F5 A5 Y9 B9 M9 E9 U9 H9 Q9 V9 W9 S2 T0 L0 K0 G0

UA477
IAD 4:45 p.m. – MSY 6:34 p.m.
Aircraft: 319
F8 A7 Y9 B9 M9 E9 U9 H9 Q9 V9 W9 S0 T0 L0 K0 G0

UA7640
IAD 10:04 p.m. – MSY11:53 p.m.
Aircraft: CR7
F6 A6 Y9 B9 M9 E9 U9 H9 Q9 V9 W9 S9 T9 L9 K9 G5

On the Washington-New Orleans United tariff, the lowest round-trip fare was LE21SFN, so we need L availability to get the $209 base price. A quick look at the inventory
shows that only the last flight for the day – at 10:04 p.m. – has
L seats left. Of course, the $209 fare will be possible only if
we find L availability on our return flight as well. Even though
the K and G fare bucket – yes, that's yet another new term –
shows 9 and 5 seats, respectively, to us they are completely
useless, because there are no K and G fares published on
the tariff.

What if we can't wait until 10:04 p.m. and want to leave at 12:15 p.m.? Then we have to pay up to an S fare, because the lower booking classes T and L show 0 seats. What does that really mean? To answer that question, we need to go back to the tariff and find the lowest S fare whose conditions we can meet. That's SE213FN, which costs $304 plus tax – or $95 more than the L fare.

Let's think more about this. We'd pay $304 if we got an S fare both on the outbound and inbound flights. But what if there were an L seat on the return? Then we'd pay half of the S and half of the L fares – $152 plus $104.50, or a total of $256.50 for the round trip. The same principle applies if the lowest available booking class on the inbound flight is higher than S – then we'd combine half of each of the two fares.

What if we have to take the 4:45 p.m. flight? The lowest available booking class is W, and on the tariff, the fare basis WE143FN has a price tag of $412. Even if we managed to get an L seat on the return – the best-case scenario – we'd still pay $206 plus $104.50, or $310.50 total. So by taking that 10:04 p.m. flight, we'd be saving at least $101.50 – again, provided there is L space on the return. If there were no L seats, the difference would be even bigger.

As with most things in life, this comes down to a choice between time and money. If you don't have time to wait until 10:04 p.m., then pay more money. If you want to save money, wait until 10:04 p.m. That's not an absolute rule, though – sometimes there is a way to get the best of both worlds, and one of this book's goals is to help you find it.

I'm often asked why we need to bother checking inventory when we can simply go to the airline's website and have it do the work. That's a good point, and if you are flying nonstop from Washington to New Orleans on a specific day, it makes sense to go straight to the airline site. I deliberately used a simple example to help you understand the mechanics of flight inventory and fare buckets while creating the minimum confusion. The real benefit of accessing inventory data is when you need to build more complex itineraries with connections, which we will discuss in the next two chapters.

Inventory management basics

As you can see from the United inventory, the maximum shown number of seats available in each fare bucket is nine, but that doesn't necessarily mean there are only nine seats left – there may be nine or 10 or 20 or even 50. When seats are sold, the respective bucket may get replenished, depending on various elements of the airline's computer model – sometimes immediately, and other times days, weeks or months later. But there is no guarantee that will happen.

While United, Delta, US Airways, Lufthansa and many other carriers show a maximum of nine seats, that's by no means a standard across the industry. American, Alaska, Turkish Airlines and others display no more than seven seats. Yet others show only four, including All Nippon, Korean Air, Asiana and many other Asian carriers. Seeing only up to four seats at a time makes it extremely difficult to estimate a flight's load. Airline agents are not supposed to give numbers of sold seats to customers, though they may give you a ballpark – they might say, for example, that the cabin is about 80 percent full. That information can be very useful if you are on an upgrade waitlist.

As I said earlier, airlines oversell flights all the time, so if you see Y2 B2 in the inventory, chances are the flight is oversold but the airline can afford to sell two more full-fare seats because there is still space in Business or First Class, and people will be moved up. We will discuss the consequences of overselling for customers in Chapter 9.

Carriers typically don't oversell First Class, though they do Business if there is a First Class cabin. As you can see in United's Washington-New Orleans inventory, the first flight for the day has five seats in F and A booking classes, which means that one seat has been sold in that six-seat cabin. How do I know the cabin's size? By looking at the aircraft type – it says CR7, a symbol for Canadair Regional Jet (CRJ-700), operated by United Express.

On the second flight, United is still selling eight seats, which is the total number of seats in First Class on the carrier's Airbus 319, so the cabin is still completely empty.

Why are the lowest coach booking classes unavailable on the first two flights on January 13, 2011? Is it because the inventory initially allocated for those buckets has been sold out? Or because it's a Thursday – a busy travel day – and United has decided that customers will be willing to pay more for those flights? Nobody knows the full and precise answer, except for United's inventory management team. I can certainly make an educated guess, but unless the people you are talking to work on that team, it might be wise not to trust them too much. Even if we knew what the flight's actual load is – many fliers try to estimate it by looking at the seat map, but that may be misleading as some passengers don't have pre-assigned seats – we still wouldn't have the entire picture.

Things get even more complicated when it comes to upgrades and award seats, and we will look at that in Chapters 13 and 14. Inventory management is the only part of the airline system I've given up on understanding fully – and possibly the only part of an airline that is a mystery to employees from other parts of the company.

International flight inventory

Let's use the Delta example from the Salt Late City-Hong Kong tariff in Figure 3 on Page 34 and look at the inventory on that route on December 30, 2010. As I said earlier, we have to connect in Tokyo and one U.S. West coast city, in order to comply with the fare rules and stay within the maximum permitted mileage (MPM) of 8,616. Below are our options, as of 8:30 p.m. on December 12, 2010, starting with the earliest departure.

Option 1: Salt Lake City-**San Francisco**-Tokyo-Hong Kong

DL4611
SLC 8:30 a.m. – SFO 9:40 a.m.
Aircraft: CR7
F8 A8 P8 Y9 B9 M9 H9 Q9 K9 L3 U1 T0

>>> connecting to >>>

DL59
SFO 12:00 p.m. – NRT 4:55 p.m. **next day**
Aircraft: 767
J9 D9 S9 I9 Y9 B9 M9 H9 Q9 K9 L3 U1 T0

>>> connecting to >>>

DL639
NRT 7:05 p.m. – HKG 11:20 p.m.
Aircraft: 747
J9 D9 S9 I9 Y9 B9 M9 H9 Q9 K9 L3 U1 T0

Option 2: Salt Lake City-**Portland**-Tokyo-Hong Kong

DL1238
SLC 8:40 a.m. – PDX 9:47 a.m.
Aircraft: 320
F9 A9 P9 Y9 B9 M9 H9 Q9 K9 L9 U9 T9

>>> connecting to >>>

DL91
PDX 12:10 p.m. – NRT 4:25 p.m. **next day**
Aircraft: 767
J9 D9 S9 I9 Y9 B9 M9 H9 Q9 K9 L9 U9 T9

>>> connecting to >>>

DL639
NRT 7:05 p.m. – HKG 11:20 p.m.
Aircraft: 747
J9 D9 S9 I9 Y9 B9 M9 H9 Q9 K9 L9 U9 T9

Option 3: Salt Lake City-**Los Angeles**-Tokyo-Hong Kong

DL4701
SLC 9:40 a.m. – LAX 10:42 a.m.
Aircraft: CR9
F9 A9 P9 Y9 B9 M9 H2 Q0 K0 L0 U0 T0

>>> connecting to >>>

DL283
LAX 12:10 p.m. – NRT 4:25 p.m. **next day**
Aircraft: 747
J9 D9 S9 I9 Y9 B9 M9 H2 Q0 K0 L0 U0 T0

>>> connecting to >>>

DL639
NRT 7:05 p.m. – HKG 11:20 p.m.
Aircraft: 747
J9 D9 S9 I9 Y9 B9 M9 H2 Q0 K0 L0 U0 T0

Option 4: Salt Lake City-**Seattle**-Tokyo-Hong Kong

DL4472
SLC 9:45 a.m. – SEA 10:56 a.m.
Aircraft: CR7
F9 A9 P9 Y9 B9 M9 H9 Q9 K9 L9 U9 T9

>>> connecting to >>>

DL295
SEA 12:45 p.m. – NRT 4:45 p.m. **next day**
Aircraft: 330
J9 D9 S9 I9 Y9 B9 M9 H9 Q9 K9 L9 U9 T9

>>> connecting to >>>

DL639
NRT 7:05 p.m. – HKG 11:20 p.m.
Aircraft: 747
J9 D9 S9 I9 Y9 B9 M9 H9 Q9 K9 L9 U9 T9

On the Delta tariff, the lowest published fare from Salt Lake City to Hong Kong was TSLHOL. So if we want to get the $970 round-trip base price, we have to take either the Portland (PDX) or Seattle (SEA) connection, since they are the only two options with T class availability.

Let's assume for a moment that transiting through San Francisco is our only option. There is one U seat left – the U base fare was $200 higher than T. What if two people are traveling together? If we put them on the same reservation, will one be booked in U and the other one is L class? No, because we will be asking for two seats at the same time, and the system will look for two seats. Since there are no two seats in the U bucket, the computer will pull them from the higher L bucket.

The only way to avoid that is to book the two passengers on separate reservations, which is a good general rule anyway. If several people are booked on the same PNR (personal name record), they have to do everything together in exactly the same way. For example, if one of them wants an upgrade, they all have to be upgraded. If there is only one seat left in First Class, none of them will get it – it will go to the next "single" passenger on the waitlist.

"Single" and "married" flights segments

You will notice that the booking-class availability on all the three connecting flights in each of the four options above is identical – in the first option, the Salt Lake City-San Francisco flight has the exact same inventory as San Francisco-Tokyo and Tokyo-Hong Kong. But let's look at it more closely. In Option 1, Tokyo-Hong Kong shows **L3 U1 T0**. In the second option, that same flight has **L9 U9 T9**. In option 3, it has **L0 U0 T0**, and in Option 4, again **L9 U9 T9**.

How can the inventory for the same flight on the same day be so different? To help us answer this question, let's look at Tokyo-Hong Kong as a standalone flight, separately and independently of the flights preceding it. Here is that inventory:

DL639
NRT 7:05 p.m. – HKG 11:20 p.m.
Aircraft: 744
J9 D9 S9 I9 Y9 B9 M9 H9 Q9 K9 L9 U9 T9

So on that particular flight, there are still plenty of seats to sell. However, when it's booked as a connection, it's influenced by those connecting to it – in other words, it's the flights from San Francisco and Los Angeles that have less availability. Since those flights have no seats in T class – and we want a "through" T fare – the presence of T class on Tokyo-Hong Kong is useless for all practical purposes.

When you book connecting flights, most airlines treat them not as "single" but as "married" segments, so they align the inventory to show identical number of available seats on all segments. Sometimes a flight's inventory as a single segment matches its availability as part of two or more married segments – but sometimes it doesn't.

Let's take a Lufthansa example from New York (JFK) to Prague (PRG) via Frankfurt (FRA) on May 26, 2011. Here is the data as of 6 p.m. on December 21, 2010.

LH405
JFK 9:40 p.m. – FRA 11:30 a.m. next day
Aircraft: 747
F7 A5 J9 C9 D9 Z9 Y9 B9 M9 H9 Q9 **V9** W0 S0 L0
>>> connecting to >>>
LH1398
FRA 4:20 p.m. – PRG 5:20 p.m.
Aircraft: 737
J9 C9 D9 Z9 Y9 B9 M9 H9 Q9 **V9** W0 U0 S0 L0 K9 T0 E0

According to this data, the lowest available booking class is V, and a look at the Lufthansa tariff from New York to Prague shows that the lowest V round-trip base fare is $965. As I mentioned in Chapter 1, the German carrier uses certain codes (U K T O) only for short-haul flights.

Now let's look at the same two flights as standalone segments.

LH405
JFK 9:4 p.m. – FRA 11:30 a.m. next day
Aircraft: 747
F7 A5 J9 C9 D9 Z9 Y9 B9 M9 H9 Q9 V9 W9 **S9** L0

LH1398
FRA 4:20 p.m. – PRG 5:20 p.m.
Aircraft: 737
J9 C9 D9 Z9 Y9 B9 M9 H9 Q9 V9 W9 U9 **S9** L0 K9 T0 E0

The lowest booking class on both flights is not V – it's S. According to the Lufthansa tariff, that's a base of $765 round trip, or $200 less than V. This is how much you'd save if you managed to book those flights as "single" – instead of "married" – segments. It wouldn't lead to "breaking" the fare in Frankfurt, because you are not stopping there, and you'd still get the $765 "through" fare. In fact, the two segments would look the same on your ticket as two separate flight coupons. You would need a multi-city booking tool to request individual segments, though not all booking systems will let you accomplish what I just described, even if they allow you to search for flights by segments.

So why is Lufthansa changing its inventory when we request "through" flights? Allocating availability for each flight segment represents the first level of inventory management. What Lufthansa has done is add another level in order to "maximize revenue," in airline lingo. In plain English, it's trying to make more money from flights that would otherwise cost less. How is it doing it? To use another industry term, by benefiting from customers' "willingness to pay."

Many airlines do this, so there is no reason to single Lufthansa out – I had to pick a carrier to illustrate the example. Some people might call the practice manipulation, while others view it simply as part of market-based pricing. The weakness of the latter argument is that this is not really pricing – airlines already benefit from free-market principles when they set their tariffs, with fares based entirely on market conditions.

Sometimes airlines tweak the inventory in the opposite direction, making available lower fare buckets on two flights if they are sold as "married," rather than "single," segments. For example, as of 8 p.m. on December 23, 2010, the lowest available booking class on United's flight from San Francisco to Seoul (ICN) on January 7, 2011, was V. However, if you originated in Washington and connected to the San Francisco-Seoul flight that day, you could get a seat in the lower W bucket on both segments.

Not all carriers manage their inventory in the manner described above. Among the exceptions is US Airways, which displays the same availability regardless of whether a flight is being offered as a separate or connecting segment, and it doesn't align the fare buckets with the same number of seats, either. Here are two connecting flights from Phoenix (PHX) to Rome (FCO) via Philadelphia (PHL) on January 7, 2011, also as of 8 p.m. on December 23, 2010:

US250
PHX 9:55 a.m. – PHL 4:35 p.m.
Aircraft: 321
F9 A9 P9 Y9 B9 M9 H9 Q9 N9 V9 W9 **L1** S0 T0 G0 K0 U0
E0 R0
>>> connecting to >>>
US718
PHL 6:25 p.m. – FCO 8:55 a.m. **next day**
Aircraft: 330
C9 D9 Z9 Y5 B5 **M4** H0 Q0 N0 V9 W9 L0 S0 T0 G0 K0 U0
E0 R0

What does this mean for booking purposes? Typically, the computer will pull seats from the fare bucket available on both flights – in this case, the M bucket. Would the price be lower if the fare is "broken"? In other words, would we pay less if we had an L fare from Phoenix to Philadelphia and an M fare from Philadelphia to Rome?

Let's compare the tariffs. First, the "through" fare: The M base fare from Phoenix to Rome was $1,645 round trip. Now let's "break" it: The L base fare from Phoenix to Philadelphia was $406 round trip, and the M fare from Philadelphia to Rome was $1,425, giving is a total of $1,831. So we are better off with the "through" fare. Sometimes, though, that may not be the case. While some systems are programmed to check whether a "broken" fare may be lower, it doesn't hurt to check that yourself.

Chapter 4 Lessons Learned

1.   An airline tariff shows what is possible if one complies with the fare rules. The flight inventory – the second pillar of airline data – shows if a particular booking class is available.

2.   Availability in a certain booking class is useless unless there is a published fare on the tariff with the same code.

3.   Seat availability changes constantly, based on airline computer models and depending on supply and demand.

4.   The real benefit of accessing inventory data lies in building more complex itineraries with connections.

5.   Accessing inventory data helps to estimate a flight's load.

6.   Some airlines allocate different inventory for flights booked as "married" segments, as opposed to "single" segments. That tactic is meant to "maximize revenue" and can result in higher prices.

Chapter 5

The Kralev Method

Now that we have covered the fundamentals of both airline tariffs and flight inventory, it's time to learn how to put them together to secure the best possible ticket prices, without relying on agents or booking websites. In other words, we are about to delve into the Kralev Method and make our own airfare "sausage." I define the method as matching tariff and inventory data to produce the ideal fare.

Let's review briefly the knowledge base we will use to master the Kralev Method. First, we learned how to access and compare all fares published by any airline on any route through the carrier's tariff. We also learned how to find and interpret the fare rules and permitted routing. Then we learned how to access and read the airlines' inventory, and how to find availability in the booking class that corresponds to the lowest fare-basis code on the tariff.

Now let the matching and "sausage-making" begin. Here are the five steps of the Kralev Method.

Identifying the lowest fare

Let's say that we need to fly from Washington to Tokyo in the first half of April 2011 for a week, with somewhat flexible dates.

We can go to ExpertFlyer or the KVS tool and request the tariffs of all airlines that publish fares on this route – all on one screen. We will get many pages of data, but the lowest fares will be at the top of the first page. In Figure 4, you can see the 20 lowest round-trip coach base fares.

Fare Basis	Airline	Base fare	Code	Effective	Expires	Min/Max
LLXUJT	AC	$648.00	L	01/10/11	04/24/11	--/6M
LLWUJT	AC	$688.00	L			
SLXUJT	AC	$698.00	S			
SLWUJT	AC	$738.00	S			
VLXEEOZ	OZ	$780.00	V	01/01/11	04/30/11	04/12M
UPRUS	CA	$810.00	U			--/2M
RECOUS	AY	$828.00	R			SU/30
SLXEEOZ	OZ	$830.00	S	01/01/11	04/30/11	04/12M
VPRUS	CA	$840.00	V			--/2M
VLPXX3M2	TK	$850.00	V	09/16/10	04/30/11	SU/3M
TLXJP2	UA	$862.00	T	01/07/11	04/24/11	--/6M
VLXJP3	CO	$862.00	V	01/07/11	04/24/11	03/6M
VLWEEOZ	OZ	$880.00	V	01/01/11	04/30/11	04/12M
ZECOUS	AY	$908.00	Z			SU/30
SLWEEOZ	OZ	$930.00	S	01/01/11	04/30/11	04/12M
VKJP3M	CA	$940.00	V	03/18/11	05/09/11	--/3M
GPRUS	CA	$960.00	G			--/3M
TLWJP2	UA	$973.00	T	01/07/11	04/24/11	--/6M
QLWJP3	CO	$973.00	Q	01/07/11	04/24/11	03/6M
OECOUS	AY	$989.00	O			SU/3M

Figure 4: Master tariff of the 20 lowest fares from Washington to Tokyo as of December 26, 2010.

Before we start comparing and analyzing, we need to keep in mind that taxes and surcharges from the United States to Asia and back will add between $300 and $400 to the base fare. As discussed in Chapter 3, the taxes may differ on each airline. So if the lowest fare on the master tariff is only $20 less than the next fare, we shouldn't ignore the slightly higher fare – in fact, after the taxes are added, that second fare may well come out lower than the first.

It's obvious from Figure 4 that Air Canada (AC) offers the best fare from Washington to Tokyo of $648 base (fare basis of LLXUJT) – actually, Air Canada has the lowest four fares. Next is Asiana (OZ) with $780, which is more than $130 higher than $648, so we can be reasonably sure that, even with the taxes, Air Canada's price will still be a better deal. This is, of course, contingent on having availability in the respective booking class on our particular travel days.

Why do we need raw airline data to find out the lowest fare? Can't we just go to Kayak.com and let the computer do the work? I created my method because most travel websites wanted me to specify dates, and then they would give me what they thought the lowest fare was on those particular dates. As we know, a major factor in determining that is the inventory on those dates. Sometimes, there would be no availability in the lowest booking class – or I wouldn't meet some of the conditions of lower fares – but those sites wouldn't tell me what those conditions were so I could comply with them. What I really wanted was to find out the lowest fare in theory on any day, and then see what I had to do to get it.

Is the fare practical and convenient?

An important point to consider when comparing Air Canada and Asiana – or any other carriers – is how a trip on either airline would be implemented in practice. It might make sense to spend a few more dollars if that would buy us more convenience and less hassle.

Let's start with the routing. Air Canada flies to both Washington and Tokyo, and we'd have to make at least one connection in Toronto (YYZ). Asiana offers service to Tokyo from its hub in Seoul, but not to Washington, so we'd have to take one of its code-share partners – most likely United – to the West Coast. This means that we'd make at least two transfers. Most people would probably prefer the single to the double connection, but if you've never been to Seoul and would like to see it for a day, this could be a good use of the 24-hour international transfer rule we discussed in Chapter 3. You could do the same in Toronto or Vancouver (YVR) on Air Canada.

The bottom line is that, if we are looking for the most direct and convenient routing with potentially the least hassle, the single connection in Toronto on Air Canada makes most sense.

Let's stray for a moment from Air Canada and Asiana and focus on two other carriers with fares in the Top 20 in Figure 4, Finnair (AY) and Turkish Airlines (TK). How practical is it to go to Tokyo via Helsinki (HEL) or Istanbul (IST)? Probably not much for most people, but if it can save you money and you have a bit more time to spare, why not? It may be worth the extra miles in your frequent-flier account, too, but more on that in Chapter 10.

One thing to keep in mind is that, while Turkish recently added Washington to its route network, Finnair only flies to New York, so you'd be adding a second connection, with a domestic code-share flight operated by American. Also, don't forget to check the respective carrier's schedule to avoid surprise inconveniences – with both Finnair and Turkish, you'd have a forced overnight in Helsinki or Istanbul on your return, because the flights from Tokyo get in too late to make the connecting flights to the United States.

Finnair frequently pops up among the airlines offering the lowest fares on many routes around the world, but that's in theory. In practice, one may never be able to use those fares without sacrificing convenience.

If convenience is our top priority and we want to fly non-stop from Washington to Tokyo, we have to take United and pay at least $862 plus taxes, or over $200 more than the lowest Air Canada fare. Actually, the Air Canada taxes are higher, so when everything is added up, the difference is $163 more on United.

As I pointed out earlier, it comes down to a choice between time and money. If you'd rather save $163, you'd have to spend a couple of extra hours flying through Toronto. By the way, All Nippon (NH) also flies nonstop from Washington to Tokyo, but its fares were not in the 20 lowest fares in Figure 4. There are, of course, other considerations when choosing the best fare, such as comfort, upgrades, frequent-flier miles and elite benefits, and we will cover those subjects in Part III.

Can we meet the fare's conditions?

We've identified the lowest fare from Washington to Tokyo – $648 with a fare basis of LLXUJT on Air Canada – and now we need to make sure we comply with its rules. This particular fare has "X" in the fare basis, so it's good only on weekdays, and if we have to fly on a weekend, LLWUJT with a "W" instead of the "X" will apply – the difference is only $40 round trip.

Next, as shown in Figure 4, both fares are valid from January 1, 2011, until April 24, 2011, so travel must begin by then, which we can do. There is no minimum-stay requirement, and the maximum stay is six months – that works for us. Looking at the other fare rules, there is a 14-day advance-purchase require-ment, and I write this in late December 2010, so that's not a problem, either. The fare also allows one stopover each way for $100.

Finding booking-class availability

Now that we are all set for the LLXUJT fare basis, we can move on to flight inventory and find seats in L booking class to secure that lowest fare. Let's aim at leaving Washington on April 5 and returning on April 12, with a single connection in Toronto in each direction. Air Canada flies only to Reagan National Airport (DCA) in Washington. Here is the inventory on our outbound flights, as of 6 p.m. EST on December 27, 2010:

```
AC303
DCA 10:00 a.m. – YYZ 11:23 a.m.
Aircraft: Embraer 175
J9 C8 D8 Z5 Y9 B9 M9 U9 H9 Q9 V9 W9 S9 T9 L9 K1 N9 A9
R3

>>> connecting to >>>

AC1
YYZ 1:15 p.m. – NRT 3:00 p.m. next day
Aircraft: Boeing 777-200LR
J9 C9 D9 Z9 Y9 B9 M9 U9 H9 Q9 V9 W9 S9 T9 L9 K0 R9
```

Looks like there is plenty of availability on both flights, and we can easily get the L fare. Now let's check our inbound flights:

```
AC2
NRT 5:00 p.m. – YYZ 3:50 p.m.
Aircraft: Boeing 777-200LR
J9 C9 D9 Z9 Y9 B9 M9 U9 H9 Q9 V9 W9 S9 T9 L9 K0 R9

>>> connecting to >>>
```

AC312
YYZ 8:45 p.m. – DCA 10:10 p.m.
Aircraft: Embraer 175
J9 C8 D8 Z7 Y9 B9 M9 U9 H9 Q9 V9 W9 S9 T9 **L9** K1 N9 A9
R6

The return looks good, too, with nine seats in L class, so our needed inventory is there, and we are ready for the final stage of the Kralev Method.

Matching tariff and inventory data

Let's review what we've done so far. We wanted to buy a round-trip ticket from Washington to Tokyo, departing on April 5, 2011, and returning a week later, on April 12, 2011. We used ExpertFlyer to identify the lowest published fare on our route by any airline – that turned out to be Air Canada, which offered a price of $648 plus tax, and it booked in L class. Then we made sure we could comply with the fare rules and allowed routing, and the proposed itinerary would be convenient and practical. Then we checked the Air Canada inventory for our dates, and L class was available both ways.

Now it's time to match the data from the airline's tariff (the fare basis LLXUJT) with the data from the inventory (the available seats in L booking class). To do that, we need a booking source, and the most natural one is the carrier's website.

I went to the Air Canada site and got what I expected – I was able to book all segments in L class, and the total price came up to $1,015, including all taxes. You can see the result in Figure 5.

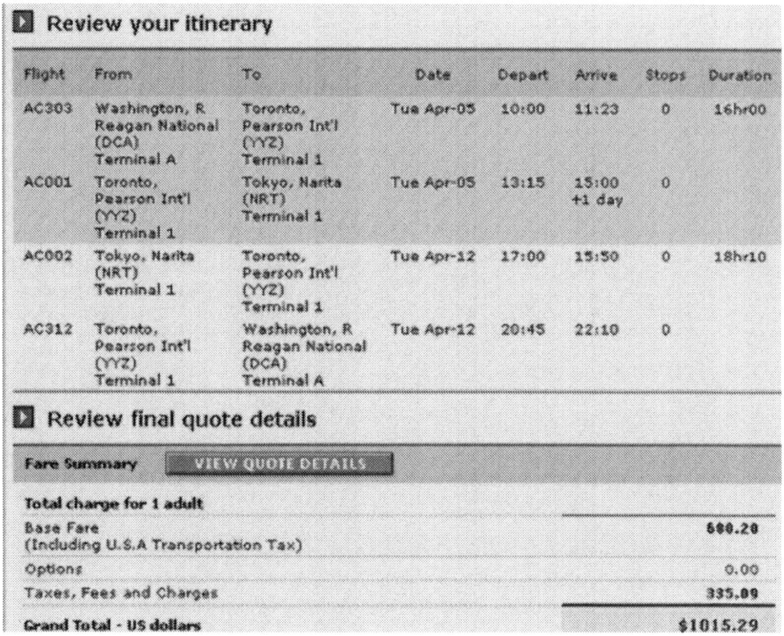

Review your itinerary

Flight	From	To	Date	Depart	Arrive	Stops	Duration
AC303	Washington, R Reagan National (DCA) Terminal A	Toronto, Pearson Int'l (YYZ) Terminal 1	Tue Apr-05	10:00	11:23	0	16hr00
AC001	Toronto, Pearson Int'l (YYZ) Terminal 1	Tokyo, Narita (NRT) Terminal 1	Tue Apr-05	13:15	15:00 +1 day	0	
AC002	Tokyo, Narita (NRT) Terminal 1	Toronto, Pearson Int'l (YYZ) Terminal 1	Tue Apr-12	17:00	15:50	0	18hr10
AC312	Toronto, Pearson Int'l (YYZ) Terminal 1	Washington, R Reagan National (DCA) Terminal A	Tue Apr-12	20:45	22:10	0	

Review final quote details

Fare Summary VIEW QUOTE DETAILS

Total charge for 1 adult	
Base Fare (Including U.S.A Transportation Tax)	680.20
Options	0.00
Taxes, Fees and Charges	335.09
Grand Total - US dollars	$1015.29

Figure 5: A screen shot from AirCanada.com, showing a round-trip itinerary and fare from Washington (DCA) to Tokyo (NRT).

Had the website given me something higher, I would have had to figure out why and make the necessary adjustments, if possible. In many cases, that involves finding and piecing together an itinerary segment by segment. If that had failed, I would have called the airline to figure out what the problem was – just a website glitch or something more serious.

What if the L buckets on our flights had been zeroed out? We'd have two options: We could reroute via Vancouver and add a segment, if we could get L seats and keep the fare low, or we could stay where we are and buy up to whatever the lowest available booking class is. If that's S class, according to the Air Canada tariff in Figure 4, the difference would be $50 more for a round trip.

Why did we need to do all this tariff-and-inventory matching? Couldn't we have gone straight to the Air Canada website or a third-party online booking engine? Wouldn't have that saved us time and given us the same result? Perhaps, but our example was deliberately simple, and there happened to be plenty of availability in the lowest booking class on our dates, because we searched for flights nearly four months in advance. Even if I get the same results through the more common ways of airfare shopping, at least I know that I'm getting the lowest possible fare.

But as you are about to see, things are much more challenging in real life, and you need to do some serious work to get the best fares.

Real-life application of the Kralev Method

As much as I recommend issuing tickets directly on airline websites, some of those sites are not always reliable when it comes to getting the best deal – so you have to force them to do it. Let me give you two examples that illustrate how the Kralev Method has saved me and others hundreds of dollars per ticket by simply having the right knowledge and skill.

Washington – Louisville

The first example is on United. In October 2010, I wanted to book a trip from Washington (DCA) to Louisville (SDF), so I went to ExpertFlyer and saw that the lowest fare – $107.09 each way – booked in S class. Once I verified that I complied with all fare rules, I moved to the flight inventory on my target dates. The only way to get from DCA to Louisville on United-operated flights is via Chicago (ORD), and I found one pair of connecting flights with S availability on the outbound and a couple of pairs on the return. Both the tariff and the inventory are shown in Figure 6.

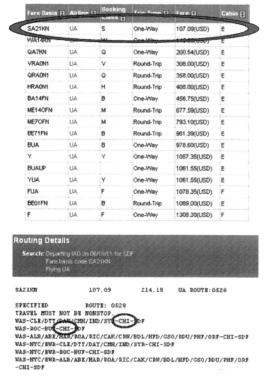

Figure 6: Screen shots from ExpertFlyer.com. The image at the top shows the United tariff between Washington, DC, and Louisville, Kentucky, as of October 25, 2010. The image in the middle shows the permitted routing. The image at the bottom shows the flight inventory on the outbound and inbound portions.

Armed with that knowledge, I went to the United website to book a ticket, expecting a base fare of $214.18 and about $40 in taxes. To my surprise, however, the lowest fare the site gave me was $563.85, as shown in Figure 7.

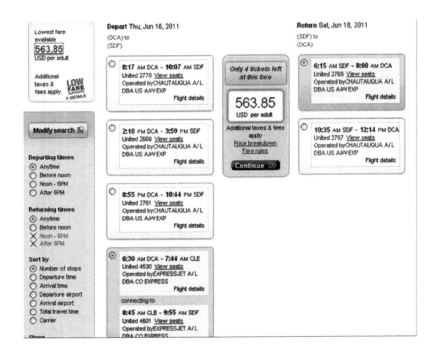

Figure 7: A screen shots from United.com. The $563.85 price at the top was offered by the website as the "lowest fare available."

No Chicago routing or true United flights were offered – instead, the only options were nonstop code-share flights operated by US Airways and code-shares via Cleveland (CLE) operated by Continental. Puzzled, I went back to ExpertFlyer to check the legal routing, and Chicago was on it, as Figure 6 indicates.

So what was the problem? Did the site try to trick me into paying more than I should have? I'm more inclined to attribute its odd behavior to software issues than a deliberate attempt to overcharge me. Whatever the reason, I knew better and wasn't going to pay more than double. The only thing I could do was force the computer to give me what I deserved by building my itinerary segment by segment, with the flights I knew had availability in S class and would hopefully price out as I wanted. The key in such cases is to use a multi-city tool, which most booking website have right next to the round-trip and one-way options.

Sure enough, after piecing them together, I got a total of $255.48, as you can see in Figure 8.

Figure 8: A screen shots from United.com. The $255.48 price at the bottom was a result of using the Kralev Method.

Washington – Punta Arenas, Chile

The second example is on American, with a more complicated trip to Punta Arenas (PUQ) in Chile, involving five connections and flights on LAN Chile, American's partner in the global Oneworld alliance.

A quick analysis of the tariff and inventory data on ExpertFlyer made it clear that the lowest fare I could get was M. The only problem was a domestic LAN flight from Punta Arenas back to Santiago (SCL) on the return, which had only full-fare Y seats available. The round-trip M base fare was $2,143, so I expected a total of about $2,500. That was a bit optimistic, given that I had a segment on a Y fare to deal with, and the challenge was to minimize the damage that segment would do on the entire ticket price.

When I asked American's website for the lowest fare, it gave me $3,801 – H class on all outbound segments, and Y class on all inbound ones, as shown in Figure 9. Every flight carried an American number, including those operated by LAN – that was precisely the reason why the fare was so high.

Why did the computer give me H class on the outbound instead of the lower M class I wanted? Looking at the inventory on ExpertFlyer, I could see no problem getting M class from Washington (DCA) to Santiago via Miami (MIA), regardless of whether the flights were on American or LAN, or American code-shares operated by LAN. The problem was the domestic LAN flight from Santiago to Punta Arenas.

When a flight is sold as a code-share by a partner carrier, its inventory is not the same as that of the actual flight sold by the operating airline. That's why the lowest available booking class from Santiago to Punta Arenas was M when booked as a "true" LAN flight, but when viewed as an American code-share number, it showed nothing lower than H class.

AA AMERICAN AIRLINES	1181	DCA Washington	Dec 25, 2010 04:50 PM	MIA Miami	Dec 25, 2010 07:40 PM	738	Economy H
AA AMERICAN AIRLINES	225	MIA Miami	Dec 25, 2010 09:15 PM	SCL Santiago	Dec 26, 2010 07:45 AM	763	Economy H
AA AMERICAN AIRLINES OPERATED BY LAN EXPRESS	7738	SCL Santiago	Dec 26, 2010 10:55 AM	PMC Puerto Montt	Dec 26, 2010 12:35 PM	320	Economy H — MODIFY
AA AMERICAN AIRLINES OPERATED BY LAN EXPRESS	7738	PMC Puerto Montt	Dec 26, 2010 01:05 PM	PUQ Punta Arenas	Dec 26, 2010 03:15 PM	320	Economy H
AA AMERICAN AIRLINES OPERATED BY LAN AIRLINES S.A.	7712	PUQ Punta Arenas	Jan 01, 2011 05:55 PM	SCL Santiago	Jan 01, 2011 09:20 PM	320	Economy Y
AA AMERICAN AIRLINES OPERATED BY LAN AIRLINES S.A.	7700	SCL Santiago	Jan 01, 2011 10:25 PM	MIA Miami	Jan 02, 2011 06:10 AM	763	Economy Y — MODIFY
AA AMERICAN AIRLINES	1054	MIA Miami	Jan 02, 2011 08:00 AM	DCA Washington	Jan 02, 2011 10:20 AM	738	Economy Y

Fare Summary ?

Average Fare per Person: Departure - 1412.00 USD   Return - 2264.00 USD

Passenger Type Used in Pricing	Adult
Departure Fare per Person	1412.00 USD
Return Fare per Person	2264.00 USD
Total Fare per Person	3676.00 USD
Additional Taxes and Fees per Person *	125.10 USD
Total Price	**3801.10 USD**

Figure 9: A screen shot from AA.com. The $3,801.10 price was offered by the American website as the lowest available fare.

As a result, even though there were available M seats on both Washington-Miami and Miami-Santiago, the American system "married" those segments with Santiago-Punta Arenas, which pushed the booking class of all segments to H. In other words, the system artificially inflated the price. If I wanted to pay less, I had to reverse that and outsmart the system. I did it by booking Santiago-Punta Arenas not as an American code-share number but as a "true" LAN flight. Now I had all outbound segments in M class, as shown in Figure 10.

Carrier	Flight Number	Departing		Arriving		Booking Code
		City	Date & Time	City	Time	
AA American Airlines	1181	WASHINGTON REAGAN	SAT 25DEC 4:50 PM	MIAMI INTERNTNL	7:40 PM	M
				Economy	Seat 20C	Food For Purchase
AA American Airlines	7661	MIAMI INTERNTNL	SAT 25DEC 9:30 PM	SANTIAGO SCL	7:55 AM	M
		OPERATED BY LAN AIRLINES S.A CHECK-IN WITH OPERATING CARRIER				
				Economy	Seat 27A	Dinner/Breakfast
✈ LAN Airlines	285	SANTIAGO SCL	SUN 26DEC 10:55 AM	PUNTA ARENAS	3:15 PM	M
		OPERATED BY ILANEXPRESS CHECK-IN WITH OPERATING CARRIER				
				Economy		
✈ LAN Airlines	990	PUNTA ARENAS	SAT 01JAN 6:05 PM	SANTIAGO SCL	9:30 PM	Y
				Economy		
AA American Airlines	7700	SANTIAGO SCL	SAT 01JAN 10:25 PM	MIAMI INTERNTNL	5:10 AM	M
		OPERATED BY LAN AIRLINES S.A CHECK-IN WITH OPERATING CARRIER				
				Economy	Seat 26L	Dinner/Breakfast
AA American Airlines	1054	MIAMI INTERNTNL	SUN 02JAN 8:00 AM	WASHINGTON REAGAN	10:20 AM	M
				Economy	Seat 17C	Food For Purchase

Receipt

PASSENGER	TICKET NUMBER	FARE-USD	TAX	TICKET TOTAL
	001	2390.00	124.90	2514.90

Payment Type: American Express		Total: $2514.90

Figure 10: A screen shot of an actual ticket booked on AA.com. The $2,514.90 price was a result of using the Kralev Method. The passenger's name, ticket number and credit card number have been erased.

I did all that while staying on the American website and booked all segments as connecting flights on the same ticket.

A similar configuration had occurred on the return, with all flights initially booked in Y class. Again, Santiago-Miami and Miami-Washington could easily be booked in M class, but Punta Arenas-Santiago had only Y seats left. So I had to split the segments – Santiago-Miami and Miami-Washington could stay "married," because they both had M availability, but Punta Arenas-Santiago had to be separated and booked as a "true" LAN flight number. Now I had a "broken" fare, combining Y and

M classes, which in this case was cheaper than the "through" fare.

As it turned out, the damage caused by the segment in Y class was minimal – I got a total of $2,514, which can be seen in the lower half of Figure 8. I often compare the Kralev Method to high science – it may take time to figure things out, but $1,300 in savings is no small feat.

By the way, in the itinerary's initial and more expensive incarnation, you can see the Santiago-Punta Arenas flight displayed as two segments. That's because it was a "direct" flight – it had two legs, with a stop in Puerto Montt (PMC). We will look more closely at the difference between "direct" and nonstop flights, as well as its significant implications, in the next chapter.

Chapter 5 Lessons Learned

1.   The Kralev Method provides a process of matching airline tariff and flight inventory data independently of automated booking systems to produce the ideal fare.

2.   The Kralev Method gives travelers the power to control the booking process from the very beginning, rather than rely on someone else's computer system.

3.   The five steps of the Kralev Method are:
   • Identifying the lowest fare.
   • Determining the fare's practicality and convenience.
   • Ability to meet the fare's conditions.
   • Finding booking-class availability.
   • Matching tariff and inventory data.

Chapter 6

Outsmarting the System

The global airline industry has had a tumultuous decade since the September 11, 2001, terrorist attacks in New York and Washington. It lost billions of dollars, went through several bankruptcies and experienced aggressive consolidation. Many carriers no longer exist. Just as the industry began to recover from the devastating losses of the early 2000s, oil prices skyrocketed in 2008, followed by the worst recession in decades. It seemed the airlines couldn't catch a break.

Understandably, they started looking for ways to increase revenues. The best-known and much-criticized method they came up with was introducing additional fees for almost everything beyond the ticket price, which used to be free, including luggage, meals, drinks, pillows, blankets and so on.

The fees, however, don't even begin to tell the whole story. The industry has also implemented various policies and practices that, while having the legitimate goal to improve airlines' bottom line, have harmed the traveling public. The main reason for that is the lack of knowledge and understanding about those practices among consumers. But even informed travelers have a hard time dealing with the current air travel system. The airlines have become very sneaky and adopted sophisticated but manipulative and less-than-honest methods to sell tickets and overcharge unsuspecting customers.

In this chapter, we will review the most widespread and harmful of those practices, some of which have existed for more than a decade but have been reinforced and expanded in recent years. They are not all bad all the time. Some of them, such as code-sharing and "direct" flights, were meant not only to help the airlines make more money, but also to offer passengers more seamless travel, with better connections and interline ticketing. Regrettably, the good intentions have given way to perversion of sorts, as is the case with "direct" flights.

In addition to marketing ploys, many airlines have resorted to refined computer models to inflate fares, which are largely unknown to the public. This chapter aims to expose them and help travelers minimize their negative effects.

Beware of "code-share" flights

I've referred to "code-share" flights several times, but they need much more attention, because passengers suffer every day from not knowing enough about this widespread practice. If you are booked on a US Airways flight number from Los Angeles (LAX) to Chicago (ORD) and go to check in with US Airways at Terminal 1, you will find out that your flight is actually operated by United, which is at Terminal 7. By the time you get there and go through all lines, your flight might have left.

Code-share flights are those operated by a carrier different from the one whose number is on your ticket. If you look closely at your itinerary, it should name the operating airline – all carriers try to do that, though some display that information more prominently than others. Another way to recognize a code-share flight is by its number – a four-digit figure is a good indication of a code-share, unless it begins with number 1.

Some airlines use four-digit numbers for their own flights, and they usually start with 1. One thing to keep in mind is that commuter flights operated by regional carriers, such as SkyWest and ExpressJet, are numbered as code-share flights, but for all practical purposes they are considered "true" flights of the network carrier for which they operate a particular flight. For example, American Eagle flights are treated as real American flights.

In the LA-Chicago case cited above, we have a United flight being marketed and sold by US Airways as its own. In fact, seven other carriers code-share United flights on the LA-Chicago route. Not surprisingly, all of them – Air New Zealand, Air China, Asiana, British Midland, Scandinavian, Turkish Airlines and Continental – are members of the Star Alliance. I can only sympathize with computer programmers and people in inventory management, who have to deal with so many airlines selling seats on the same flight in booking classes that don't always correspond to United's fare buckets.

Code-sharing is one of the practices I mentioned at the beginning of the book that have been implemented to help airlines increase revenues. Unfortunately, passengers didn't get the memo – the industry hasn't found a mechanism to educate customers, and most of them haven't taken the initiative to educate themselves, either. As a result, even though there is a silver lining about code-sharing, travelers usually experience its negative consequences.

Before we get to the silver lining, let's examine the negatives more closely. In addition to potential hassle, you may not be able to upgrade a code-share flight, and you may not receive elite-qualifying miles or bonus redeemable miles for being an elite flier. We will talk more about this in Part III.

A much bigger problem is paying for Business Class on a code-share flight and ending up in coach. In late 2009, I received an e-mail message from Lance Cygielman, a travel agent from Jackson Hole, Wyoming, who had bought Business Class tickets for clients from Chicago to Costa Rica for travel in March 2010. He purchased them from LACSA, the Central American country's national airline, which sold the flights as its own, though they were operated by United.

"When I called United [to get] seat assignments, they advised me that the tickets were not actually confirmed in Business Class," but in coach, Cygielman wrote me. "It made me look like an idiot in front of my clients." No wonder he felt that way – he could have had the same coach seats for a third of the money his clients had paid.

When Cygielman called LACSA, he was told everything was booked correctly and he shouldn't have problems with United. But United agents continued to insist that the reservation was made in Economy and refused to move up the passengers.

So what had happened? I decided to write a column about the case at the time and looked into it. The problem came from the difference in booking classes LACSA and United use. The tickets in question were booked in I class on LACSA, which is a revenue Business Class code. However, United was selling its premium cabin not as Business, but as First Class, which was peculiar, because on all other Central American routes, that cabin has long been sold as Business. When LACSA's I class converted in the United system, it did so into a coach booking code. At that point, there was nothing either airline could do, so Cygielman got a refund and rebooked the tickets in coach.

After my column ran and he filed a complaint with the Department of Transportation, LACSA realized that its code-sharing agreement with United wasn't working as it should have. Since then, it has been selling only coach tickets on those code-share flights, although United still sells First Class.

It's usually a good idea to stay away from code-share flights, though sometimes they are difficult to avoid, and some of them – especially connecting short hauls from intercontinental jaunts – are rather harmless. If I have a United ticket flying from Washington to Munich (MUC) on United and then connecting to Venice (VCE) on Lufthansa, I don't mind the short segment booked as a United code-share number. There is no difference in the miles I'll earn, and upgrading on intra-European routes rarely makes sense.

If you fully understand the implications of booking a code-share flight and know what you are doing, sometimes you could actually save money by going that route. Let's say you need to go from LA to Miami, and your preferred carrier is US Airways because of your elite status. As of January 21, 2011, the lowest fare on the US Airways tariff was $182 each way, while United was offering $79 one way. If you managed to book US Airways-operated flights with United code-share numbers, you would pay the United fare but would actually fly on US Airways.

To summarize, unless you are saving money or benefiting from a seamless connection, book a flight with the number of the airline actually operating it.

Fake "direct" flights

Did you know that hundreds of fictitious flights inhabit U.S. airline schedules every day? They don't exist in real life – just on paper, or on computers, I should say. They are meant to make more money for the airlines by tricking customers into thinking they are booking a nonstop, and perverting a practice that was actually started to make a long trip a bit easier for travelers. In fact, they spell nothing but trouble for passengers.

Those fictitious flights are labeled "direct" by the airlines, which years ago decided to rewrite the dictionary and use that term for flights that weren't nonstop but made at least one stop on the way to their final destination. Originally, those flights were operated on the same aircraft, but later a "plane change" was introduced. The U.S. Department of Transportation (DOT) has allowed the airlines to abuse the practice any way they like – something not permitted in most other countries.

In September 2010, I was returning from a trip to Boston (BOS) on United flight UA897, which the purser announced repeatedly was "a nonstop service to Washington Dulles (IAD), with continuing service to Beijing (PEK)." I immediately cringed, because there was nothing "continuing" about the two flights, except for their number. The plane I was on was a two-cabin Boeing 757 with 182 seats and arrived at gate C19 at Dulles.

The plane destined for Beijing was a three-cabin Boeing 777 with 253 seats and departed from gate C3. So the passengers connecting to Beijing did exactly what others did connecting to flight UA803 to Tokyo (NRT) at gate C1 – or any other flight for that matter. They left the first plane and walked to their new gate.

Did the Beijing-bound travelers benefit in any way from the fact that their tickets showed one Boston-Beijing "direct" flight? Absolutely not. In fact, many of them were surprised to discover they were on two separate flights. Then why does United even have that fictitious "direct" flight? Because it wants customers to think that they can fly from Boston to Beijing without the hassle of a connection – a competitive advantage no other carrier offers.

Let's say you have two options: a "direct" flight on United and two connecting flights on American via Chicago. Wouldn't you be willing to pay extra for the "direct" flight to avoid the hassle of a connection? That's exactly what United hopes you would do. In reality, both options are identical.

There is nothing that customers gain from this dishonest and deliberately deceptive practice. They actually lose. Many airlines will give you mileage credit for a "direct" flight as if it were a nonstop, which could be thousands of miles less than the two or more segments you actually fly.

Upgrading a "direct" flight can be a nightmare – not just for passengers but also for those who work in inventory management. They have to create inventory for a flight that doesn't exist and to balance the load of two separate flights on different aircraft types, with a different number of cabins and hugely different number of seats. As a result, the lowest booking classes and upgrades are often unavailable on "direct" flights.

In addition, if you have a domestic and an international segment booked as one "direct" number, the domestic flight likely won't be eligible for a complimentary elite domestic upgrade. Why? Because that domestic segment won't exist on your ticket. There is a way to break a "direct" flight into its real segments, but most agents either don't want to do it or don't know how, so be insistent if you find yourself in such a position.

Almost every international United flight has a domestic tag attached to it, but United is by no means the only U.S. airline abusing the system. All major carriers do it. According to the winter 2010-2011 schedule, Delta pretends to fly "directly" from Minneapolis (MSP) to Moscow (DME), Continental from Amsterdam (AMS) to Denver (DEN) on UA-operated codeshares, US Airways from LAX to Zurich (ZRH) and American from Tokyo (NRT) to Boston (BOS).

United and Delta are the biggest abusers, while American seems to be the most prudent in that most of its "direct" flights are operated with the same aircraft. American is also the only one whose website displays a "direct" flight as two separate segments at the very beginning of the booking process.

I've written several columns about these fake flights, and after one of them reader Steve Boress commented that "this practice is particularly troubling when an older passenger realizes they now have to navigate a strange airport and find a connecting flight they did not expect to take. Couple that with a reduction in airline staff to assist passengers in need, and it's not hard to see why airlines are viewed as villains."

In the rare cases when foreign carriers, such as Lufthansa and Singapore Airlines, operate "direct" flights, they are flown on the same plane, so there is no danger you will miss your "continuation," which happens regularly on U.S. airlines. If my flight from Boston to Washington had been late, United wouldn't have held the plane for Beijing just because the two flights share the same number. Of course, such decisions depend on many circumstances, including how many connecting passengers are on the delayed flight, but there are numerous examples of unfavorable outcomes for customers.

Case in point: At about 9 p.m. on October 6, 2008, Delta flight DL9 was over eastern Canada on its way back from Cairo (CAI). At the same time, Delta flight DL9 took off from New York (JFK) en route to Los Angeles (LAX). That same day, the "continuation" of United flight UA902 from Washington (IAD) to Munich (MUC) left two hours before the first leg even took off from Denver (DEN).

Airline	Flight	Departure	Arrival
	Flight 846 Arrived at Gate More details	Ezeiza, Argentina (EZE) Fri, Nov 26 Scheduled: 10:05 PM Actual: 11:31 PM Reason: Schedule change due to Aircraft Servicing Gate: 2	Washington, DC (IAD) Sat, Nov 27 Scheduled: 6:41 AM Actual: 7:58 AM Reason: Schedule change due to Aircraft Servicing Concourse C Gate: C5 Baggage claim: --
United	Flight 846 Arrived at Gate More details	Washington, DC (IAD) Sat, Nov 27 Scheduled: 8:10 AM Actual: 8:12 AM Reason: -- Concourse C Gate: C6	San Francisco, CA (SFO) Sat, Nov 27 Scheduled: 11:12 AM Actual: 11:29 AM Reason: -- terminal 3 concourse 1 Gate: 86

Airline	Flight	Departure	Arrival
	Flight 881 Cancelled More details	Boston, MA (BOS) Sun, Dec 12 Scheduled: 9:05 AM Actual: Flight cancelled Reason: -- Gate: --	Chicago, IL (ORD) Sun, Dec 12 Scheduled: 10:56 AM Estimated: Flight cancelled Reason: -- Gate: -- Baggage claim: --
United	Flight 881 In Flight More details	Chicago, IL (ORD) Sun, Dec 12 Scheduled: 12:06 PM Actual: 12:22 PM Reason: Schedule change due to Weather Gate: --	Narita, Japan (NRT) Mon, Dec 13 Scheduled: 4:15 PM Estimated: 4:53 PM Reason: Schedule change due to Weather Gate: -- Baggage claim: --

Figure 11: Screen shots from United.com. The first screen shows fake "direct" flight UA846. The second screen shows fake "direct" flight UA881.

Figure 11 shows the status of two fake "direct" flights. In the first screen shot, you can see that United flight UA846 was late arriving from Buenos Aires (EZE) on November 26, 2010, leaving passengers only 14 minutes to clear immigration and customs, go through security and reach their next gate. That, of course, is not humanly possible, especially at Washington Dulles – yet, the fake "continuation" of UA846 departed without waiting. Perhaps there were no connecting passengers, but you get my point. The second screen shot is self-explanatory – the first "leg" of United flight UA881 was canceled on December 12, 2010, but the second flew normally.

"Direct" flights have been around for more than two decades. But because the Department of Transportation never provided a legal definition, airlines have bent the concept to the point where the advertised benefits of "seamless travel" for passengers have all but vanished. "Somewhere along the line, airlines started using 'direct' flights for purely marketing purposes and skipped the most important part – avoiding plane changes," said Samuel Black, a frequent traveler from the San Francisco Bay area.

False fare advertising

Remember that mysterious "Twin Peaks" revelation, "The owls are not what they seem"? I'm always reminded of it when I see airfare advertising in the United States. One of its permanent features is the stipulation that fares are "each way, based on a required round-trip purchase, plus taxes and surcharges." The most logical question is: If a round trip is required, why on earth is only half of the actual base fare being advertised? Doesn't it seem that the airlines want to trick customers into thinking they will pay less than they actually do?

"Halving fares and advertising them as if you could buy one-way travel is confusing to the customer, unfair to the competition and ethically wrong," said Mike Borsetti, a frequent traveler from San Francisco. "Just like if Disney started advertising half-priced [entry] tickets that required the purchase of a similarly priced exit ticket."

In March 2011, United became the first major U.S. carrier to change its policy and advertise predominantly round-trip fares on its website – the only exceptions seemed to be last-minute weekend specials. The airline was promoting five domestic and four international sakes on its site, and they all included round-trip prices and fuel (YQ) surcharges – though some taxes and fees were excluded.

For example, a Business Class fare for a round trip from Los Angeles (LAX) to Shanghai (PVG) was shown as $3,513, while the total final price was $3,572, if booked on nonstop flights. A round-trip Business Class fare from Washington (IAD) to Rome (FCO) was displayed as $2,411, and the final price was $2,460, if purchased today on nonstop flights. As you see, the differences were not that big

At the same time, Continental and US Airways displayed some fares as round trips, but most of their advertising was still being done the old-fashioned way, as was American's and Delta's. Southwest, Alaska Airlines and Virgin America showed one-way fares but didn't require round-trip purchases.

Although the Department of Transportation has looked into the issue and called on the industry not to deliberately mislead consumers, it has done little to stop the controversial practice. Finally, In April 2011, it issued the following guidelines: "Prohibits carriers and ticket agents from advertising fares that are not the full fare and impose stringent notice requirements in connection with the advertisement of 'each-way' fares available for purchase only on a round-trip basis."

The European Union (EU), on the other hand, has been much more proactive on behalf of travelers. That's why fares in Europe are advertised with the full ticket price. Some of the European carriers that fly to the United States, such as Spain's Iberia, are honoring the EU rules globally and displaying actual full prices on their U.S. websites as well. But others, such as British Airways, Air France and Lufthansa, while observing the rules on their home turf, have given in to the pressure from their U.S. competitors and adopted the "one-way based on a round-trip purchase" policy.

In January 2011, all four above-mentioned European airlines offered the same fares from New York to London. The last three advertised $199, while Iberia showed $584, which is what the actual fare was. Singapore Airlines, also having the guts to be honest with its customers, promoted a $586 fare from New York to Frankfurt that was truly the final price.

When it comes to sales, there is another peculiar practice in the U.S. industry: Airlines often advertise "sales" prices that are higher than the lowest published, but unadvertised, fares at the time. In July 2010, United promoted $109 each way between Washington and Boston, but when I looked at the tariff, I saw $49, $54, $64, $74, $84 and $99 fares. Moreover, they all had fewer restrictions than the $109 "sales" price. That same month, the advertised fares between Denver and LA in two separate United "sales" were $99 and $89 each way. However, I found $68 each way. In addition, Denver-New Orleans was on "sale" for $123 each way, but there was also $109, and even $89.

How airlines overcharge customers

When I talked about flight inventory in Chapter 4, I mentioned the "married segments" tactic many airlines use to artificially increase fares by zeroing out lower fare buckets on connecting flights, even though those buckets have availability on the individual segments, before their "marriage." Apparently, that wasn't enough for some carriers, and they have been looking for new ways to overcharge unsuspecting customers – or, as they call it, to "maximize revenues."

In October 2010, Amadeus, the Global Distribution System (GDS) I've also mentioned before, proudly announced the launch of "Active Valuation," an "IT solution that enables airlines to maximize revenues across multiple channels." Amadeus was surprisingly open about how it will help airlines take more of your money, although it made marketing sense to point that out in order to attract airlines to sign up. Its first "Active Valuation" contracts were with some of its largest customers, including Lufthansa, Singapore

Airlines, Brazil's TAM, the United Arab Emirates' Etihad and Air Baltic.

"'Active Valuation' works by enabling the application of sophisticated business logic to dynamically adjust the yield (revenue expected) of an airline product, according to the context in which a booking is made," Amadeus said in a statement at the time. "These yield modifiers are used in a seamless manner in order to perform an origin and destination calculation. This allows a dynamic segmentation of customers, taking into consideration their characteristics, the point of sale used and any connecting flight data, in order to better capture their willingness to pay."

On one hand, Amadeus obviously deserves credit for developing a new product that will no doubt boost its business. On the other hand, "Active Valuation" sounds like a recipe for screwing consumers over – big time. How does this work? For example, if you live in the United States and want to buy a plane ticket between two European cities, you may be paying more than someone who makes the purchase in Europe. The airlines are banking on your lack of knowledge about European fares and betting on your willingness to spend more money than a European traveler, who can distinguish a good fare from a bad one.

As Amadeus pointed out, airlines have been doing similar tricks for years through their inventory management and are now simply expanding them. "For example, when a customer requests availability information for a multi-leg journey, the solution automatically considers the complete value of the trip and delivers appropriate availability information to the customer," the Madrid-based company said, in an apparent partial reference to "married segments."

How would you fight all those airline attempts to "maximize revenue"? Demand an addition to the Passengers Bill of Rights? Complain to your congressman or member of Parliament? As you might have guessed, my approach is education – learn as much as possible about what the airlines do, and about the entire air travel system, and beat them at their own game. If you don't know that something is happening, how would you know how to avoid it? The Kralev Method, of course, comes in handy in this case as well.

When fares jump on you for no reason

Airlines have gone to great lengths in recent years to encourage customers to book tickets on their websites, and that can certainly save travelers time and hassle in the event of any changes to a ticketed reservation. However, to their utter shame, many carriers haven't built reliable and user-friendly sites.

In fact, some airlines, such as Asiana, have outsourced their entire online booking process – at least in the U.S. market – to a third-party travel agency, which charges its own booking fees. Other airlines have made their sites so difficult to navigate that one needs a day off to figure out basic booking features and frequent-flier program rules. Not to mention that many, such as Qatar Airways (QR), don't display the most important element of a reservation – ticket numbers – as of January 2011.

And then there are those carriers whose sites look all modern and dandy, only to go nuts on you once you begin using them. A case in point is Air Canada's site, which went out of control when I tried to build the Washington-Tokyo example in Chapter 5.

At first, I got the $1,015 fare I quoted at the time, with L class on all four segments. After describing the process here and finishing the chapter, I returned to the site to copy the screen shot and save it in my records. However, the site canceled the pricing page automatically after 10 minutes and sent me back to the home page. So I thought I'd simply rebuild the same itinerary. To my astonishment, this time the site "broke" the fare into W and S classes, producing a total of $1,612, as shown in Figure 12 on Page 88. I checked the tariff and the inventory on ExpertFlyer to make sure nothing had changed in the past 15 minutes, and it hadn't. I also called Air Canada to verify that. There was no reason for the site's odd behavior.

I started a new search with the same parameters, and a new surprise followed. Now the booking classes were M on the outbound and L on the return, for a total of $3,795. I tried again, and this time I got a "through" M fare on the outbound and a "broken" S/W fare on the way back, for a total of $4,089.

I've always brushed off suggestions that airline websites are deliberately programmed to increase the fare if you don't buy the initial price they offer immediately and continue searching. I've been skeptical because I know how airfares work – and now you do, too. For a particular fare to change, one of two things has to happen: a change in the tariff or in the flight inventory. If they both stay the same, there is no reason for the price to jump by hundreds, or even thousands, of dollars within minutes.

So what was the Air Canada website doing? Did it remember my data and play tricks on one? I tried closing my browser and reopening it, but that didn't help. I checked back a couple of days later, and the same shenanigans repeated. Then I rebooted my computer, and I finally got the initial and proper fare of $1,015. I decided to do the same experiment again and performed three additional searches, just a couple of minutes apart. Sure enough, the fare came back higher every time: $1,612, $3,795 and $4,089.

I called Air Canada and spoke with a very polite reservations supervisor named Monalisa. At first, she thought I was doing something wrong and confirmed the $1,015 fare on her system, and also verified the tariff and the inventory, which still showed nine seats in L class. Then she went to the website and did exactly what I'd done – she was as surprised as I was to see those outlandish prices. She promised to report the problem to the appropriate department.

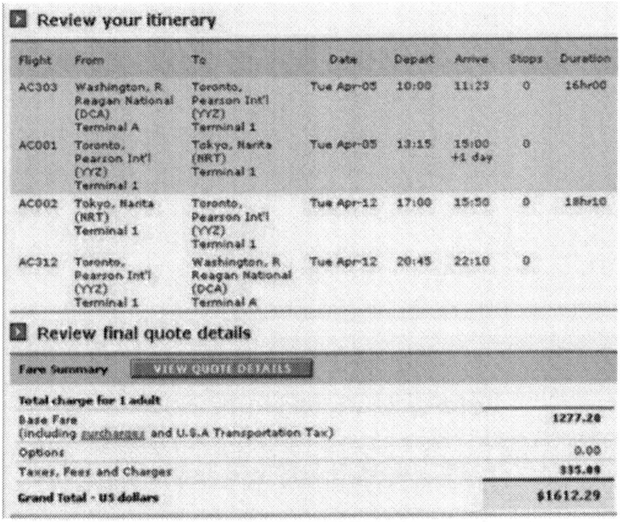

Review your itinerary

Flight	From	To	Date	Depart	Arrive	Stops	Duration
AC303	Washington, R Reagan National (DCA) Terminal A	Toronto, Pearson Int'l (YYZ) Terminal 1	Tue Apr-05	10:00	11:25	0	16hr00
AC001	Toronto, Pearson Int'l (YYZ) Terminal 1	Tokyo, Narita (NRT) Terminal 1	Tue Apr-05	13:15	15:00 +1 day	0	
AC002	Tokyo, Narita (NRT) Terminal 1	Toronto, Pearson Int'l (YYZ) Terminal 1	Tue Apr-12	17:00	15:50	0	18hr10
AC312	Toronto, Pearson Int'l (YYZ) Terminal 1	Washington, R Reagan National (DCA) Terminal A	Tue Apr-12	20:45	22:10	0	

Review final quote details

Fare Summary VIEW QUOTE DETAILS

Total charge for 1 adult	
Base Fare (including surcharges and U.S.A Transportation Tax)	1277.20
Options	0.00
Taxes, Fees and Charges	335.09
Grand Total - US dollars	$1612.29

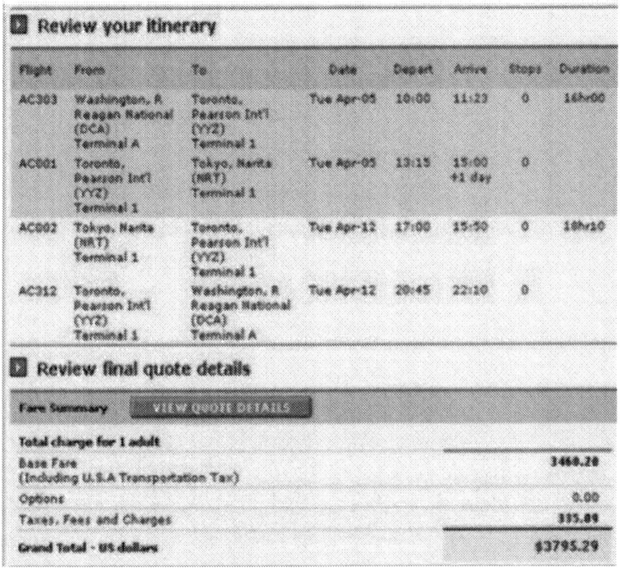

Review your itinerary

Flight	From	To	Date	Depart	Arrive	Stops	Duration
AC303	Washington, R Reagan National (DCA) Terminal A	Toronto, Pearson Int'l (YYZ) Terminal 1	Tue Apr-05	10:00	11:25	0	16hr00
AC001	Toronto, Pearson Int'l (YYZ) Terminal 1	Tokyo, Narita (NRT) Terminal 1	Tue Apr-05	13:15	15:00 +1 day	0	
AC002	Tokyo, Narita (NRT) Terminal 1	Toronto, Pearson Int'l (YYZ) Terminal 1	Tue Apr-12	17:00	15:50	0	18hr10
AC312	Toronto, Pearson Int'l (YYZ) Terminal 1	Washington, R Reagan National (DCA) Terminal A	Tue Apr-12	20:45	22:10	0	

Review final quote details

Fare Summary VIEW QUOTE DETAILS

Total charge for 1 adult	
Base Fare (Including U.S.A Transportation Tax)	3460.20
Options	0.00
Taxes, Fees and Charges	335.09
Grand Total - US dollars	$3795.29

Figure 12: Screen shots from AirCanada.com, showing by how much the website increased the fare during two searches with identical criteria, only seconds apart.

It could be just a software glitch – if deliberate, I imagine the fare difference would be more subtle than $600 or more – but it certainly looks suspicious. If Air Canada doesn't want to drive customers away and into the arms of third-party sites, such as Expedia and Travelocity – or worse, other airlines – it should offer a much more stellar booking experience on its own site.

Unreliable airline websites

The out-of-control fares weren't Air Canada's only problem. I also noticed that the penalties for changes and cancellations displayed under the priced itineraries were unusual for heavily discounted international tickets. Moreover, they never changed even as the fare kept going up. They said that the tickets were refundable for C$200, and "cancellations can be made up to 45 minutes prior to departure." Changes could be made "prior to day of departure" for US$100 each way, "plus applicable taxes and any additional fare difference." On the departure day, changes were permitted at the airport for C$100 "plus applicable taxes (no charge for fare difference) for same-day flights only."

I didn't trust what I saw, so I checked the actual fare rules on ExpertFlyer, which are published by none other than Air Canada. As I suspected, the L fare was nonrefundable, and the change fee was US$250. I went back to the carrier's website and discovered a hardly noticeable link at the bottom of the page to the proper fare rules, which matched the information on ExpertFlyer.

These were big discrepancies, and I suspected they were causing serious problems for unsuspecting customers, so I mentioned them to Monalisa. Unlike the out-of-control increases, she was aware of this one. "I've made several complaints in the last several months to the website people, but they said this wasn't a priority for them," she told me. She also explained that the rules shown on the Air Canada site are typical for domestic Canadian tickets, and they use the same template for the much more diverse international rules, instead of creating new content. If a customer who has booked a nonrefundable ticket on the website wants to cancel it, Monalisa said they will honor the incorrect rules displayed on the site.

If they haven't bothered to fix the problem by the time you read this – fixing it could actually be more expensive than refunding tickets – perhaps you could take advantage of the mistake. Just make sure to print out the rules on the carrier's website.

Similar examples can be found on many other airline websites. Delta, for instance, has put the following text on a page titled "Ticket Changes": "For travel outside the United States, the change fee is typically $250, but can vary based on location and type of fare. Changes are usually permitted only to the return portion of an international itinerary."

No issue with the first sentence, assuming travel originates in the United States. As for the second, I can't even imagine who came up with such a misguided blanket statement and why. All you need to do is read the actual rules of any international Delta fare to realize that, if any changes can be made, they are in fact allowed on both the outbound and return portions.

In March 2010, I wrote a column about the US Airways website's inability to display many itineraries, even when booked directly with the carrier, which airline officials told me at the time happened because the site didn't recognize some foreign airport codes. I thought it was an embarrassing excuse for a major airline belonging to a global alliance (Star). The officials promised to fix the problem, and to my surprise, they actually did a couple of months later. The US Airways site is still one of the less advanced in the industry, but I thought the willingness of its officials to take seriously a journalist's complaint and do something about it was rather impressive.

Airfare mistakes

Like any human activity, publishing fares in an airline tariff is prone to significant errors – a few times a year at most, which is too much for the airlines, but not enough if you ask bargain-hunting travelers. The question is, will the airline that makes a particular mistake honor it?

FlyerTalk is usually the place where I first learn about fare anomalies, though word quickly spreads on Twitter and various blogs. As helpful as that is for travelers, it also alerts the airlines and leads to the suspiciously low fares at issue being corrected. So one must react almost immediately, and while the time to book tickets is often very limited, a fare mistake could still end up costing a carrier a lot of money.

The history of honoring tickets issued at such extremely low prices in recent years is mixed. In 2007, United did honor a mistake Business Class fare from the U.S. West coast to New Zealand of about $1,600 round trip, as Alitalia had done a year earlier, when it published a base fare of $33 – instead of $3,300 – from Toronto to Cyprus, also in Business Class.

However, the tide seemed to turn in 2009. The year had barely begun when Swiss International Airlines found itself in a bind. In the middle of the holiday week, the carrier had filed a Business Class fare from Toronto to several European and Indian cities for $0 plus tax. It was available on several sites, including that of the airline. The news first spread by word of mouth but soon hit FlyerTalk, where I saw it while I was – ironically – in Switzerland. Airline spokeswoman Jacqueline Pash told me at the time that dozens of people bought tickets, paying only about $300 to $400 in taxes, in the few hours before a travel agent noticed the online posts about the fare and alerted the airline, which corrected the fare as soon as it could.

A couple of days later, Swiss canceled the issued tickets. Some travelers, however, decided to put up a fight. Arguing that the airline should bear the consequences of its mistake, a few even threatened litigation.

"I entered into a binding contract for air transportation," traveler Matthew Klint wrote in a letter to Travelocity, on whose Canadian site he'd bought a ticket to New Delhi (DEL). "Swiss' and Travelocity's efforts to modify, vary or call into question the terms of the contract more than two days after its execution is not acceptable and will be considered a material breach of contract."

Klint contacted the Canadian Transportation Agency, which asked Swiss to resolve the issue. The airline relented, agreeing to fly Klint in Business Class from Los Angeles to Zurich and on to New Delhi at no extra cost. The new routing meant that Swiss didn't have to pay Air Canada for flights between Toronto and Montreal in the original itinerary, and it worked out well for Klint, who lived in LA and had booked a separate "positioning" flight to Toronto.

Most other affected customers, however, didn't get their tickets restored or alternatives offered. Swiss agreed to honor bookings on Travelocity.ca as a Canada-based site after being contacted by the Canadian authorities, but those who used the Swiss site were out of luck. I suppose this should be another exception to my rule to book directly with an airline.

"Imagine if I had purchased a nonrefundable ticket and decided 48 hours later that I no longer wished to travel, so I called the airline and asked for my money back," Klint told me after returning from India. "Do you think they would be receptive? Of course not – they would laugh at me. It sets a dangerous precedent when an airline can unilaterally cancel a contract because they decide they no longer like the terms."

Joseph Schwieterman, a transportation expert at DePaul University in Chicago, says that airlines "usually honor" mistake fares, because the public relations "fallout makes it not worth fighting for," even though they may not be legally required to do so.

But it turns out some carriers don't care about public perceptions too much. In October 2009, British Airways published an unusually low coach fare from New York to India. The base was $40 round trip, plus a $370 fuel surcharge and $150 in taxes, with slight variations depending on the actual city pairs. So while the total $560 price was several hundred dollars less than a regular advance-purchase fare to India, it didn't seem an obvious mistake like the Swiss error.

The British fare was corrected in less than a day, but hundreds of tickets were purchased anyway. Three days later, the airline decided that a mistake had been made and unilaterally canceled all those tickets. Some of the affected travelers made a complaint to the Department of Transportation (DOT). They said they had made nonrefundable hotel and car-rental reservations and even had bought other plane tickets in conjunction with what they had thought would be their main trip to India.

DOT determined that the carrier's "unilateral cancellation" of all tickets had "caused financial harm to a large number of consumers." It also said that "all airlines should accept some responsibility for even the erroneous fares they publish. Thus, we believe that British Airways should compensate affected consumers to make them whole." However, the department's Aviation Consumer Protection Division refused to force the airline to restore the canceled tickets.

British Airways offered customers a $300 discount on new tickets to India, but it imposed strict rules. It also said it would reimburse "those passengers who necessarily incurred added airfare costs in restoring a preexisting booking or reservation from the United States to India, if that booking or reservation was abandoned as a result of making the canceled booking."

In early 2010, it was American Airlines' turn, with a rather peculiar mistake. It filed a $1,200 fare from LA to Sydney (SYD) with a coach fare basis, but it booked in First Class. Similar fares were available from other U.S. cities. Because American doesn't fly to Australia, it offered code-share flights operated by its Oneworld partner Qantas, which it would have to pay for the booked seats. Qantas had recently started flying the Airbus A380 on the route in question, and its lowest published First Class fare was about $20,000.

American spokesman Tim Smith told me at the time that the issued tickets were "in the very low three figures," and they were all canceled. Affected customers were offered several options. They could take the trip in coach or get a full refund and be reimbursed for expenses associated with the planned trips they had already incurred, such as nonrefundable hotel or rental car reservations. They could also buy new tickets in First or Business Class at about two-thirds of published fares. As a "good will gesture," American threw in $200 vouchers for future travel anywhere it flies, valid for a year.

"While we regret the error, we feel this situation clearly falls into the category of an obvious mistake that most people would view as something that is too good to be true," Smith said. American's decision was "based on precedent and procedures established by other airlines in similar incidents," he said, in an apparent reference to the British Airways case.

A more common and less painful mistake by the airlines is forgetting to include fuel (YQ) surcharges in ticket prices, which they usually honor. In November 2010, American sold tickets from New York to Europe for less than $300 round trip, apparently dropping the YQ charge.

Three weeks later, American's Oneworld partner Iberia did the same, and in another two weeks, Iberia offered fares from New York to Morocco for less than $350. Before that was corrected to $513, I did a sample Morocco booking, and the price breakdown was $180 base and $159 in taxes – both of these amounts are too small to have included fuel surcharges. In fact, when I clicked on tax breakdown, there was no mention of such a charge at all.

Chapter 6 Lessons Learned

1. "Code-share" flights are marketed and sold by one airline as its own but operated by another carrier.
2. Unless booking a flight as a "code-share" leads to saving money, it should be booked as a "true" flight number of the airline actually operating it.
3. A "direct" flight consists of two or more segments operated by the same plane.
4. A fake "direct" flight consists of two or more segments that have nothing in common but their number – they are regular connecting flights, deliberately marketed by airlines as "direct" to trick customers into thinking they would be avoiding the hassle of transfers.
5. Upgrading a "direct" flight is very difficult, because of the challenges of balancing the fictitious inventory created for such a nonexistent flight.
6. Most U.S. airlines engage in false fare advertising by promoting only half of a base fare with the stipulation, "each way, based on a required round-trip purchase, plus taxes and surcharges."
7. In addition to marketing ploys, many airlines resort to refined computer models to inflate fares, which are largely unknown to the public.
8. Some airline websites provide incorrect general information about fare rules, so it's best to check the rules of each fare basis separately.
9. Occasionally, airlines make mistakes when publishing fares, and the history of honoring tickets issued at mistake fares in recent years is mixed.

PART II

CREATING A SEAMLESS JOURNEY

Chapter 7

Between Booking and Travel

Most travelers consider all their flight-planning work done once they buy a plane ticket, and they don't think about it again until it's time to fly. In most cases, that's a recipe for trouble. There are many things that could go wrong and ruin your trip long before you arrive at the airport, and paying just a little attention and knowing how to handle those issues in advance could prevent a travel disaster.

I'm no fan of scare tactics, but I have to warn you about possible failures of the air travel system, so you can be prepared for anything. My fondest wish is for your journey to be smooth, fun and hassle-free. So here is one thing to consider: Even though you may have a ticket, if it was issued by one airline but includes a flight on another, the partner carrier may have never confirmed your seat. That doesn't happen very often, but even once is too much if it happens to you. A more likely occurrence is a schedule change that could turn your travel plans upside down.

What can you do to salvage your trip? This chapter will try to give you the answer to that question and many others, so you have the knowledge and the tools to deal with just about anything that might threaten to derail your journey.

What's a pricing record?

Let's recall the matching of airline tariff and flight inventory data we discussed in Chapter 5. The Kralev Method is not the only one to do such matching – that's how an airline reservations system produces the final fare for a particular itinerary. Once the taxes have been added, we have our full ticket price.

This is all combined in a so-called pricing record, and that is the basis on which a ticket is issued. Most of the time, the pricing record is built automatically, but occasionally it has to be done manually. Every time a ticket is reissued, a new pricing record is necessary. Here is the pricing record of a Malaysia Airlines (MH) coach round trip from Los Angeles (LAX) to Kuala Lumpur (KUL) in February 2011.

LAX MH KUL 428.50 VLLF6MUS MH LAX 428.50 VLLF6MUS NUC 857.00 END ROE 1.00 XT 5.50YC 7.00XY 5.00XA 32.60US 2.50AY 16.60MY 370.00YQ 4.50XF LAX4.50

Let's decipher this. First, we have the routing in each direction, with the airline's two-letter code between the origin and destination airports (LAX MH KUL). That's followed by the base fare and the fare basis each way ($428.50 and VLLF6MUS). Next, these fare components are added up to $857 in the so-called Neutral Unit of Construction or Neutral Unit of Currency (NUC) – if the fare is published in local currency, it's converted in this special airline currency governed by IATA, which is pegged approximately to the U.S. dollar. In this case, the fare is published in U.S. dollars, so the Rate of Exchange (ROE) is 1.00. Finally, we have a breakdown of the taxes, fees and surcharges, which I explained in Chapter 3.

Your trip-planning process shouldn't end with issuing a ticket. I'm constantly amazed by how many people still wait to get a seat assignment at check-in even when they can get one ahead of time for free – and then complain about being stuck in a middle seat or separated from their traveling companion. Even famous people do that. In 2010, actor Don Cheadle complained to NBC's Jay Leno that a certain airline, which he didn't name, hadn't "given" him and his wife seats together when they checked in at the airport on a recent trip. Why did he have to wait for the airline to give him seats? He could have selected them as soon as the reservation was made. I suppose he doesn't book his tickets, but his assistant or travel agent could have done it. How difficult is it to access a seat map these days, especially in First Class, where the Cheadles sat?

'Gardening' your reservation

As you may have discovered, sometimes there are no seats available for you to select at ticketing. That could be a result of overselling the cabin, or the only seats left may require an additional fee. Most travelers simply leave it at that, hoping for a seat on the departure day. It doesn't take much to do better than that. Whether you have no assignment or are stuck in a middle seat, chances are a decent seat will open up before your travel day, as other passengers get upgraded or cancel their reservations. All you have to do is check the seat map from time to time.

Securing a better seat is part of what I call the "gardening" of an airline reservation. Convenience and comfort are extremely important to me during a trip, and I don't like to leave anything to chance. That means there are certain things I have to do to "tend" to my bookings, so that any potential issues can be resolved in advance.

For example, I request upgrades as soon as a ticket is issued – there is no point in waiting until check-in. If my itinerary includes flights on carriers different from the ticketing airline, I call them for four reasons: to confirm that they have me on their flights; to ensure they have my frequent-flier number so I receive mileage credit; to get seat assignments, if that can't be done on their website; and to make sure they have the ticket number, because if that number wasn't transmitted, they will likely cancel my seats. That may be a rare occurrence, but it has happened to me.

In 2007, I issued a United ticket with segments on Saudi Arabian Airlines from Sharm el Sheikh, the Egyptian Red Sea resort, to Dubai via the Saudi city of Jeddah. It was a paper ticket, so I thought I had sufficient protection and didn't bother to call Saudi Arabian to verify whether it had received the ticket number from United – until the day before my flight. The Saudi carrier had no trace of me on those flights, and now the first segment was sold out. For the first and only time in my life, I was holding a worthless airline ticket. At least I didn't wait to find that out at the airport and had a day to make alternative arrangements. My only option was to buy a new electronic ticket on EgyptAir and Emirates via Cairo, and get the paper ticket refunded when I got back home.

Another part of my "gardening" is to keep an eye on my upgrade requests and get a seat in my new cabin when an upgrade clears. I also watch out for any schedule changes to my reservation – in the flight times, routing, aircraft type and seat assignments. Why aircraft type? Because different planes even on the same airline may offer different seats and comfort levels.

Changing and canceling a ticket voluntarily

We talked about domestic and international penalties when it comes to changing or canceling a ticket in Part I. Now let's look at the mechanics of those procedures.

If you need to change your **outbound flight**, your entire ticket must be re-priced based on the fare available on the day you are making the change. If the new fare is higher than the original one, you will be charged the difference plus the penalty. So if you paid $300 for a domestic ticket, and the fare now is $350, you will pay $50 plus the $150 change fee. In case the new fare is lower – say $250 – the $50 difference will be credited against the penalty and reduce the amount you need to pay to $100. A notable exception is US Airways, which will charge you the full $150, even if your new fare is hundreds of dollars lower than the original price.

Even if you want to buy up to a higher fare, most major airlines will still charge a service fee. The same rule applies if the fare for your itinerary drops and you are eligible for a voucher with the difference.

If you need to change just your **return flight** – and your fare rules allow changes after departure, which is not always the case – it might be better to wait until you've taken the outbound flight. In that case, you will only need to pay the penalty and no re-pricing is necessary – provided your original booking class is available on your new flight. If you meet these conditions but the airline agent still insists on re-pricing, ask to speak with a supervisor – or hang up and call again.

What if your original booking class isn't available? Then re-pricing will be necessary, using the lowest available booking class on the new flight. This could get messy, and three agents could give you three different quotes. It can be confusing. For example, if you have to go from an S fare up to a W, how exactly do you use the tariff? Do you take the W fare as of today, or do you go back to the W fare that was valid on the day the ticket was issued? Do you waive the advance-purchase requirements?

There is no formal industry standard and every carrier sets its own rules, but most go by the tariff as it was on the day the original ticket was purchased, except that advance-purchase rules don't apply. Agents usually consult their rate desk, because re-faring a ticket that includes a past flight often requires manual re-issuance. While those working on the rate desk are more knowledgeable than the customer-service agents, they make mistakes, too. So if you know you are right, don't give in. Having done your homework will help immensely.

If you cancel a nonrefundable ticket, do you lose its entire value? No, as along as your fare rules allow changes, and you cancel it before the first ticketed flight departs. The only part of the ticket you will lose is the penalty amount, and the rest you can use for a future ticket, which must be issued within a year of your original purchase. So if you paid $350 for a domestic ticket, you will have a so-called residual value of $200 after the $150 penalty. Is there anything you need to do? Yes, you need to make sure you keep your original receipt with the ticket number – that number will be used by an airline agent to search for your residual value in the airline's system when you are ready to book another trip.

What if your new ticket is cheaper than the amount you have left from the previous one? You won't lose the difference – it will be given to you in the form of a voucher to use for yet another ticket, within a year from the voucher's issue date. US Airways is again an exception – you would be forfeiting the difference if your new fare is lower than the original price.

Change-fee waivers

How can you avoid paying penalties for voluntary changes? By having a good reason. The first thing you need to know is that many airlines allow a 24-hour grace period to cancel your ticket for free after issuance, but only if it was booked directly with the carrier. That said, some online travel agencies like Expedia also offer penalty-free cancellations within 24 hours on most airlines, though there are a few exceptions.

If a medical problem prevents you from taking a ticketed trip, you may need to fax an airline supervisor a letter from your doctor. In most cases, you won't get your money back – what you will get is the ability to use the entire amount you paid toward a future ticket, since the change fee will be waived. Your original itinerary will be canceled, but your reservation will be "kept alive" artificially, so when you call to rebook, the agent will see the supervisor's waiver authorization.

Whether any other reasons for requesting a fee waiver will fly depends on several factors, including your story, your elite status and the supervisor you speak to. Let's say you paid $200 for a domestic ticket, but a more important international trip came up at the same time that would cost $2,000. I'd call the airline and explain to a supervisor why I need to postpone the domestic trip. Then I'd politely suggest that I'd book the new trip on the same airline if they are willing to waive my domestic ticket's change fee. Many supervisors will probably refuse to do it, but some will realize that it makes good business sense to forfeit a $150 fee in order to make $2,000.

What if the change is not a voluntary one, but the airline is responsible for it? I'm not talking about delays and cancellations on the day of travel, but about schedule changes made weeks or months in advance. In such cases, the penalty section of the fare rules usually say, "Waived for schedule changes."

Advance airline schedule changes

When it comes to working the air travel system, knowledge is power, and the lack of knowledge among travelers about their rights in the event of schedule changes makes their lives unnecessarily difficult. I don't blame them, because someone has to educate them – they just have to be willing to be educated.

How many times have you had an itinerary you barely recognized as a result of a schedule change? Before the end of 2010, I already had a dozen tickets booked for 2011, and each of them had at least one flight vanish from the respective airline's schedule. One example was a United ticket from Washington to Spokane (GEG) via San Francisco, which was issued in the fall for spring travel. A few weeks after the purchase, United axed my San Francisco-Spokane flight, and I rerouted through Seattle. Several weeks after that, the carrier discontinued its Seattle-Spokane service altogether.

What many travelers don't know is that it's up to them to decide how much they can put up with in the event of changes imposed on them. You don't have to accept the new flights on your itinerary if they are unreasonable. Almost all rebooking is done by computers. Even though airlines use sophisticated software that looks for an alternate routing to get you to your destination as close to your original arrival time as possible, machines are not humans, and sometimes they do illogical things.

So the next time an airline alters your itinerary, take a look at what other options you might have and ask an agent to put you on the flights that would minimize the inconvenience caused by the change – and don't worry about the booking class. An available seat in any booking class would do, since the rebooking is not your fault. There will be no extra charge, of course, because the change is involuntary.

You have many rights that you probably don't even suspect. After all, when you want to change a nonrefundable ticket, you pay a penalty. An involuntary schedule change puts you in the driver's seat. Did you know that most airlines allow a full refund even on nonrefundable tickets if your flight has been moved significantly? I wouldn't be surprised if you've never been offered that option. The specific requirements vary – for example, the change in either the departure or arrival time must be at least 90 minutes on American and 2 hours on United – so check with your carrier.

In addition, both American and United permit refunds if your original routing has changed. American also "allows customers to be rebooked to/from any city within an approximate 100-mile radius of the origin/destination city," according to its website.

Of course, you have to be aware of the change in order to react to it. Although most carriers try to notify passengers by e-mail, relying on them is not a good idea. It's best to log on to your account on the airline's website from time to time, and if your membership number is in your reservation, you should be able to bring up all your active bookings. There should be an indication if there has been a schedule change.

While some carriers try to notify customers as soon as the change has occurred, others wait until closer to the travel date. In 2009, US Airways spokeswoman Valerie Wunder told me that the Phoenix-based airline doesn't inform affected passengers until about a month before departure to avoid having to reissue the same tickets multiple times, in case of more changes. That makes sense for the carrier – it saves it money. I've had many tickets that underwent several schedule changes during the course of their life, and several agents, supervisors and rate-desk specialists spent a lot of time dealing with them. For a customer perspective, however, the sooner one learns about a change the better – the alternatives for rebooking may be much more limited closer to the travel date. That's particularly true with mileage tickets, which we will discuss in Chapter 14.

It's much easier to deal with schedule changes and get rebooked on the flights you want if your ticket is booked directly with an airline than through a third-party agency – online or traditional – because you are skipping the middleman. Agencies are given less leeway by the airlines and won't risk possible fines to accommodate you.

For example, United authorizes travel agencies to rebook customers only one booking class higher than the original class. So if your original flight was booked in T class, an agency can put you on a new flight if it has availability in S class, but not in W or higher. The airline itself, on the other hand, will give you the flight as long as it's selling seats in any booking class – again, at no extra charge. In theory, travel agencies can call the airline to ask for an exception, but most don't bother to do it.

A student of mine in Phoenix, Jason Carns, booked a Business Class ticket to New Zealand in the fall of 2010 for travel in the spring of 2011 on Expedia – that was before he knew me – using United ticket stock. The outbound itinerary included a United flight to San Francisco, connecting to Auckland (AKL) on Air New Zealand, United's Star Alliance partner.

In December 2010, United took the first flight off its schedule and rebooked him on an earlier flight he couldn't take. He found a better connection via Los Angeles, still on United and Air New Zealand, with availability, but Expedia still refused to reroute him – something United would have done in a second. While the Expedia agent kept him on hold for a long time, he went to the Air New Zealand website, priced out the itinerary he wanted, and got $120 less than he had originally paid. As soon as the Expedia agent came back, he asked for a refund and took care of the rest himself.

Missing a flight segment

Now a little practical theory. An airline ticket consists of flight coupons. In the old days, those were paper coupons that were detached from your booklet every time you checked in for a flight. Today, the coupons are electronic, but they work in a similar way. When you check in, the airline system looks for the correct coupon on the basis of which it issues a boarding pass.

Why is this important? Because if you miss a segment from your itinerary, the rest of your ticket is automatically voided. Many travelers have arrived at an airport thinking they are holding a seat on a certain flight, only to find out they need to buy another ticket if they want to fly.

In the summer of 2009, I wrote in my column about Michelle Renee, an author and former bank executive, who paid $586 for a ticket from Los Angeles to Melbourne, Australia on United. After flying to Melbourne (MEL), she backpacked around the country and ended up in Sydney (SYD). Her ticket had her flying back home from Melbourne, with a connection in Sydney on the same flight number (UA840), but she saw little sense in going to Melbourne only to turn around right back to Sydney. Not bothering to at least call United to check if that would be an issue, she showed up at the check-in counter in Sydney and expected to receive a boarding pass.

The agent had every right to make her buy a new one-way ticket home, but all he required was that she pay the standard $250 change fee. Instead of her gratitude, he received a thrashing by Renee in a Huffington Post blog. "I felt like I had just been cornered and robbed in an alley by a bully that looked a lot like the United counter guy," she wrote in her post.

The way Renee thought about the circumstances that day is common among travelers. Why should flying from Sydney to LA be more expensive than flying from Melbourne to Sydney to LA? Because airfares are based not on distance but on market pricing. In addition, the $250 fee applies to any change, regardless of what you are changing.

If we could get technical for a moment, let's go back to the flight coupons. When Renee tried to check in for her flight in Sydney, the system automatically looked for the next unused flight coupon of her ticket. That coupon was for the Melbourne-Sydney segment, which didn't match the flight she wanted a boarding pass for, which was Sydney-LA. When that happens, an agent has to override the computer – provided there are active flight coupons left. In Renee's case, the Melbourne-Sydney flight hadn't taken off when she tried to check in, so the Sydney-LA coupon hadn't been voided yet, and the agent was able to use it.

"I learned a lot from this lesson, especially from reading the comments on my blog [and] won't be making that travel mistake again," Renee wrote me in an e-mail message at the time.

What if you miss a segment involuntarily? A traveler wrote a post on FlyerTalk in 2010 about a United Express flight from Washington Dulles with a mechanical delay, which dragged on for so long that he decided to rent a car and drive to his destination instead. When he showed up at the airport for his return flight, he was shocked to find out that his ticket had been canceled.

Why did that happen? Even though the passenger had a boarding pass at Dulles, it wasn't scanned at the gate when the flight finally boarded and he wasn't on the manifest. For the

airline system, that meant he was a no-show, and his flight coupon was never detached from the ticket. Had he told a United
agent he was going to drive, they would have put an "I indicator"
– "I" stands for involuntary – that would have salvaged the rest
of his itinerary.

I was in a similar position in the summer of 2008, during
a crew strike at a couple of Lufthansa regional subsidiaries. I
didn't take one of my outbound flights, but an "I-indicator" saved
my return coupons.

What if you deliberately skip the last flight on your ticket?
Some travelers do that to lower their fare. Let's say you need to
fly from Houston to New York, but prices on that route are too
high. You discover that it's much cheaper to fly to Boston, so you
buy a ticket to Boston with a connection in New York, and when
you get to New York, you stay there. Your ticketed flight from
New York to Boston becomes what is known as a "throwaway
segment." That trick is prohibited by most airlines in their "conditions of carriage," but in reality it's difficult for them to enforce
the ban.

Requiring credit cards at check-in

Do you always pay for your airline tickets? If not, what would you
do if you are denied boarding unless you show the credit card
used for the purchase at check-in? It may sound unreasonable,
since many companies buy tickets for their employees with corporate cards that all of their travelers cannot possibly carry with
them. It happens often enough, however, for all of us to keep our
eyes open. Usually, there are alerts about such requirements
during the booking process, but sometimes they can be missed.

A column on this topic on my website is the most-read travel-
related article. I wrote it in Frankfurt in July 2009, on my way to
India on Lufthansa. While Lufthansa customers have reported
problems with credit cards at check-in, the carrier has no specific rules on handling such situations. "We have no official policy

that dictates a passenger needs to present the credit card at check-in," said spokesman Martin Riecken. "In some instances, if something seems suspicious, then it is possible that a passenger may be asked to produce the card."

Unlike the German carrier, Singapore Airlines has a strict blanket policy. About a month before I wrote that 2009 column, I booked a ticket to Indonesia for a colleague on the Singapore website. I was asked if I was the passenger, and when I proceeded to enter my credit card number, this message appeared on the screen: "Please note that, since you are not part of the traveling party, you will be required to sign a Letter of Indemnity (LOI) and submit it to the nearest Singapore Airlines ticket office. Please bring your credit/debit card used for this booking for verification purpose." It also said that, if I fail to comply with the requirement, the passenger "will be denied boarding."

The airline doesn't have an office in Washington, and the nearest one is in New York, which I had no plans to visit soon. At the time, however, I thought I'd be flying through Singapore before my colleague's trip and present my card and letter to an airport agent there, so I issued the ticket. My plans later changed, and my only option was to fax the paperwork to the New York office. It worked in my case, but it's up to each office whether a fax will be honored.

Some airlines don't have a blanket policy – their requirements are on a case-by-case basis, usually generated automatically by their computer systems. All carriers with such a practice cite security reasons for it, such as credit card fraud.

In my column, I wrote about Abdul Samad, a frequent traveler from New York, who bought a United ticket for a friend. When the friend tried to check in at the Atlanta airport, she was "asked to produce the card that was used" for the purchase "or buy a new ticket at current price, which was at least three times the original amount," Samad said. His friend missed her flight, although later an agent at the counter "took pity on her" and let her on the last flight for the day. "I, the credit card holder, was traveling in Asia at that time and was not contactable," Samad said. "I was really surprised to hear [about it] when I came back."

The most likely reason for his experience is not that the name on the card didn't match the one on the ticket, but that he used a discount certificate when issuing the ticket online. That has happened to me as well, even when I'm the passenger. The following message appears as part of the receipt in red letters: "The credit card used for this purchase must be available at check-in." If you purchase a ticket from an agent on the phone, they should see the same message and are supposed to read it to you and make sure you hear and understand it.

The United system doesn't let you know about the requirement until the ticket is issued. That makes the practice difficult to predict, although using an electronic discount certificate seems almost a certain bet. What you need to do in such cases is show your card to any airport agent at any time before the trip at issue, and they can remove the alert from the reservation. Don't leave the counter before they have done it. I've had agents at several airports who didn't know how to do it and had to call their support desk.

Chapter 7 Lessons Learned

1.   An airline ticket is issued on the basis of a "pricing record," which includes the base fare, taxes, fees and surcharges.

2.   The "gardening" of an airline reservation consists of checking for better seat assignments, monitoring upgrade requests and keeping an eye on possible advance airline schedule changes.

3.   When changing an outbound flight, the entire ticket must be re-priced, based on the fare available on the day the change is being made.

4.   When changing just a return flight, it might be better to wait until the outbound flight has been taken. Then no re-pricing is necessary – though any penalties still apply – provided the original booking class is available on the new flight. If it's not, re-pricing will be needed.

5.   If a nonrefundable ticket is canceled, the only part of the ticket that will be lost is the penalty amount – as along as the fare rules allow changes, and the itinerary is canceled before the first ticketed flight departs. The rest of the ticket value can be use for a future ticket.

6.   Advance airline schedule changes are planned weeks or months before departure. Irregular operations (IRROPS) are not schedule changes, as they are unplanned.

7.   In case of schedule changes, customers don't have to accept the new flights if they are unreasonable. They should look at what other options are available and ask an agent to rebook them on the flights that would minimize the inconvenience caused by the change.

8.   An airline ticket consists of flight coupons. At check-in, the airline system looks for the correct coupon on the basis of which it issues a boarding pass.

9.   If a passenger misses a segment from the ticketed itinerary, the rest of the ticket is automatically voided.

10. Some airlines occasionally require passengers to show the credit card used for the ticket purchase at check-in.

Chapter 8

The Travel-Booking Business

In late 2010, American Airlines banned Orbitz from booking seats on its flights. In early 2011, Expedia stopped selling American tickets. Within days, Delta removed its data from eight less popular sites, including Airfare.com, CheapOAir.com and OneTravel.com. Thus began a very public spat between airlines and online travel agencies – the latest battle in a much quieter war that has been going on for years.

American flights were taken off Orbitz and Expedia because the airline wanted those sites to change their data source. Instead of using Global Distribution Systems (GDS) – Sabre, Amadeus and Traveport – American insisted that its data be accessed and bookings made through its new "Direct Connect" channel. The dispute signaled the start of a significant trend in the distribution and sales of air travel products. This chapter will help you make sure you don't get caught in the crossfire and pay more than you should be for your flights.

Various trade groups and companies claim that American is trying to suppress fare transparency and comparison-shopping. But is that a fair criticism? Let's find out.

The war over airline data distribution

Why does American want that change? First, because its data distribution costs would be significantly lower than its current expenditures. Second, because its revenue would increase as a result of selling not only airfare, but additional products like priority check-in and boarding, which bring in hundreds of millions of dollars in additional annual revenue.

Why are Orbitz and Expedia resisting the change? Because they would lose revenue. Although it's not publicly known how much American has offered to pay the two sites in fees for using "Direct Connect," that amount apparently would be much lower than the kickbacks they get from Sabre. If several other airlines followed American's example, online travel agencies would see slimmer profits.

Those that stand to lose the most, of course, are the GDS companies. In January 2011, Sabre, which ironically was founded by American four decades ago, said it would remove American data from its offering in the summer. Litigation followed, but later the two companies decided to let things cool down and negotiate.

The GDS companies and their supporters, which include several trade groups, have argued that the "Direct Connect" model is bad for consumers, because it makes it more difficult to compare prices. Kevin P. Mitchell, chairman of the Business Travel Coalition (BTC), described it in January 2011 as a "threat to consumers of being denied full access to airfare and ancillary fee information and to comparison shop among competing airline offers."

But is that really the case? Let's look at the current system and then at the proposed new model.

A GDS hosts an airline's data and controls its content, delivery, display, and most of its sales. The airline gives the GDS its data in parts, but it's the GDS that in effect manufactures the airline's product. When an airline is so much dependent on a GDS, it ends up paying a high price. With all the money the industry has been losing in recent years, it was no surprise that airline executives began looking for ways to lower distribution costs.

In the meantime, technology companies, such as Farelogix and Datalex, were hard at work trying to build channels through which airlines could distribute and sell their products directly to buyers – a capability that would free them from the grip of their GDS and significantly reduce costs.

In January 2011, I visited Farelogix's main office in Miami to learn more about the company's game-changing products. Jim Davidson, the president and CEO, told me that a dozen airlines now use a "Direct Connect" channel, including American, United, US Airways, Air Canada, Lufthansa, Emirates and Singapore Airlines. So far, that direct channel has been implemented on the carriers' websites and in their reservations departments.

However, that's not where the majority of airline tickets are sold. According to Farelogix, about 60 percent of the roughly 1 billion tickets issued worldwide each year are sold through indirect channels, and virtually all of them use a GDS. The average GDS fee paid by the airlines is about $12 per ticket, or more than $7 billion a year in distribution costs, Davidson said. In contrast, Farelogix's "Direct Connect" offers a carrier the opportunity to spend only between $2 and $3 per ticket, saving about 80 percent of the current costs. Does it then surprise anyone that American wants to expand usage of its direct channel to third-party providers, such as traditional and online travel agencies?

The latest case for the Kralev Method

BTC's Mitchell said that the "independent distribution system anchored by the GDS is a successful, efficient and low-cost one," and the "managed travel community in particular has technology and business-process requirements that cannot be satisfactorily met on required scales by any other solutions currently offered in the marketplace other than by GDS."

Farelogix's Davidson agreed that the GDS system offers significant benefits and is not going anywhere anytime soon, because airlines need that system's capability to reach the vast and lucrative business market. But he predicted that the future standard will probably be a hybrid model.

Airlines don't need to outsource the "manufacturing of their products" to a GDS anymore, Davidson said. They can host their own data and do all the packaging through "Direct Connect," and then deliver their final product to the GDS, which can just display and sell it. The carriers will still have to pay GDS fees, but they would be much smaller than $12 per ticket, because the GDS function would be much more limited.

"Direct Connect" can be easily integrated into a GDS, Davidson said, with some airlines taking advantage of all current GDS functionalities, and others using only the ones they need. Not only have the GDS companies rejected that, but they have begun penalizing travel agencies and other providers that use direct channels in addition to their GDS. In turn, American has started imposing fees on GDS bookings.

If one examines the direct model closely and see how it works, which I've done, one will see that integrating "Direct Connect" properly with or in a GDS would do nothing to prevent comparison-shopping.

Interestingly, in early April, a few days after I completed this manuscript, Expedia agreed to carry American data again, using a hybrid model – it will access that data through the carrier's "Direct Connect" channel, with the help of GDS aggregation technology. Until that system can be implemented, Expedia will use the existing GDS model to display and book American flights.

There is one thing about "Direct Connect" that concerns me. Remember when I wrote about how airlines are finding new ways to overcharge unsuspecting fliers in Chapter 6? One of the direct model's features is that it allows carriers to display search results based on "who's asking," as Farelogix puts it. I fear that when they have full control of their product-making and distribution, the airlines might come up with even more ways to "maximize revenue" by taking advantage of our "willingness to pay."

In that case, you'd need a really good grasp of the Kralev Method to make sure you beat the airlines at their own game and don't leave money on the table. We all have to become more knowledgeable and sophisticated travelers if we don't want to be taken for a ride.

Finding the best booking process

What do the recent and likely future changes in airline data distribution mean for the way you search for fares and book travel? I find that there are typically three main types of booking: you know where and when you need to go; you know where but the dates are very flexible; you know when but the destination is undecided. Let's look at the best way to handle each of these scenarios.

Scenario 1: Known destination, known date

If you are looking for a simple, nonstop itinerary on specific dates, start with ITAsoftware.com or Kayak.com. ITA, which is one of Kayak's data sources, is more sophisticated, provided you know where to click. You will get a similar matrix to the ones you see on Orbitz or Expedia, but it will be more comprehensive than those sites, since they no longer carry American Airlines data. ITA has another very useful feature: It can check actual seat availability on your specific dates, or it can just tell you what the lowest fare could be in theory, without factoring in availability.

After you choose an itinerary on ITA, there will be a link at the bottom to details you can rarely find anywhere else. They include the fare basis for every segment with another link to the fare rules, the most comprehensive and accurate breakdown of taxes, fees and surcharges I've ever seen, and – even more impressively – the actual fare construction, or pricing record, of your future ticket.

Once ITA or Kayak has helped you identify the lowest fare, you can go to the respective airline's website and book a ticket. However, if the fare still seems a bit too high for you, it might be worth visiting ExpertFlyer for a quick look at the tariff for your route to make sure that what you are getting is, in fact, the best deal. If it's not, perhaps the problem is in the flight inventory, so take a peek at it and see what you can do to secure the lowest fare.

Of course, if your trip involves connections, stopovers, open jaws (arriving in one city and departing from another) and other complications – or if you need a particular booking class for upgrade purposes or mileage credit – ExpertFlyer or the KVS tool is what you need. Use the Kralev Method to construct your itinerary step by step, as suggested in Chapter 5.

Scenario 2: Known destination, unknown date

Suppose you live in Boston (BOS) and one of the places you'd like to visit in the next year is Palm Springs (PSP) – perhaps you have family or a client there, or you just always wanted to go – but the dates are entirely up to you. In that case, the best thing to do is keep an eye on Boston-Palm Springs fares and book a ticket when they hit bottom.

How do you do that? First, open a free account with FareCompare and add the Boston-Palm Springs route to your saved city pairs. You can specify an airline, if you have a preferred one, but don't specify dates. As I mentioned in Chapter 2, you can also subscribe to e-mail alerts when the fare drops.

Those alerts aren't always reliable, though, so log in to your account once a week, if possible – Tuesday through Thursday is best, as I explained earlier – and check where the fare stands. If you click on the fare details, you can see a graph of the fare's fluctuations over the past year, which will give you an idea what to expect. Another site, BingTravel, has a "price predictor" that tells you whether the fare is likely to go up or down in the next seven days, though not all routes are included.

Let's say that, after keeping track of Boston-Palm Springs fares for a month or two, you see it drop to $220 and decide that it's good enough for you. In the fare details on the "My Trips" page in your FareCompare account, it will show which airline offers it, so you can go to that carrier's website and check availability on various dates that work for you. Finding flights at the lowest fares can sometimes turn into an exercise of futility. ITA can show you a calendar with the best prices for the next month, but because it's automated, it will be looking for the most obvious connections, as well as for "married" segments, which could prevent it from finding the lowest fare you saw on FareCompare.

So what's left to do? I'd find the fare in question on the airline's tariff on ExpertFlyer or the KVS tool, read the rules and legal routing, then go to the flight inventory, dig up flights with the necessary booking-class availability and build my own itinerary. In fact, for international tickets, I'd go straight to ExpertFlyer and use this strategy from the beginning, as FareCompare's main strength are U.S. domestic fares.

Just a reminder: If you need help with this or anything else covered in the book, you are welcome to attend my seminars or request a private training session. Remember, you can get a discount equal to the full amount you paid for this book.

Scenario 3: Known date, unknown destination

In this scenario, imagine you are planning a vacation or a weekend getaway, but the price is more important to you than the destination. I'm not suggesting you go to Pittsburgh just because it's cheap – the point is that you can choose among several appealing places. If you have specific ideas, check out ITA or ExpertFlyer. If you don't, start by visiting FareCompare. In addition to the features I already mentioned, that site can produce a list of the cheapest destinations from your home airport.

Another thing you could do is bookmark the "Mileage Run Deals" forum on FlyerTalk or subscribe to e-mail alerts when new threads are posted in that forum. The people who post there usually find those deals randomly, but some of them are truly amazing – and the fact that the forum's purpose is to share good opportunities to earn many frequent-flier miles in no way diminishes their value. We will talk about how to maximize miles in Chapter 10.

There are other sites where human beings keep an eye out for fare deals, such as AirfareWatchdog. Although I've noticed that it gets some of its information from FlyerTalk, AirfareWatchdog scours the airfare landscape rather seriously and does a great job spreading the word about various deals through social media, so make sure you follow it on Twitter or Facebook. TravelZoo's weekly Top 20 list is worth subscribing to, as well.

Booking flights on third-party sites

Why do airline reservations agents usually refuse to change tickets issued by travel agencies and third-party websites, such as Expedia and Orbitz? Dealing with those companies' agents can be frustrating, and many fliers call the airlines for help directly, only to be sent back to the "original booking source."

Once the airline takes control of a ticket, it effectively releases the original booking source from its responsibilities as the issuing agent – and when the booking source loses control of the ticket, it will no longer keep track of your reservation. So if there is a schedule change, that source won't alert you, because it won't know itself that a change has affected you. In other words, the link between the booking source and the airline will be broken, and the source won't act as your agent. Instead, the airline will have to assume responsibility not only for notifying you of any changes, but also for rebooking you and reissuing your ticket.

Airlines don't want that responsibility. The reasoning they offer customers usually is that the issuing agency may not have transmitted the passenger's correct and full contact information, and they don't want to be blamed in case you weren't informed of any changes. That can be easily taken care of when the customer calls to voluntarily change a ticket, but there is a more serious reason, which airline agents almost never mention.

It comes down to money. Here is the airlines' argument: They will be happy to keep track of your reservation, notify you of schedule changes (whether they actually do is another issue), rebook you and make any other changes, if the particular fare allows them. But if this is what you want, you should book your ticket directly with them. They pay web travel agencies to display and book their flights. If you bought your Delta ticket on Orbitz, why should Delta, which is paying Orbitz, have to bear the labor and other costs of changing your ticket?

Now, Delta will charge you the $150 or $250 change fee either way, depending on your fare rules, but that's a different issue. This is about spending the time of a reservations agent – and possibly other airline employees. Delta prefers to use those employees' time and effort to help direct Delta customers, not those booking through a middleman. So don't be surprised if an airline agent declines to deal with your reservation and sends you back to Travelocity or Priceline – or wherever you booked your ticket. That other agent may not be as well-trained as an airline employee and may have a limited capacity to help you, so you should think about that before you buy a ticket.

When might an airline agent agree to help you? Most likely, after travel has begun or if you are affected by severe weather and the airline has issued a change-fee waiver. Some agents may take mercy on you if you've been battling in vain with an online agency's outsourced customer-service representatives in India or other overseas locations. As with any exceptions you want made for you, your chances of succeeding are much higher if you are an elite member of the airline's loyalty program. Just ask politely – not as if you are entitled – and ensure the agent that you understand it's your responsibility to check your reservation's status from time to time and stay informed about any schedule or other changes.

Do web agencies offer cheaper tickets?

It always amazes me how many people think they always pay less for plane tickets on third-party sites than if they book directly with an airline. Now that you understand how airfares work, you know that, if the lowest available booking class on an Air France flight is Q, and the lowest published Q fare on the tariff is $800, you'd pay $800 – regardless of where you book your ticket – with a possible small difference in taxes.

Some airlines, such as JetBlue and Virgin America, sometimes offer special fares only on their websites and don't officially publish them. In January 2011, Spain's Iberia had an incredible sale from the United States to various international destinations – for example, New York to Johannesburg (JNB) for $689 total – but it was only available on its own site. Those fares weren't listed on any GDS or ExpertFlyer, and some of them may have been mistakes, resulting from the site's dropping fuel surcharges, which we discussed in Chapter 6.

Although booking directly with the airline is a good general rule, there are a few exceptions that are limited in application but worth keeping in mind.

In general, the only meaningful way to lower fares consistently on a large scale is through negotiated discounts, which of course are determined by the airline. Those discounts may be corporate – usually given directly to large companies and organizations with millions of dollars in travel spend a year – or provided to travel agencies as an incentive to book clients on the airline's flights.

There are also travel-industry consolidators, which offer wholesale prices on specific airline and hotels. Most online agencies are hotel and rental car consolidators – but they are not airline consolidators. That's why when you price out a flight on Expedia, you get a message saying that adding a hotel room would save you money. It's not because your flight will suddenly become cheaper, but because Expedia has negotiated lower rates with various hotels.

If you only need a plane ticket, the best use of online agencies and non-booking sites like Kayak is to compare prices across airlines. Once you've identified the best deal, go to the airline's site. Hopefully, it will work better than the Air Canada site did in my Washington-Tokyo case. You'd be saving yourself potentially serious hassle, and possibly even money.

That said, there are rare occasions when you may be able to get a lower fare on Orbitz, Expedia or another similar site. Let's say that it's an hour after the 8 p.m. fare-filing feed – the last for the day – and Alaska Airlines has just taken a very low fare off its tariff. You can no longer buy that fare on the carrier's site, but for another half-hour – until the data updates – you may still be able to book it on a third-party site. In addition, such a site may sometimes drop the fuel (YQ) surcharge from the ticket price, making it hundreds of dollars cheaper. But as we saw in Chapter 6, airline websites occasionally forget to include those surcharges, too.

Something airline sites usually don't do – but web agencies do – is combining flights operated by different airlines on the same ticket, regardless of whether the carriers are partners or not. The American site will book you on fellow Oneworld members British Airways and LAN, but not on Star Alliance member United. The United site is even less flexible. Most of the time, it will let you book partner flights only if they have a United code-share number. Most major carriers have interline e-ticketing agreements with each other, but if you want to book non-partners like American and United on the same ticket, your best bet is a third-party site.

It should be noted that booking non-partner airlines on the same ticket is a double-edged sword. It may be cheaper sometimes, but missing a connection could turn into a nightmare. While in theory airlines have some responsibility in such cases, getting one carrier to rebook you for free because another's delay caused you to miss your original flight will likely be very challenging. Still, if you know what you are doing and can protect yourself in needed, there is nothing wrong in combining non-partner airlines on one ticket.

Airline consolidators

Now let's talk about actual airline consolidators. There are many out there, though those with online booking engines, such as Airfare.com, are fewer. Their main limitation is that they usually work only with certain airlines. In addition, they typically book into a special fare bucket that may be ineligible for mileage accrual and upgrades.

Remember that $1,015 Air Canada fare from Washington to Tokyo in Chapter 5? Airfare.com gave me the same flights for $890. Predictably, it didn't show me the booking class. I also priced out a United itinerary on the same route and got $1,277. Then I did the same on the United site and – surprise – it was $1,177, as shown in Figure 13.

So the Air Canada ticket was more than $100 lower, but on the same site, the United price was $100 higher. No one site should be used all the time, and it's good to know where to go under different circumstances – and knowing the intricacies of the system no doubt helps. There are plenty of lists floating on the Internet of a particular airline's consolidators, so if you are interested, check them out to get a broad idea who and where they are. But the best way to use them might be on a case-by-case basis.

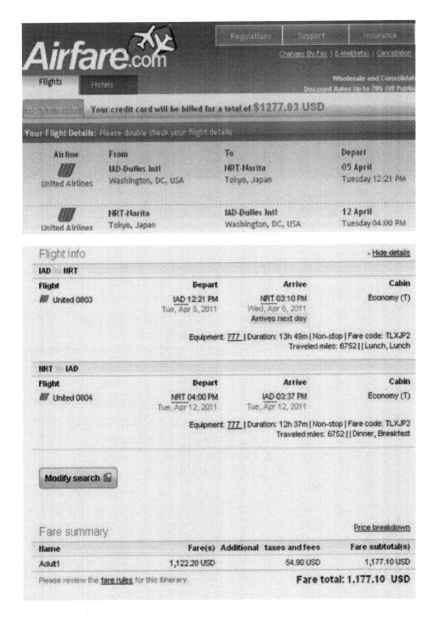

Figure 13: Screen shots from Airfare.com and United.com. The first screen shows the United fare for a coach round trip from Washington to Tokyo on Airfare.com, a consolidator. The second screen shows the fare for the exact same trip if purchased on the carrier's website.

The problem with travel agencies

When was the last time you used a travel agent? Perhaps you don't even remember the time when that was the only practical way to book a trip. While many consumers today book their own travel, using travel agencies is still quite prevalent in the corporate world. However, most business travelers I know are unhappy with their company's travel agency. It's clear the current system isn't working well anymore for a variety of reasons. Without taking sides, let's look at those reasons from the perspective of travel agencies and their customers.

If you are a traveler – for work or pleasure – you probably have at least one of the following problems with travel agents:

- They don't always offer you the lowest fares or best itineraries;
- They only book tickets and leave the rest to you;
- They know little, if anything, about frequent-flier programs, elite status, miles and upgrades;
- They are not familiar with on-board products and don't know which airlines have flat beds in Business Class;
- They don't travel frequently, if at all, but sit in an office and rely on computers to tell them what to do;
- They are inflexible when schedule changes affect your tickets;
- They don't take care of all your travel needs.

As the air travel system has become more complex and customer-unfriendly in recent years, the needs of the modern traveler have grown and diversified enormously. The traditional travel agency model has so far survived the Internet threat, but its relevance has diminished significantly, because it hasn't caught up with the changes in travelers' needs and demands.

Booking a ticket is no longer even close to enough. You have to be able to compare fares and products of different airlines and alliances, and to offer your customers the options that provide the best combination of price, comfort, convenience, maximizing frequent-flier miles, progress toward elite status, best upgrade opportunities and the most effective use of elite benefits.

For this to happen, you need a wealth of knowledge, which most travel agents don't have. For example, you need to know what booking classes are eligible for upgrades and which don't earn miles. It's certainly unreasonable to expect one person to be familiar with each airline's requirements, but there are ways to deal with that – an agency can have employees or teams specializing in the different alliances or groups of carriers.

Probably the two most important and consequential weaknesses of the agency model are its use of limited data and booking sources (often just one GDS) and its almost exclusive reliance on automated systems to do all the work. If you've reached this part of the book, you already know more than the average travel agent – and you realize why those two weaknesses result in millions of customers paying much more than they could be. Automation is no doubt vital for the travel-booking process, but given the intricacies of airfares and the tricks airlines have adopted to "maximize revenues," sometimes we need to rely more on our brains than on machines.

For years, I've been booking tickets for friends and colleagues, who usually come to me because the fares they find through both traditional and online travel agencies are too high. Using what are considered unconventional methods I've learned from my own experience, I've saved them thousands of dollars.

Let me give you two examples. The first is from 2009, when two colleagues had to go from Washington to Mongolia at a week's notice, and the lowest round-trip Business Class fare available through any booking source was $8,700 per person. In just a few minutes, I saved them almost $5,000 each. In 2010, three friends had only three days to arrange a trip from Washington to Tahiti. A travel agent had quoted them a last-minute coach round-trip fare of about $5,000, so they asked me to help. I got them tickets for about $2,300 each. So some serious money is at stake here, though those large amounts by no means fill my entire record – sometimes, the savings would be several hundred dollars, but that's still pretty good for most people, and I've had no complaints.

One other thing to keep in mind when dealing with a travel agency is whether it has contracts with specific airlines. Airline commissions were discontinued years ago, but large agencies still have contracts. How does that affect you? The purpose of those contracts, of course, is to encourage agencies to send more business to the respective carrier. If your agency receives its biggest commission from American Airlines, it might book you on American even if Delta has a lower fare.

Now let's look at the above-described picture from a travel agency's perspective. Most agencies don't have the pull of American Express and Carlson Wagonlit, and they don't receive airline commissions. They do get GDS kickbacks, as well as transaction fees for provided services directly from clients – about $35 on average. For what you pay them, they have decided that it's not worth more than several minutes of an agent's time to work on booking you a ticket. Then how do you expect them to do more than letting the computer do all the work? Would you pay them more to take care of your upgrade and other needs? I suppose it depends on whether you trust that agent to do a good job. There is no point in paying for something that you later have to fix yourself.

So what's the solution? Should everyone stop using travel agencies? Of course not – they do have a place in the travel industry. Many companies simply can't handle their travel volume without outside professional help. At the same time, the gap between agency services and travelers' needs keeps widening.

One solution could be for agencies to have teams dedicated to high-end, high-demand executives, who are willing to pay more for additional services. Some large agencies already have such teams, but their tasks usually don't include creative ways to save on airfare or any of the frequent-flier services described above.

There is another solution, which was suggested to me by – ironically – travel agency owners. They shared my observation about the gap between what they do and what their clients want, and urged me to bridge it. How? First, by educating their clients in seminars and private training how to do for themselves what the agencies don't offer. Clients who don't have the time or patience to learn can ask me to provide those additional services to them.

As it happened, I was already doing that for myself and a small number of other people. When I book a ticket, trying to beat the computer and find a lower fare is only the first thing I do. Keeping in mind travelers' frequent-flier particulars, I try to maximize the mileage they will earn to bring them closer to achieving or maintaining elite status. I also take care of upgrades – if they are unavailable at the time of booking, I determine the upgrade chances and select flights on which those chances are higher. I keep an eye on any schedule changes, and if travelers are stuck in bad seats, I monitor the seat maps and move them to better seats when they open up, which is always the case as other passengers change plans or get upgraded.

On the travel day, I track where the aircraft assigned to my people's flights are coming from, and in case of delays or cancellations, I try to rebook them before they head to the airport. I also give them tips about how to navigate the airport more easily – which security checkpoint to avoid and which business lounge to visit, if there is more than one.

So to bridge the gap and fill the void this chapter in about, I started a company, Kralev International LLC, which now offers these services, along with training and consulting. As one of my clients says, we can do your homework if you don't have time to do it yourself.

Mind the fees, please

I've already mentioned airline fees several times, but they deserve more attention. They have mushroomed in recent years, and the industry seems to come up with new ones all the time. Why wouldn't it, when it makes billions of dollars a year in so-called ancillary revenues?

There are fees you must pay – unless you are exempt from them because of your elite status, full-fare ticket or an airline co-branded credit card – and there are fees you don't have to pay if you don't want to, such as those for priority boarding or seating.

Let's first look at the non-elective fees. All airlines charge for booking a ticket with an agent on the phone and at the airport, though top-tier elite fliers are usually exempt. Those fees are as much as $30 in the United States. While in the U.S. market there are generally no booking fees on airline websites – except for Spirit – that's not the case in Europe.

In fact, the same carrier may have difference policies in different countries. Lufthansa has no booking fees on its U.S. website, and a $20 phone fee. But here is what its German site says: "The level of charge is based on the destination, i.e. for continental flights (Europe including Germany), there is a charge of €10 for a booking made online at lufthansa.com, whilst a €15 charge is made for intercontinental flights. The ticket service charge is reduced by €20-€30 for online bookings compared with bookings made by telephone or at a ticket counter. The level of the ticket service charge can also vary depending on the market or point of sale."

Except for Southwest Airlines and JetBlue, all U.S. carriers now charge extra for all checked luggage on domestic flights, usually $25 for the first bag and $35 for the second. Southwest allows two free bags and JetBlue one. Spirit Airlines sank to a new low in 2010 by charging for certain carry-ons. Most airlines also want more money for certain seats on the plane, such as those in the first few coach rows or in exit rows.

Then there are those that have imposed additional fees simply for selecting a seat – any seat – in advance. Those carriers include Air Canada, AirTran, Allegiant, Continental, Spirit and US Airways. I should note that many low-cost airlines around the world don't allow advance seat assignments at all, and even major carriers like Lufthansa and Austrian Airlines don't offer pre-assigned seating in coach on short-haul flights.

Many airlines waive those charges on full-fare tickets, but generally the best way to avoid them is to have elite status. We'll talk about how to do that in Chapter 12.

Now let's move on to fees you don't have to pay, such as those for pillows and blankets, which were introduced in the U.S. market by American ($8), JetBlue ($7), Allegiant ($15), US Airways ($7) and Virgin America ($12). American and United offer priority check-in and boarding for an extra fee, as well as the opportunity to double or triple the frequent-flier miles you earn for your trip.

Websites like SmarterTravel and FareCompare have comprehensive guides to various airline fees, which can change without notice.

U.S. domestic First Class

One doesn't hear many good things about domestic First Class these days. There is no trace of the luxury and glamour of decades past – in fact, some airlines now use plastic cups instead of glasses, serve meals without tablecloths and offer no entertainment at all, even on five-hour flights. Still, most travelers agree that even bad First Class is better than coach. Who can argue with that, given the current state of coach cabins?

What about the front cabin's name? Shouldn't the First Class designation be reserved for international First Class – the cabin that's better than Business Class? How could one possibly equalize the two? Every time I mention this to airline employees, they tell me it's a legacy thing – domestic First Class existed long before Business Class was invented, and Americans are used to it. It's no secret that U.S. carriers are resistant to change, but why not have Economy and Business on two-cabin planes, and First Class only on three-cabin aircraft? After all, that's exactly the arrangement on international flights, following accepted practice around the world.

But this is not just about the name. It can get confusing when booking tickets. All you need to do is take a look at flight inventory for different airlines. Virgin America (VX), which has the best premium cabin in the U.S. market, calls it First Class, but it sells it as Business, using J, C, D and I booking classes. Pre-merger Continental (CO) and AirTran (FL) mix booking codes for First and Business in the same cabin – Continental offers F, C, D and Z buckets, while AirTran has A, J and D.

It gets really confusing on those fake "direct" flights I wrote about in Chapter 6. As I said, most United international flights have a domestic tag, which means that the tag's fare buckets have to match the international inventory. International flights have three cabins and domestic only two. So how do you align them? By selling the single premium cabin on the domestic tag as two cabins – both Business and First Class. Here is the inventory for two United flights from Seattle (SEA) to Washington (IAD) on February 6, 2011, as of three days before departure. The first flight has two cabins and regular domestic inventory – First Class (F and A booking classes) and coach.

UA260
SEA 1:28 p.m. – IAD 9:16 p.m.
Aircraft: 320
F5 A5 Y9 B9 M9 E9 U9 H9 Q9 V9 W9 S9 T9 L9 K9 G9

The second flight is flown on the same aircraft type (Airbus 320), which of course also has two cabins. However, as you can see below, the inventory shows three cabins – First (F A), Business (J C D Z) and Economy. Why? Because this is the domestic tag of UA916 from Washington (IAD) to Frankfurt (FRA). As you might have guessed, United sells Seattle-Frankfurt as a "direct" flight, so it has to align the inventory artificially and create a fictitious third cabin on the two-cabin Seattle-Washington segment.

UA916
SEA 7:22 a.m. – IAD 3:14 p.m.
Aircraft: 320
F5 A5 J5 C5 D5 Z5 Y9 B9 M9 E9 U9 H9 Q9 V9 W9 S9 T9 L9
K9 G9

American Airlines, the only other U.S. carrier to operate three-cabin planes, usually has just one fake "direct" intercontinental flight on its schedule – Tokyo (NRT) to Chicago (ORD) to Boston (BOS). It allocates its inventory differently from United on the domestic segment. Instead of creating a fictitious third cabin, it sells it as any other two-cabin domestic flight.

Delta has plenty of fake "direct" flights, and it handles its inventory differently from American and United. On stand-alone domestic flights, it sells the front cabin as First Class, but on those that are domestic tags of intercontinental "direct" flights and have international numbers, it sells it as Business Class. For example, out of five daily flights from Miami (MIA) to New York (JFK), two have Business and three have First Class.

Wouldn't it make more sense and be less confusing if there were Business Class on all flights?

Chapter 8 Lessons Learned

1.   A GDS hosts an airline's data and controls its content, delivery, display, and most of its sales. The airline gives the GDS its data in parts, but it's the GDS that in effect manufactures the airline's product.

2.   According to Farelogix, a technology company, airlines incur more than $7 billion a year in distribution costs through the GDS model.

3.   An airline's "Direct Connect" channel allows it to control its data distribution and customize its products based on "who's asking."

4.   Farelogix's "Direct Connect" offers a carrier the opportunity to spend only between $2 and $3 per ticket, saving about 80 percent of the current costs.

5.   A hybrid model may be the future of airline data distribution. Carriers can host their own data and do all the packaging through "Direct Connect," and then deliver their final product to the GDS, which can just display and sell it.

6.   A good grasp of the Kralev Method will ensure that customers are not caught in the crossfire of any disputes between airlines and data distributors, so they don't leave money on the table.

7.   Airline reservations agents usually refuse to change tickets issued by travel agencies and third-party websites. Once the airline takes control of a ticket, it effectively releases the original booking source from its responsibilities as the issuing agent.

8.   Booking directly with an airline is a good general rule, except when a customer can use a negotiated discount, an consolidators or when buying an airfare-and-hotel package.

9.   Probably the two most important and consequential weaknesses of the traditional agency model are its use of limited data and booking sources (often just one GDS) and its almost exclusive reliance on automated systems to do all the work.

10. Except for Southwest Airlines and JetBlue, all U.S. carriers now charge extra for all checked luggage on domestic flights, usually $25 for the first bag and $35 for the second

11. Labeling the only premium cabin on U.S. domestic flights operated by two-cabin aircraft First Class instead of Business creates confusion and a series of problems.

Chapter 9

The Travel Day

So many people have come to dread their travel day that you have to wonder what happened to the time when flying was among the best experiences of one's life. For some of us, that is still the case, but now we have to work to make air travel more comfortable and less of a hassle. As with airfares, we need to know the system well in order to make it work to our advantage.

Dealing with delays and cancellations is one of the worst parts of the travel experience – it has the potential to ruin a trip, and to turn a customer against an airline. I often feel sorry for passengers waiting in long lines at the airport to speak with an agent, only to be offered terrible options, if any, in the end. I wish they knew better.

As much as I'd rather not remember, once I was one of those travelers. Now I know from experience that most agents wait for their computers to tell them what to do, without applying the slightest effort to find creative solutions to our problems. I've had agents tell me there weren't any available seats to my destination for two days, but when I got online and put my brain to basic use, I found seats on less obvious flights that most likely hadn't come up on the agents' computer screens.

So let's see how we can make the travel day a less stressful, more pleasant and even memorable experience.

Predicting delays and cancellations

Do you wait until you get to the airport to find out that your flight has been delayed or canceled? You'd be much better off if you are a proactive flier and learn how to predict disruptions, so you can get rebooked before anyone else on your flight, with a minimum impact on your travel plans. Although there is no guarantee that your prediction success rate will be 100 percent, because airlines often swap aircraft, the method I've adopted works most of the time. It's actually rather simple: I track the planes assigned to my flights by matching arrival and departure gates. Continental makes it even easier by providing the most advanced data in the industry, but more on that later.

Here is one recent example: The aircraft for one of my United flights from Washington to San Francisco came from São Paulo, Brazil (GRU). Had the flight from Sao Paulo been late, I would have known hours in advance, which would have allowed me to get rebooked on the phone before even leaving home. Why do you need to waste time tracking planes and matching gates, when airlines usually send e-mail and phone alerts in case of delays and cancellations? Unfortunately, those systems often fail.

United passenger Tamar Abrams wrote in a Huffington Post blog in October 2010 about being surprised to discover upon arrival at the Singapore (SIN) airport that her flight to Tokyo (NRT) had been canceled. She later told me she had problems getting rebooked by an airport agent, and I suggested that she didn't have to put herself in that agent's hands. In fact, she could have known about the cancellation about 12 hours earlier, before she had gone to bed, because her plane didn't make it to Singapore from Tokyo the previous night. How did I know? The plane was a Boeing 777, which is the only such United aircraft arriving in Singapore daily, and it comes from Tokyo.

Was it Abrams' responsibility to track her plane and predict the cancellation? No, but it would have helped her a lot and saved her hassle and an unpleasant experience. United usually contacts passengers regarding flight disruptions if it has their contact information, though Abrams said she didn't get notified in advance.

Even when the airline alert systems do work, I find that I'm often ahead of them, because they can take too long to update their systems. If I see that UA952 from Washington to Frankfurt is four hours late, I know immediately that the return UA953 will be delayed, too. But I've seen United take hours to reflect that in its system, perhaps hoping that the plane will make up time in the air. That can be a valid reason, as can be the possibility that another aircraft may be found to replace the delayed one

So why am I so sure UA953 won't depart on time if UA952 is four hours late? There is only one United Boeing 767 flying to Frankfurt daily, and it operates both UA952 and UA953, which leaves no room for aircraft substitution. In addition, the turn-around time for that plane on the ground in Frankfurt is less than two hours, so there is no way the plane will leave Frankfurt on time after arriving from Washington four hours late. True, United could decide to put a Boeing 777 on that flight, but then it has to cancel that plane's originally scheduled flight, which makes such a scenario very unlikely.

Knowing the type of aircraft assigned to your flight would make the gate-matching exercise much faster, especially at a hub like Washington Dulles or Chicago O'Hare (ORD). To make it even easier, you can use your departing airport's website, which will display all arriving flights in a certain time frame with their gates on the same page. If you know your flight leaves from Gate 72 at LAX, save yourself time by going to the LAX website, rather than the United site.

What about aircraft replacement? That's another reason to do your homework. That flight from Washington to San Francisco I mentioned earlier was scheduled to be operated on a Boeing 767 – with a domestic seat configuration, which means two cabins and those utterly unimpressive domestic First Class seats. As soon as I learned my plane was coming from São Paulo, I knew there had been a swap to an internationally configured, three-cabin Boeing 777, so I'd sit in a much more comfortable Business Class seat. Since the substitution changed seat assignments, I quickly logged in and grabbed my favorite seat in the Business cabin.

All major U.S. carriers' websites show gate information, but Continental beats them all to the punch by displaying much more valuable data – it actually shows the tail number of the specific aircraft assigned to your flight and tells you where it's coming from, including the inbound flight's number. For instance, if you flew from Newark (EWR) to Berlin (TXL) on CO96 on October 5, 2010, your Boeing 767's tail number was N158CO, and it's coming from Zurich (ZRH) as CO79. Right next to that information on the Continental site is a link to the real-time status of that flight

Continental goes even further, offering descriptions of beverage and meal services for that particular flight, as well as data on in-seat power, entertainment, aircraft features and seat configuration. This is a great example of a customer-friendly policy, which I hope the merged United will adopt on its website. In fact, all airlines should provide that information – it would certainly make our lives much easier.

Handling disruptions and rebooking flights

It's part of today's airline reality that employees care little for non-elite customers, and I've seen many of them mistreated and not being offered the flight protections they deserve. But I thought that elites get better treatment by default. Naturally, I was very disappointed when I first became a top elite flier more than a decade ago. While in many areas the benefits are significant and truly meaningful, as we will see in Chapter 12, when it comes to rebooking on the day of travel, few agents go the extra mile, beyond what their automated system tells them – unless you take the initiative and propose a solution.

This is the key for me: No matter how high your elite status is or how much you've been inconvenienced or disserviced by an airline, blindly trusting strangers and putting your entire trip in their hands is a very bad idea. Sure, those strangers work for a company you've paid to provide you with air transportation, but customer service is what it is. Even if an agent wanted to spend half an hour looking for better options for you, with 100 people waiting behind you, it's unrealistic to expect such attention to one customer.

Doing your homework is what I advocate throughout this book, but it's particularly essential when it comes to rebooking. I like to be in control of my journey, and if I know what I want and how to ask for it, I can be on my new flight while my fellow passengers are still waiting in line. Of course, waiting in line is almost never a good idea. I realize that when non-elite fliers call reservations, they may get an agent in India, the Philippines or at another outsourced call center, which can be a frustrating experience. But if you know what you want, you may save valuable time.

If you have Internet access, there are plenty of tools you can use to find an alternate flight. ExpertFlyer, the KVS tool, ITA Software, your airline's website and many others will show you any available flights. If you find yourself at a gate or on a plane with no online access or an Internet-enabled mobile device, a very helpful tool to have is your airline's electronic timetable, which you can download to your computer in advance. Even though that timetable won't show you actual availability on other flights, it will give you enough information to ask the right questions when you call reservations to get rebooked.

In 2008, I was on my way to San Juan (SJU), on one of the very few truly "direct" flights in the United system, as opposed to the fake ones I described in Chapter 6. My plane stopped in St. Thomas (STT), on the U.S. Virgin Islands, and was then scheduled to continue to San Juan. On landing in St. Thomas, one of two engines experienced a mechanical problem, which meant that the Airbus 320 wouldn't leave St. Thomas until the problem was fixed. The only way to accomplish that in St. Thomas was for mechanics to be flown in, most likely from United's maintenance base in San Francisco, and that wasn't happening anytime soon.

So what were the passengers to do? We weren't allowed off the plane and were told that a "customer service representative" would come on board instead. The United ground staff in St. Thomas is outsourced, with limited capabilities, so I immediately called my dedicated elite line. The agent who answered couldn't help me, because the flight was still showing as being on time in the United system. I asked for a supervisor and offered to hand my phone to the captain to confirm that we had a mechanical problem. I knew there was a plane coming in from Chicago (ORD) about an hour later, which also would continue to San Juan, and within a couple of minutes, I was rebooked on that flight, with my upgrade preserved. The passengers around me who overheard my conversation were stunned.

U.S. airlines have plenty of faults, but when it comes to handling irregular operations, they are usually much better than most foreign carriers. I've heard various explanations of that difference. Some say that American companies have learned valuable lessons from frequent weather-related problems resulting from operating in a vast country with very different climates. Others suggest that U.S. carriers experience more disruptions because of their fleets' old age, which often causes mechanical problems. Whatever the reason, the important thing is that it has been beneficial.

In general, airport agents in the United States – whether at check-in counters, gates or even business lounges – can do almost anything a passenger needs, including rebooking, rerouting and reissuing tickets. In contrast, agents in other countries are much more specialized, and thus less helpful.

I always try to have my tickets issued by a U.S. carrier. That doesn't mean that I don't fly on foreign airlines – in the era of code-sharing, global alliances and other partnerships, that limitation is no longer an issue. What it does mean is that, when something goes wrong during a trip, I don't have to queue up for hours and be at the mercy of airport agents with questionable training in another country. Instead, I can call my original ticketing carrier in the United States and have my ticket reissued in minutes. Even if my new flight is operated by a foreign airline, thanks to electronic ticketing, I can simply walk to the check-in counter or kiosk to get my boarding pass.

In March 2010, I wrote in my column about Alex Cohen, a frequent traveler who lived in Reno, Nevada. A month earlier, he'd had an unpleasant experience with Lufthansa. He was on his way home from Venice, Italy (VCE), when his flight to Munich (MUC) was canceled because of bad weather. Although he was already in the gate area, the customer-service line in the terminal was too long, so he went back to the check-in counter outside. To his surprise, the agents there told him they couldn't rebook him on another flight and sent him to a ticketing office in a different part of the lobby.

To those of us in the United States, that sounds rather puzzling. Why aren't agents in Europe and elsewhere trained to perform all major tasks needed at an airport? Why waste even more of passengers' time when they have already been delayed? If carriers care little about passenger convenience, perhaps they should care about their own efficiency?

Finally, Cohen was booked on a Lufthansa flights to Frankfurt (FRA) and on to Denver (DEN) – he had missed his original connection from Munich to Philadelphia (PHL) – and then to Reno (RNO) on United. Lufthansa and United, both founding members of the Star Alliance, have one of the industry's closest partnerships. That, however, wasn't the end of it. Cohen's flight to Frankfurt was delayed, and he missed his Denver connection. As a Star Alliance Gold member, he went to the Lufthansa lounge, hoping that an agent there could rebook him again. After all, Frankfurt is the carrier's main hub, so perhaps the agents there are better trained than in Venice, he thought. Of course, he was wrong.

"The agent in the lounge sent me to the service center in the terminal, but the person managing the long queue there said I'd be better off going outside to the check-in area," Cohen recalled. He obliged, only to be told again by the check-in agents that they couldn't rebook him, and he need to go "upstairs to the ticketing office" and wait in yet another line, he said. By then his only option was to take a United flight to San Francisco (SFO), if he wanted to make it home that day. With less than half an hour left before that departure, he decided he'd had enough of Lufthansa.

He called United, which had issued his ticket, and as a top elite member of its Mileage Plus program, he got a U.S.-based agent – not one in India. The agent instantly figured out what had happened to his original itinerary and put him on the San Francisco flight he wanted, with a connection to Reno, within seconds. Then he walked to the United counter to quickly get his boarding passes and arrived at the gate just as it was about to close. "It was stunning how efficient the United agent was," he said. "When things go wrong [during a trip], it's gratifying to deal with U.S. agents."

Actually, Cohen was incredibly lucky to have a United-issued ticket. He purchased his original ticket from US Airways, but his very first outbound flight from Reno to San Francisco was on United. That flight was canceled, and United ended up reissuing the ticket on its own ticket stock. Had that not happened, he most likely would have come home a day later than he did.

As I said, this is hardly a Lufthansa issue. Most foreign carriers have similar customer-unfriendly policies, but hopefully they can learn from their U.S. colleagues. That said, not all U.S. agents are to be praised, especially those at airports. I've met some who didn't know basic things despite their seniority. Even so, they still tend to react faster and be more empowered than others.

Making the best of the airport experience

Many people have told me that they dread air travel in large part because of the hassle and unpleasantness they experience at airports. I can certainly understand and relate to that sentiment, even as I wish the reality were different. Just like with the airline system, the airport experience has changed for the worse in recent years, and there is little we can do about it. However, there are things we can do to minimize hassle and create as much comfort and convenience for ourselves as possible – and even a bit of fun.

Here are my main rules:

▶ Complete as many tasks as possible before getting to the airport and leave only those you can't take care of by yourself.

▶ Maintain elite airline status to minimize the time spent in various lines.

▶ Secure business lounge access, which often comes with elite status, as the best way to keep your sanity and not waste time and nerves.

▶ Try to remember an airport's particulars, so you can save time rediscovering them next time – and if you are going to a certain airport for the first time, put a little effort in learning how to navigate it efficiently by reading up on it online.

Here is how these rules have worked out for me: I always check in online when the airline allows it, which is almost every time – and of course I do my upgrading and seat selection in advance as well. For the life of me, I can't possibly comprehend why millions of travelers still queue up to check in at the airport when they don't need to. You can do it online and still check luggage, though I usually pack economically and confine myself to a carry-on. What that means is that I go directly to security, bypassing the hassle of the check-in lobby.

As you know, security lines at big airports can be rather long. That's why it helps to know shortcuts – perhaps there is a checkpoint less known to passengers. At Washington Dulles, for example, that's the so-called Diamond Checkpoint on the arrivals level, which is not at the most logical place and most people have no idea it exists. The wait time there is usually several times shorter than that in the main security area.

The security checkpoint, where I usually use the priority line if there is one, is where I first interact with an employee. My second interaction is at the business lounge, if available, where my credentials have to be checked. It helps to know which lounge to visit if there is more than one. Some are smaller and more crowded than others. Some are better for getting work done, and others for getting some rest.

My last contact is with the gate agent who scans my boarding pass – or who watches me scan it myself if I have a mobile boarding pass on my BlackBerry, instead of a paper one. United was the first to introduce red carpet boarding for premium passengers – you literally walk on a small red carpet in a dedicated line – which makes a huge difference. Even if you are not at the gate when boarding begins, there is no danger there won't be overhead bin space for your carry-on. Whenever you get there, you can simply bypass everyone else waiting in the regular line.

Having a tested routine and positive attitude about this also helps, especially if your flight is delayed. We all want to vent sometimes, but rather than badmouth airlines or abuse agents, I try to make things work.

I'm not arguing against constructive criticism – in fact, a columnist often has to be critical, and I'm no exception. I've been particularly critical of U.S. airports, beginning with my home one, Washington Dulles. If you've even been there, you know it deserves to be criticized. I've gone as far as to call it a disgrace for the capital of the world's richest and most powerful country. Its many limitations include the archaic people-movers officially known as "mobile lounges," and the depressing interior of the "midfield terminal." Still, Dulles is slowly joining the modern age. In 2009, it opened a new international arrivals hall, and the long-delayed AeroTrain linking terminals finally began operations in 2010. The train has its problems, but at least it's faster and more presentable than the people-movers.

I've also criticized airports in other Western countries, which sometimes remind me of the Third World. Many travelers often complain about London's Heathrow, but I find Frankfurt no less frustrating. I especially detest the so-called "remote" gates – a fancy term used when a plane is parked away from the terminal and you are driven there by bus. I've had more than 100 takeoffs and landings in Frankfurt, and I can hardly remember a trip that didn't involve at least one bus ride. I've even boarded Boeing 747 aircraft that way, and they have never left on time.

Finding an oasis in a busy terminal

Although I'm no fan of the Frankfurt airport, it has one undeniable advantage – the Lufthansa First Class Terminal. You must travel in Lufthansa or Swiss First Class to experience it. It's simply unsurpassed – even by the likes of Singapore Airlines and Cathay Pacific – and no competition is evident on the horizon. The only problem is that Lufthansa has restricted access even to eligible passengers.

When you arrive at the First Class Terminal, you are met by an agent assigned to be your personal assistant during your stay. You go through the terminal's security checkpoint, usually without waiting, and then you are faced with more choices than you know what to do with: sleeping rooms, mini-offices with wireless Internet, a bar, a restaurant with a chef ready to cook anything you want, and showers with jacuzzi.

At boarding time, your assistant comes to collect you and takes you to the terminal's passport control booth if you are flying outside Europe's Schengen passport-free area, before handing you over to a chauffeur who drives you to your plane in a Mercedes or Porsche. That's right, you avoid all the hassle of the main terminal, which in Frankfurt can be overwhelming and rather unpleasant. You are usually the last person to board the plane – as soon as you step in, the door closes behind you.

When I first started using the unique facility in 2006, upon arrival at the First Class check-in area in the main terminal, a call was made for one of those chauffeur-driven cars to come and take you to the First Class Terminal. Later, the car service was replaced by a shuttle bus, but now there is no transportation at all. You are supposed to find your own way to the somewhat remote location. You can get there by taxi, if your driver knows the way, but if you use the train to take you to the airport, your only option is to walk – and that walk is certainly not a proper part of the First Class experience.

As for other world-famous airport lounges, Virgin Atlantic's Clubhouse at London Heathrow (LHR) is among the most impressive. Thai Airways' Royal Orchid Spa at Bangkok's Suvarnabhumi Airport (BKK) is one of the most delicious treats a traveler can ask for. First Class passengers enjoy a complimentary one-hour full-body massage, while a Business Class boarding pass gets you a half-hour neck-and-shoulders or foot massage. Cathay Pacific's The Wing lounge in Hong Kong (HKG) also offers a superb experience. Its Business Class area sports the famous Noodle Bar, while the First Class section has an impressive library, as well as luxurious shower and bathing facilities called The Cabanas.

Top-tier elite members of frequent-flier programs often get free access to Business lounges, no matter in which class of service they are traveling, as we will see in Chapter 11.

Although many airlines limit lounge access to departing and connecting – not arriving – passengers, some carriers have separate arrivals lounges. Admission is usually restricted to paying First and Business Class fliers. Those lounges are very few around the world, and some of the world's best carriers like Singapore Airlines don't have any even at their hub airports. Those that do have them include American, United, Virgin Atlantic, British Airways, Lufthansa and Emirates, among others. Most arrivals lounges are open only in the morning, when the majority of their long-haul flights arrive. Many business people use them to take a shower and have breakfast before heading to the office.

Companies like Priority Pass have their own networks of lounges, though they often contract with airlines as well. They charge annual or per-visit fees – or a combination of both.

Some lounges can also be accessed for free with certain credit cards that provide such benefits. For example, U.S. holders of American Express Platinum cards can use American, Delta and US Airways lounges at no charge, as well as most Priority Pass lounges around the world. Having access to airline lounges makes a huge difference, but there are other lounges less known to the traveling public. They serve U.S. military personnel and their families, even when they are on personal trips. Those so-called airport centers are operated by the United Services Organization (USO), a private, nonprofit group whose mission is "to support the troops by providing morale, welfare and recreation-type services to our men and women in uniform." Like the airline lounges, USO's airport centers provide peace and quiet, along with drinks, snacks, newspapers and Internet access. But those are just the basics. Some centers have sleeping rooms, shower and laundry facilities, said USO spokeswoman Tiane Harrison.

"If you sleep, you don't have to worry about missing your flight, because someone will wake you up," she said in reference to a service provided by the staff upon request. "Even if you do miss your flight, we'll help you make other arrangements." Although there are paid employees at the centers, most of the staff are volunteers, Harrison said. They usually escort their guests to the gate, "but before that happens, they announce that troops are deploying and ask passersby to help give them a hero's farewell," she added.

The lounges are only part of USO's network of facilities in more than 20 states and 10 countries. The group is also well-known for organizing entertainment tours for troops with comedians, musicians and other artists. "The USO currently operates more than 135 centers worldwide, including 10 mobile canteens located in the continental United States and overseas," according to the organization's Web site.

Army Reserve Capt. Malia Du Mont, who has served in Afghanistan, said she was "stuck" at the Bagram Air Base outside the capital Kabul "on more than one occasion for two or three days awaiting onward transportation, and had nowhere to go except the USO, where I could telephone home for free, have access to the nicest bathrooms on the base, watch movies and relax." The USO center at Bagram is named after former Army Ranger and Arizona Cardinal player Pat Tillman, and his framed football jersey hangs on the wall, she said. Cpl. Tillman was killed by friendly fire in Afghanistan in 2004.

"Military people travel a lot and spend a lot of time waiting, particularly when connecting from a military flight to a commercial flight or vice versa. Often, we travel with a lot of luggage too," Capt. Du Mont said. "USO lounges are a haven for service members," she said. "They vary widely – some of them have big-screen TVs and Internet, while others resemble more typical waiting areas. What they have in common is that they are all staffed by enthusiastic, friendly volunteers and offer a quiet place to relax between flights both for active-duty service members and their families."

What a difference a captain makes!

On many of my flights, the passengers don't hear from a pilot until it's time to turn off the seatbelt sign after takeoff. Captain Dennis J. Flanagan, a legendary United pilot, couldn't be more different. If he ever piloted any of your flights, you most likely still remember the experience.

Long before I met him in November 2009, I had heard a lot from fellow travelers about his attentive customer-service approach. I had also spoken with him on the phone with the intention of writing about him. But our actual encounter wasn't planned. As I boarded a plane in Phoenix (PHX), I saw a pilot greeting passengers at the door and handing out small information cards about the Boeing 757 we were about to fly. I had no idea what Flanagan looked like, but I immediately thought it might be him. A minute later, the purser confirmed my suspicion.

Because I tend to arrive at the gate just at boarding time, I missed Flanagan's initial interaction with customers. He usually introduces himself in the gate area, thanks everyone for flying United and says a few words about the flight. Actually, he later told me he starts thinking about his passengers even before he gets to the airport by "pre-writing thank-you notes" on his business cards. After takeoff, when the plane has reached cruising altitude, he "adds the names of customers in First Class, including any employees" sitting in the front cabin.

"I thank customers for their business and ask how we can exceed their expectations. I thank fellow employees for their dedication and hard work," he said. "If time permits, I also send thank-you notes to my customers in coach. I target those in the middle seats first, with the intent to emotionally and physically make their seat bigger."

Flanagan, who is better known as Captain Denny, has been flying for United since 1986, although his flying began in the Navy 14 years earlier. He commutes between his base in Chicago and his home near Cleveland, Ohio, and spends quite a bit of time in passenger seats, so he is well aware of the "middle-seat syndrome," as he calls it.

"Have you ever tried to get control of an arm rest once it's occupied?" he asked. But when "a flight attendant stops at your row, leans over and says, 'Excuse me, I have a note for you from the captain,' your neighbors would like to know who you are and what the captain had to say. So one leans left and the other leans right, and the two armrests are yours for the taking," he said. "My flight attendants witness the experience and later call and start telling me the fantastic story of the person in the middle seat using the arm rests. They are shocked."

Passengers who get the captain's card often e-mail him back. "I have never in my years of travel received a personal note from the captain of the aircraft I was flying," David Spires wrote in a message Flanagan forwarded to me. "Everything you did today to add a personal touch to an otherwise mundane business trip was outstanding."

You can listen to Flanagan's interaction with air traffic controllers during a flight, thanks to United's Channel 9, a service much loved by airline junkies, but which some pilots choose to turn off for various reasons. Dennis Bent, who listened to the tower communications during a flight to Iowa once, said that Flanagan "complimented the ground crew for their work on de-icing the plane and was extremely personable to all of the traffic-control personnel he spoke with."

After we landed in Chicago (ORD), Flanagan went back to the aircraft door to say goodbye to his passengers. On his way down the cabin, he picked up trash and looked for any items left behind on the seats to help out the cleaning crew.

"We were struck by his relational skills and approach to his role versus the very transactional approach evidenced by most service leaders," said Jimmie R. Alford, founder of a consulting firm in Evanston, Ill. "His warmth, authentic caring and concern for others stood out dramatically in this time of pressure, cutbacks and bottom-line focus."

Flanagan said he tries not to get involved in management and labor controversies, but simply to do his job and leave his customers satisfied as they get off his plane. "The recipe is easy for things like this to happen every day and everywhere. Just choose your attitude and exceed your customers' expectations," he said. "I heard a saying once: 'Choose your attitude for the altitude you wish to maintain during the day.'"

Flanagan was the one who told me about the Captain Jason Dahl Scholarship Fund, established in honor of his fellow pilot who was at the controls of the fatal United Flight 93, which crashed in Pennsylvania on September 11, 2001. Each year, the fund awards $5,000 grants to two aviation students – one at Dahl's alma mater, San Jose State University, and one at Metro State University in Denver, where Dahl lived.

Creating on-board enjoyment

I'm often asked how I spend my time on board, so let me tell you about my routine on long-haul flights. As I mentioned in the foreword, the last time I sat in coach on a domestic or intercontinental flight was in 2002, so the pastimes described here are spent in international Business or First Class. Don't think this doesn't apply to you because you fly mostly in coach – that's about to change after you finish reading this book. Every traveler should find his or her own comfort level, but this is what works for me.

I try to board my flights early, if possible. If not, there is often a red-carpet lane or something similar for premium passengers. Because I usually don't check luggage, securing overhead bin space for my somewhat sizable carry-on is important. Once I've done that, I inspect my seat to make sure that all its functions work properly. I certainly don't want to spend 12 hours in a seat that is supposed to become a flat bed but doesn't recline.

By this time, a flight attendant has usually offered to hang my coat, if I have one. In the past few years, I've collected excellent plane pajamas I've been given in First Class on some of the world's best airlines, including Swiss, Lufthansa and Singapore Airlines. I always carry a pair on international trips, and my next order of business is to visit the lavatory and put on the pajamas. I used to do that after takeoff, but I decided there is no point in waiting until then. It may be a while before the seatbelt sign is turned off. By that time, the flight attendants will most likely have begun the service, and I'd rather not be in their way.

Now that I'm in my in-flight clothes, I relax in my seat with a newspaper and a pre-departure drink (usually water). I also glance at the menu and make my main-course selection. Once in the air, I finish up my reading and start my first movie – or if there is no on-demand entertainment, the purser starts it for me. I actually watch most of my films on planes, not on the ground. Unless I'm on a late-night flight, I usually put on a second movie and hope I'll fall asleep in the middle of it. I watch the ending when I wake up for the second meal service, or on longer flights to and from Asia or Australia, there is time for a third film and possibly a couple of TV shows.

Naturally, on certain airlines the experience in Business and First Class is better than on others. Asian carriers' crews are exceptional in the way they take care of their premium passengers, with incredible attention to detail.

During a flight in First Class on Singapore Airlines a few years ago, I stood up from my seat to go to the lavatory, which was behind me, and when I turned around, I saw a flight attendant hurrying to open the door for me. I had just enjoyed black caviar as part of a five-course dinner, and I loved the pillows, sheets and blanket on my fully flat bed, but for some reason that thoughtful gesture meant more than the luxuries.

On-board meals are also an important part of the flying experience. Asian carriers generally excel in that department, too, though European airlines like British Airways, Swiss and Lufthansa, as well as Turkish Airlines, Emirates, Etihad and Qatar Airways, also have great offerings.

On U.S. carriers, dining is not the luxurious experience it once was. Still, if you are a frequent traveler with a confirmed seat in domestic First Class, you probably rely on those meals to save you the time and hassle of trying to grab a bite before boarding.

How do you make sure you get your meal choice? Airlines today rarely load more meals than the number of seats in the front cabin, and they can't predict every passenger's preference, so someone is bound to be disappointed – particularly on domestic flights, where there are usually only two meal options. If you fly consistently on one carrier, you are no doubt familiar with its meal-choice policy. But if you travel on different airlines, and if you care about the food on board, it's a good idea to learn those policies in advance, because they are much less alike than you might expect. While most carriers simply start taking orders from the first row, some don't.

On United, top elite customers and full-fare passengers get priority. American begins from the front on even-numbered flights, but from the back on odd-numbered flights. US Airways has been exploring yet another model – front to back on eastbound flights, and back to front on westbound ones. Hector Adler, the carrier's vice president for in-flight services, shared that idea with a pilot who contacted him in 2010 about an experience I had during a flight to Costa Rica.

As soon as I boarded that US Airways flight in Charlotte, North Carolina (CLT), I asked the purser about the meal choices in First Class and mentioned that I'd like a salad, rather than a sandwich, if possible. I sat in the last of three rows, and by the time the purser came to me, she had only a sandwich left. I was obviously displeased and tried to tell her about United's system, which is much less arbitrary, hoping that she could share it with her management. But her only response was, "This is not United."

Although the purser had no interest in any of my suggestions, a female pilot sitting next to me was much more curious, so I explained the United model of giving priority to elite passengers. In a letter to senior management, the pilot wrote that the carrier's current meal-choice policy "does not seem to recognize and reward the very passengers we value most." Recounting my experience as a witness, the pilot called me "most polite and courteous, although clearly disappointed" and asked, "Don't you believe it would be worth revisiting the food-service policy to reflect the [elite] and fare status of the first-class passengers when honoring meal choices?"

Two US Airways executives responded immediately. Elise Eberwein, executive vice president for people and communications, was very impressed that the pilot took the time to write a letter, which showed that she had "great empathy for our customers," in Eberwein's words. "Many times we don't know exactly who is up front…, but the suggestion makes good sense and we'll look at it," she said, adding that she would "pass it along" to Adler, the other vice president. He, however, wasn't convinced the United model was the best. "Consistently offering first choice to [top elite] customers within hearing range of others can get very tricky. Many people become quite vocal about this, so it's always a balancing act," Adler wrote.

How do airlines right a wrong?

It's hardly breaking news that many things can go wrong when dealing with an airline. The carrier may be responsible for some of them, but not for others. There aren't many government regulations that require the airlines to right a wrong, and they set their own rules. You might have heard of the so-called Rule 240, which applied to the entire industry before deregulation. That rule no longer exists officially, though it's still used in reference to individual airlines' "conditions of carriage."

Let's first look at the cases in which the problems we experience are not the airline's fault. They usually have to do with the weather, political violence, labor strikes or acts of nature, such as earthquakes and active volcanoes.

When any of these occur, most airlines waive the change fees otherwise required to rebook your trip. It's a good idea to take advantage of those waivers – and to read the rules carefully. Some carriers will let you move your trip by weeks or months, as long as your new dates are within the life of your ticket, meaning one year from the issue date. Others, however, will want you to fly within seven days of your original flights. Some will insist on putting you only on flights that have availability in your ticketed booking class, while others will be more liberal.

All carriers typically require keeping the "same itinerary." What does that mean? Some agents may not allow you to change the routing, but the same itinerary usually means the same origin and destination – not connecting point. So if an agent gives a hard time on the phone, hang up and call again.

Another important thing to remember is that, if any of your flights are canceled, many carriers will give you a full refund even on a nonrefundable ticket. If you choose to go to the airport and take care of rebooking there, the agents will try to help, but they are not required to go out of their way for you. Of course, if you have high elite status, they may be more inclined to do so. When delays and cancellations are not the carrier's fault, it has no obligation to pay for meals or accommodation, though some do provide those to top elite customers.

Recent Department of Transportation (DOT) rules "prohibit most U.S. airlines from allowing a domestic flight to remain on the tarmac for more than three hours," with a couple of exceptions, according to the DOT's "Fly Rights: A Consumer Guide to Air Travel," which is a very useful read and is available on the DOT's website. When it comes to international flights, airlines "must each establish and comply with their own limit," the guide says.

Now let's move to problems caused by the airlines. "Contrary to popular belief, airlines are not required to compensate passengers whose flights are delayed or canceled," the DOT guide says. Even so, the airlines do have policies designed to right a wrong – again, depending on your elite status. For example, if your airline is unable to offer you a satisfactory alternative to your canceled flight, it's supposed to put you on another carrier. Most agents won't offer you that option and will resist if you ask for it. That doesn't mean they are right.

Depending on how much later than your originally scheduled time you will arrive at your destination, and on your elite status, you may be eligible for a "goodwill gesture" – they don't like to call it "compensation" these days. That may be a discount voucher or bonus miles.

Another recent trend is not to offer these "tokens of appreciation" at the airport, but to have customer relations departments do it after travel has been completed. Of course, those departments are almost never proactive in reaching out to passengers. In fact, most fliers don't even know that they are entitled to a "goodwill gesture," so they don't call to ask for one. In some cases, there is no one to call, as many airlines are moving to using solely e-mail in handling customer complaints and other issues.

Delays and cancellations are not the only reason to ask for compensation. If your seat was broken and you couldn't recline it on a six-hour flight, they might give you a little something – or a bigger something if you are an elite flier.

I've never volunteered to give up my seat on an oversold flight, but that's a great way to save on a future trip. Bumping passengers from such flights is the only time the airlines are required by law to offer compensation. That's why they ask for volunteers first – instead of paying you money, they prefer to find someone willing to take a voucher. Before you give up your seat, make sure you know exactly what you will be getting in exchange. When will your new flight depart? Will you receive a discount voucher or a free domestic ticket? Will the voucher have any restrictions? Can you use it for international travel? Will you earn frequent-flier miles?

Most airlines waive their airport ticketing fees when you use bump paper vouchers. American Airlines, however, kept charging $30 fees for years, effectively reducing the compensation passengers received for helping the carrier out by giving up their seats. In February 2011, DOT fined American $90,000 for that practice. "When passengers volunteer to give up their seat on an oversold flight, they are entitled to be fully compensated – not to find out later that they are getting $30 less," Transportation Secretary Ray LaHood said at the time. "Passengers deserve to be treated fairly when they fly."

Fliers have even more rights when they are bumped involuntarily. In that case, they are entitled to a check instead of a voucher, according to the DOT guide cited above. If your new flight takes you to your destination within an hour of your original arrival time, you are not entitled to compensation. If that time is between one and two hours (one and four hours on international flights), "the airline must pay you an amount equal to your one-way fare to your final destination that day, with a $400 maximum." For a delay of more than two hours (four on international flights), the compensation doubles to 200 percent of your one-way fare, with an $800 maximum.

In April 2011, DOT increased these amounts. For delays of up to two hours, the new compensation is 200 percent of the fare, with a $650 limit. For longer delays, it's 400 percent, with a $1,300 ceiling.

Airlines are exempt from these rules if the offloading of passengers is due to substituting the scheduled aircraft with a smaller plane, or if the plane has fewer than 30 seats. The rules don't apply to international flights inbound to the United States, though the European Commission has even stricter rules for flights originating in the European Union.

Chapter 9 Lessons Learned

1. Tracking an aircraft's path can help to predict delays and cancellations, which can allow a passenger to get rebooked even before heading to the airport.
2. All major U.S. carriers' websites show gate information, which can be used to find out where a plane is coming from before turning around to operate its next flight.
3. In case of delays or cancellations, blindly trusting airline agents to rebook a passenger on the best alternate flight is a bad idea. Doing one's homework is essential when it comes to rebooking.
4. U.S. airlines handle irregular operations (IRROPS) better than most foreign carriers.
5. Completing as many tasks as possible before getting to the airport is crucial for ensuring a seamless airport experience.
6. Business lounge access is essential to minimize hassle at the airport. Such access can be gained through flying in a premium cabin, having elite airline status, holding certain types of credit cards or paying for membership.
7. Lufthansa's First Class Terminal in Frankfurt and Thai Airways' spa in Bangkok offer two of the most luxurious airport experiences in the world.
8. Creating an in-flight routine makes the time spent on board more efficient and enjoyable.
9. There aren't many government regulations that require the airlines to right a wrong, and they set their own rules.
10. A passenger who has experienced a delay, cancellation or an inconvenience during a flight, such as a broken seat, may be eligible for a "goodwill gesture." That may be a discount voucher or bonus miles.
11. Discount vouchers can significantly reduce travel costs if used smartly.
12. A passenger may receive a voucher of up to $400 for volunteering to give up his or her seat on a U.S. domestic flights, and up to $800 on an international flight.
13. Passengers bumped involuntarily are entitled to a check instead of a voucher.

PART III

MASTERING THE FREQUENT-FLIER GAME

Chapter 10

Frequent-Flier Programs

Many people question the value of frequent-flier programs, and I've written columns pondering whether being loyal to an airline is worth it. I've quoted travelers complaining that they worked hard to accumulate miles, only to see their airline significantly increase the mileage required for award redemption or slap new fees on supposedly "free" tickets. I've received numerous angry e-mail messages about Delta's devalued elite benefits, United's blocking of award seats made available by its Star Alliance partners, and American's ban of stopovers on award tickets.

While these complaints are perfectly reasonable, others are less so. For example, I keep reading stories in the media about passengers bad-mouthing an airline just because they didn't get a free upgrade.

The reality is that the frequent-flier game, along with the entire air travel system, has become very complex and often confusing in recent years. If you don't know how to play the game well, you will no doubt feel cheated and utterly frustrated. But if you are a knowledgeable and experienced player, you can reap tremendous benefits. As I said in the foreword, even in my wildest dreams, I never imagined that I'd fly in First Class on the world's finest airlines.

The airlines certainly didn't invent frequent-flier programs to satisfy customers – they did it to make more money. There is a reason these programs are known as "loyalty businesses." In the process, however, they have added some worthwhile incentives and outstanding rewards. True, they have erected barriers to many of those rewards, but barriers are to be broken down – and hopefully this chapter will help you do so.

Choosing the best program for you

If you are reading this book, you are most likely a member of at least one frequent-flier program. But it's worth spreading the word to anyone you know: It's a really good idea to be earning miles or points from almost everything you do in life. Whether shopping, dining or financing a home, if you don't get miles or points, you might as well be leaving money on the table. Sometimes people tell me they never fly on the same airline enough to justify having an account. That is completely irrelevant – you don't have to fly to earn miles.

Choosing the best program for you is probably the most important decision you have to make. It will determine how happy you are as a traveler, how much you spend on flying, and even how much you travel. Chances are, you made your choice long ago, but as you read this part of the book, it may be good to reevaluate that choice and see if it still makes the best sense for you.

Selecting the right program depends on a variety of criteria, and the first is your method of earning miles – with or without flying, or most likely both.

Let's first focus on the flying option. For most travelers, their location plays a major role in choosing an airline. In the United States, living in or near a city that is a hub for a certain carrier usually means being part of that carrier's program. As I said in Chapter 2, if you live in Atlanta, you are probably a Delta flier. If you are in Dallas, chances are you are with American. That makes a lot of sense – a business traveler who is on the road all the time no doubt prefers nonstop flights, and no one has more nonstops from Atlanta than Delta.

However, if you fly less often, other criteria may be more important to you. Perhaps you are unhappy with Delta's award availability, and American will offer you more redemption opportunities. Or maybe Delta's system-wide upgrades are too few and too restrictive for you, and United offers a better international upgrade policy. Also, remember the fare wars we discussed in Chapter 2? Both American and United often "attack" Delta's Atlanta hub with lower fares – and Delta does the same to their hubs. Flying an airline that doesn't have a hub in your city can actually save you money.

So before determining where to place your loyalty, it would help to decide what your priorities are. Do you care most about using your miles for award tickets? If so, you might want to compare redemption requirements and find out which airline has the best award availability – or the most generous partners. Do you want to avoid sitting in coach as often as possible? If that's the case, it's a good idea to compare various carriers' upgrade policies – both domestic and international. If you end up in coach most of the time, is it important to you to have access to an Economy section with more legroom? Not all airlines have such sections. Is one of your priorities to fly on one of the three global alliances – Oneworld, SkyTeam and the Star Alliance? If it is, you'd pick a carrier that is a member of the respective group.

Many of us join a certain frequent-flier program by accident, manage to achieve elite status, and find it difficult to leave even if we see better opportunities elsewhere. It's much wiser to weigh our options before we make a significant investment.

My first membership was in United Mileage Plus, just because my first employer out of college had booked me on a United flight in my first week on the job in 1998. Until then, I didn't even bother to open an account anywhere, although I'd already done more flying than most people do in a lifetime. I was living in New York at the time, where both American and Delta have a stronger presence, but I didn't think about that.

A year later, I moved to Boston for graduate school – again, not a particularly strong United market – but I kept flying United or crediting my flights on partner carriers to my Mileage Plus account. Finally, I moved to Washington and experienced the benefits of living in a United hub. I must admit, it has been hard to defect. Fortunately, despite some problems, Mileage Plus has become one of the best programs in the world.

If you live outside the United States, you probably feel even more limited in your choices. Most countries have one major carrier, and a large majority of their travelers belong to its program. If you live in Germany, you are likely a member of Lufthansa's Miles&More. If you are in Hong Kong, you must be a member of Cathay Pacific's Marco Polo Club. Partly because of a lack of competition, foreign airline programs haven't been nearly as innovative, generous and customer-friendly as those in North America. In fact, many European and Asian travelers who fly regularly to the United States are members of U.S.-based programs.

I'm often asked if it makes sense for U.S. residents to sign up with a foreign airline program. It does, even if you never fly on that airline, but usually as a second or third membership. It really depends on your reasons – some of the obvious ones include a more generous award chart than those of U.S. carriers, big credit card bonuses, lower thresholds to achieve elite status, and free access to airport lounges, for which you typically have to pay in the United States.

In the last couple of years, in addition to my top elite status with United, I've had Gold status with British Midland International (BMI), Britain's second largest carrier, because it was relatively easy to achieve and maintain that status. BMI is a Star Alliance member, so my Gold card has given me free access to all United, Continental and US Airways lounges, which otherwise require paid membership.

That raises the question how many programs one should belong to. As far as flying is concerned, my first priority is always securing top elite status in my main program. As long as that goal is achieved, I can have as many other accounts as I want. If one of those other carriers has a great promotion that doesn't involve flying – a huge credit card bonus or selling miles at a significant discount – it certainly doesn't hurt to have an account with it.

I've been a non-active member of the American AAdvantage program for years, with not a single mile in my account. That all changed in 2010, when American offered extremely generous 75,000-mile bonuses for its personal and business credit cards. I got one of each, earning a total of 150,000 miles.

Having several accounts sometimes becomes a problem for many travelers because of the time and effort it takes to monitor and manage them, especially with most airline miles expiring at some point. Luckily, websites like AwardWallet.com, UsingMiles. com and MileageManager.com can do the monitoring and managing for you.

If you earn most of your miles from non-flight activities, choosing the best program for you should be a different exercise from the one I've been describing. Location and airline hubs are irrelevant in this case, and your best bet is to find the program that offers the best combination of earning lots of miles and being able to use them for quality trips – or anything else you might want to redeem them for. I realize that's easier said than done, but if you read carefully the rest of Part III, things will become much clearer.

Earning flight miles

Unless you are a super-frequent business traveler, you most likely care about getting the most number of miles for the money you spend on flying – whether to gain elite status or book a dream trip in international First Class. We will discuss elite-qualifying miles in more detail in Chapter 12, and it's very important to distinguish them from the so-called redeemable miles, which can be used for free tickets, upgrades and other awards, but which don't count toward elite status. That said, the strategies for maximizing mileage apply to both elite and redeemable miles.

Airline	Discounted Economy	Full-Fare Economy	Business Class	First Class
American Airlines	100% miles/points H K M L W V 100% miles/50% points G Q N O S	100% miles 150% points Y B	100% miles 150% points D I J R	100% miles 150% points F A P
United Airlines	100% M E U H Q V W S T L K G	150% Y B	150% J C D Z	150% F A
Delta Airlines	100% H Q K L U T	150% Y B M W	150% J C D S I	150% F A P
Lufthansa	100% G H K M Q V 50% L S U W	150% Y B	200% J C D Z	300% F A
Air France	75% H 50% L T V 25% G N Q U	125% S W 100% A Y B K	175% C J 150% D I 125% Z	300% F P
Korean Air	100% K M E T H L S B 80% X G 70% Q V	100% Y W	135% J 125% C Z O	200% R 165% P 150% F

Figure 14: Earning schedule for elite-qualifying base miles on long-haul flights.

When it comes to earning miles, U.S. carriers are typically more generous to coach fliers than their foreign peers. As shown on Figure 14, with very few exceptions, they allow mileage accrual on all revenue booking classes, and in most cases the credit is at least 100 percent. The contrast with the European and Asian airlines included in the table is obvious. Foreign carriers reserve their generosity for paying Business and First Class passengers, offering bonuses of up to 200 percent – four times the amount awarded by U.S. carriers.

Things can get tricky when it comes to partner flights. The credit for those flights is determined differently from what you receive when you fly on your own airline. If you fly from Seoul to Los Angeles on Asiana but credit the flight to your United account, you need to check on the United website how many miles you will receive, depending on your booking class. United has a separate earning chart for each partner-carrier.

What if the Asiana (OZ) flight was booked as a United code-share number? In other words, what if your ticket shows UA1060 instead of OZ202? The same method applies in that case as well. It doesn't matter how the flight is marketed – what matters is who operates it. The code-share UA1060 number will convert into the "true" OZ202 number when the flight posts to your account, which means that the United booking class will convert into an Asiana booking class, and they may not be the same. So you need to be very careful.

The code-share earning rule is exactly the opposite on American and Delta. It doesn't matter which airline operates the flight – what matters is how it's marketed, or whose number it carries. Whether you fly on British Airways (BA) or Qantas (QF), as long as your flight was booked as an American (AA) code-share number, you will get the same miles as if you flew on American. However, if those flights appear on your ticket with their BA or QF numbers, they will follow different earning rules.

As you see, things can get very confusing, and you can do nothing but learn the differences and keep your eyes open. What makes that difficult is that most carriers either don't explain their code-share earning policy on their websites or, if they do, they make it very difficult to find. Accrual policies generally follow alliance rules, so the United way of earning miles applies to the other Star Alliance carriers as well. The same goes for American's Oneworld partners, and Delta's fellow SkyTeam airlines.

Strategies for maximizing miles

The suggestions below to boost your account balance through flying apply to both elite-qualifying and redeemable miles.
▶ The first strategy is **finding creative routings** that will give you many more miles for no extra money. In fact, using the Kralev Method, you may even end up saving money. Why? Think about it. Most people choose the most obvious − meaning direct − routing, which is likely to translate into more scarce availability in the lowest booking classes on those supposedly logical flights.

For example, the most direct routing from Washington to Anchorage on United is via Chicago. Because of high demand for that least time-consuming routing, the lowest fare buckets may be zeroed out by the time you try to book your trip. However, if you build your unconventional − but still legal − routing, you may get a lower booking class, and you will definitely receive more miles.

I booked that exact trip in the spring of 2010 for travel that summer. Looking at my options, I compared the single Chicago connection (6,870 round-trip miles) to what I'd done a couple of times before, which was transiting in San Francisco (8,874 miles). Getting more than 2,000 extra miles isn't bad at all, and I was just about to book that San Francisco connection, when something prompted me to look at the legal routing for the lowest fare, which was $400 plus tax.

I was shocked to discover that I could go to San Francisco, then backtrack to Denver (DEN), and from there fly to Anchorage. Typically, backtracking of almost 1,000 miles is not allowed, but Alaska fares are considered special and tend to be more liberal than other U.S. domestic fares. The Washington-San Francisco-Denver-Anchorage routing adds up to 11,582 miles. With my elite bonus of double redeemable miles, that's over 23,000 miles − only 2,000 miles short of a free domestic round-trip coach ticket.

As I've said before, convenience and comfort are very important to me during travel, and I'm almost never willing to sacrifice them for more miles or even a little less money. So before I bought my Anchorage ticket, I had to think about the consequences of the unusual routing. I decided to do it only if it didn't make me suffer.

My first condition was that upgrade space be available on all flights, and I could confirm seats in First or Business Class as soon as the ticket was issued. That was indeed the case. Then I figured all my meals on my travel days would be taken care of – I'd have my breakfast on the flight from Washington to San Francisco, my lunch from San Francisco to Denver, and my dinner from Denver to Anchorage. I know what most people think about airline food, but United First Class meals have improved dramatically in the last year, and most of them are actually rather decent. An added bonus was that my Washington-San Francisco flight was operated on a three-cabin Boeing 777, so I'd have an international Business Class seat much better than the domestic First Class hard product.

In my analysis, the only downside of my unconventional routing was that I'd spend a few extra hours flying. That didn't really bother me – it was the July 4th weekend and I wasn't in a hurry. Plus, unlike most people, I actually like being on a plane (not in coach, of course). Moreover, I had a $400 discount voucher to use, so I paid about $50 for my ticket. At the end of the day, I spent $50, flew in Business and First Class all the way and back, and got 23,000 miles. Wouldn't you do it?

I should point out that United no longer allows that routing, because its merger with Continental has increased the connecting options to Anchorage. However, all is not lost. Now you can transfer in Houston (IAH), which will actually give you more miles (8,912) than if you routed only through San Francisco. You could also do a double connection in both Houston and San Francisco and earn 9,686 miles. It's not 11,582, but it's much more than the 6,870 miles most travelers get on the most logical Chicago routing.

While United, Delta and US Airways allow no more than two connections between Washington and Anchorage, American lets you make up to three. When trying to maximize your mileage, if you are flying east to west, it's best to choose connections that will take you south, then north. Transiting in Houston will result in more miles, but going through Chicago or Denver will give you almost the same mileage as a nonstop, because those two cities are on your natural path. On Delta, connecting in Salt Lake City is not nearly as lucrative in terms of miles as is flying via Atlanta.

▶ The second strategy for maximizing mileage is to secure a **good price-per-mile ratio (PPM)** when shopping for airfare. The Kralev Method can help you achieve a favorable balance between minimizing spending and maximizing miles. In addition, FareCompare, which I've mentioned several times before, can give you a list of destinations from your home city – or any other city – arranged according to PPM. It usually calculates the shortest distance between two airports, so you can often get even more miles than what the site shows you, if you come up with a creative routing. About 3 or 4 cents per mile is a great ratio, though 5 or 6 cents is very good, too.

▶ The third strategy is **using discount vouchers** to lower your spending, which means that you could buy more tickets and accrue more miles on your travel budget. For example, if you've allocated $300 for airfare during the summer, you most likely wouldn't be able to get more than one ticket for that amount. However, if you have two $200 vouchers and apply them toward two $300 tickets, you'd only pay the difference of $100 for each and still have $100 to spare from your initial $300.

We talked about how to get vouchers in Chapter 9, but it's worth repeating that you should contact customer relations when something goes wrong during a trip. Don't just shrug off a three-hour delay – if it's the airline's fault, they could very well give you a "good-will gesture." The higher your elite status, the better the gesture – and some carriers are more generous than others – but even a $100 voucher helps. On that Anchorage trip I mentioned above, not only did I use a voucher when buying my ticket, but I came home with another voucher I got because of a significant delay.

▶ The fourth strategy for maximizing mileage is **converting discounted booking classes into full-fare codes**. Remember, full fare often gives you bonus miles that also count toward elite status. So how do you convert your W or lower class into full Y? You don't – an agent has to do it for you. If you recall, I said in Chapter 9 that, if you get rebooked because of flight disruptions, or irregular operations, most agents will rebook you in Y class. That also happens when you volunteer to take a bump if your flight is oversold. Some agents may book you in the lowest available booking class, so to make sure you are rebooked in Y class, you might want to do a little research, find flights that have only Y seats available, and ask the agent to put you on those flights.

▶ The fifth and last strategy applies mostly to people living, or spending a lot of time, in the United States. In order to minimize spending and maximize mileage, **buy domestic tickets and use your miles for international trips**. Because of taxes and fuel surcharges, international prices fail the PPM test miserably. If you fly from New York to London and back, you will get about 7,000 miles for the round trip, and given all those London taxes, you will pay at least $600 – if you are very lucky – unless the airline files a mistake fare. Compare that to flying from New York to the U.S. West coast and back. With a creative routing, you could earn the same 7,000 miles, but you could find a $200 fare – it may not be a frequent occurrence, but it's probably more frequent than a $600 fare to London.

Earning miles without flying

If you like to travel but can't afford to pay for all of it, your best bet is earning miles without flying, and redeeming them for award tickets. Even those of us who fly all the time like to accrue miles for non-flight activities, so we make sure that everything we do in life enriches our frequent-flier accounts by at least a few miles. The easiest way to churn miles is through **credit cards**. The basic principle of co-branded airline credit cards is that, on average, they award one mile for every dollar spent on the card, and two miles for purchases made with the airline. The biggest allure of those cards is their sign-up bonus, which is usually tens of thousands of miles. As long as your credit card is linked to your frequent-flier account, the miles should post automatically at the end of each billing cycle. If you want to use those miles for award tickets, you have consult the airline's award chart to determine the mileage required for your award, which is based on your destination and class of service.

I'm one of the more cautious travelers when it comes to applying for credit cards just to get miles. In addition to the two American AAdvantage cards I mentioned earlier, I've had six more credits cards in my entire life. I was very tempted by British Airways' 2010 sign-up bonus offer of up to 100,000 miles, but BA award tickets come with such high taxes and fuel surcharges that the prospect of spending $1,000 on what is supposed to be a free ticket was too painful. I suppose I could have used the miles for hotel stays or other non-flight products, but I was also worried that I'd hurt my credit score. As you probably know, scoring is widely accepted by lenders as a reliable means of credit evaluation.

You may have seen TV commercials featuring American Express or Capital One credit cards that promise points or miles with the clout to get you any seat on any airline without blackout dates. Those financial services companies try to distinguish their own loyalty schemes from airline programs, which restrict access to award seats. Non-airline programs are not affected by award seat limits, because they don't need award availability to book you on a flight. Instead, they sell you a regular revenue ticket, charge the ticket price on your credit card, then credit the cash amount back to your card and take miles or points out of your account, whose number is based on a standard formula.

Let's say that you want to use your Capital One miles for a free ticket. The Capital One website performs a flight search and you choose a flight that costs $100. Once the ticket is issued, 10,000 miles will be deducted from your account. While Capital One values $1 at 100 miles, the American Express Membership Rewards program converts $1 into about 80 points. By any measure, that is a lot of points. If we assume that the average U.S. domestic round-trip ticket costs about $500, Capital One will charge you 50,000 miles and American Express 40,000 points. In comparison, you need only 25,000 miles from most airline programs – if there is award availability, which is a big if.

Of course, the airlines will also give you any open revenue seat on any flight, but for double the miles required for a "saver award" – they call it "standard" or "anytime" award. If you need a First or Business Class ticket, the airlines will actually give you a better rate even on a standard award. Such an award from North America to Europe in Business Class will be about 200,000 miles. Assuming that the average revenue ticket costs about $5,000, Capital One will charge you 500,000 miles and American Express 400,000 points.

The advantage of the tickets purchased with non-airline miles or points is that they earn miles, because they are in effect revenue tickets – the airlines will never know that you didn't pay money for them. That model, however, is not unique. It's used by some hotel loyalty programs, which allow points to be redeemed for flights. Even some airlines offer such options, in addition to their regular award redemption opportunities. For example, United's Mileage Plus Choices program is very similar to Capital One's scheme, valuing $1 at 100 miles – only miles earned from Mileage Plus co-branded credit cards can be used for such tickets.

I'm not an expert in this area, so I asked someone with much more experience than me: Richard Ingersoll, who writes a blog called "Frugal Travel Guy." Although he agreed that "your credit is one of your most important assets," he has still managed to "churn over 100 credit cards in the last 11 years at an average of 25,000 miles or points per card."

"Good credit allows us the ability to buy homes and cars, and pay for education," he said. "If used properly, it can also reduce your cost of travel significantly. Card-churning is not for everyone. It takes discipline, education on the process and commitment to know when to stop or pause your applications to always protect that most important asset. Each application you make hits your credit score by two to five points. There must be significant return in value for that ding to your credit score. Each person's situation will determine how many applications he or she can handle in a year. If the result is a five-point drop per application, and your current score is 750, I would say 10 cards spread out throughout the year would be maximum. I always recommend that individuals strive to keep their FICO scores in the 700+ range."

A FICO score – the name comes from the Fair Isaac Corporation – can range from 325 to 850. The median score in the United States is about 720.

A less profitable way to earn miles is through airline **dining and shopping** programs. If you eat out frequently, why not find a restaurant that's on your airline's partner list? If you shop online at major vendors, why not use your airline's portal to go to the respective site? You'd receive a certain number of miles per dollar spent, plus you'd get additional miles for using your airline co-branded credit card. Many carriers also have relationships with specific vendors, such as wine or flower companies, which come up with various promotions from time to time. Check your airline's website for a full list of its partners.

Some of the most lucrative mile-earning opportunities are **unintended deals**. In 2006, American Express, the fourth-largest U.S. credit card issuer, began what company officials called a pilot program that allowed customers to use their cards to buy traveler's checks without the standard $15 fee. The limit was set at $1,000 a week per card.

Several months later, reports surfaced on the Internet that those transactions appeared as regular purchases on card statements, and if you had a co-branded American Express card from travel companies such as Delta Airlines, Hilton or Starwood, you could earn miles or hotel points. Having figured out that they could amass thousands of miles or points at no cost, scores of cardholders descended on American Express offices around the country to buy traveler's checks, even though they didn't really need them. Although some of them used the checks for various purchases, most simply deposited them in their bank accounts and then paid their credit card bills with those same funds. For many customers, a stop at their local American Express office became a weekly habit. It was a great deal – you circulated your own money between your bank and credit card accounts, and a few months later, you got a free plane ticket or hotel stay.

It took American Express two years to catch up with its inventive customers, closing the loophole in November 2008. The company said it never intended for this to become a points gold mine. In fact, no points should have been awarded for those purchases, said Desiree Fish, vice president for public affairs. "Those have been our terms and conditions for years, and we seek to enforce them," she told me at the time. "We may reinstate the program in the future, but customers will not be able to earn points."

Some of those who benefited from the unintended deal were angry at American Express for ending it, but most were understanding and just happy about all the points they earned. "Although I'm sad to see this point opportunity end, I don't blame Amex at all," said Bob from Long Island, N.Y., who asked that his last name not be used for fear of retribution. "It certainly makes sense to allow cardholders to buy traveler's checks if they actually need them, but to give away points at a loss makes no business sense."

If you thought those who visited an American Express office every week went too far in pursuit of points, you probably will find the next deal that enticed some people even more peculiar.

In the summer of 2008, the U.S. Mint announced a "circulating $1 coin direct ship program," making it "easy for retailers, financial institutions and other interested parties to obtain smaller quantities of $1 coins than can otherwise be obtained from the Federal Reserve." It also said the coins "will arrive in boxes of 25-coin rolls within about two weeks, and the United States Mint will pay the standard shipping and handling costs," the agency said at the time.

The free shipping and the credit card payment option caught the attention of point-seekers. They realized that, in order to earn enough points to make it worth the effort, they would have to order quite a few boxes, and because they wouldn't be able to spend the coins, they would have to deposit them in the bank.

Christopher Beck, a University of Alaska student, learned about the deal on FlyerTalk. "I was skeptical at first, waiting for feedback from others on if it truly worked," he said. "It sounded positive for the most part, except for some customer service issues, so I decided to try it out. I ordered $250 of the Andrew Jackson dollars first, and they showed up in a week. My second venture was a little more adventurous. I purchased $500 of George Washington, Thomas Jefferson and John Adams coins. I deposited them at my Credit Union with no problems, but they did wonder where I got the coins."

Revenue-based programs

Although most frequent-flier programs are mileage-based – what counts are the miles you fly, not the money you pay – there are a few schemes that reward customers according to the money they spend. As few and unpopular among travelers as those programs are, they deserve at least a mention.

In the U.S. industry, the low-cost carrier JetBlue first introduced such a revenue-based program (TrueBlue). It gives fliers three point for each dollar spent, and three additional points if they book a ticket on the airline's website. It also offers bonus points for every 3,000 earned.

Southwest Airlines also moved to a revenue-based model in March 2011, stirring quite of bit of controversy. Its Rapid Rewards program used to be known for its simplicity. This is how the carrier's website described the old policy: "Simply fly just eight round trips in 24 consecutive months, and get one free." Well, it's more complicated than that now. Under the new policy, fliers get points for every dollar spent, and the number of points depends on the fare – the higher the fare, the more the points.

Among non-U.S. carriers, Australia's Virgin Blue uses an earnings model similar to that of JetBlue and Southwest. Others, such as Emirates and Air New Zealand, have adopted a mixed model – they reward miles based not on actual flown distance between two cities, but on flat rates according to geographic zones, as well as paid fare. In a way, that approach is an extension of the more widespread practice of giving fewer miles for lower fares and more miles for higher fares, even in distance-based programs.

For example, BMI gives fliers a 200-percent credit for flights in paid Business Class and 300 percent in First Class. Several European programs offer similar bonuses, while at the same time reducing the earned mileage on discounted coach fares to less than 100 percent, and in some cases to no miles at all. In comparison, most major U.S. carriers reward at least 100 percent mileage for all coach fares, and 150 percent for full Economy, Business and First Class, as we saw in Figure 11.

Some airlines, such as Singapore and United, have added a revenue-based mechanism to their otherwise mileage-based programs, in order to reward big spenders. We will look at those tiers in Chapter 12.

The airline loyalty business

As I said at the beginning of this chapter, the main reason frequent-flier programs exist is not to make us happy, but to make money – and most of them do. I've never considered that a problem in principle. A successful business deserves all the rewards it can get. My problem has been with the way airlines have been trying to make money through their so-called loyalty businesses.

For decades, airline executives have had an utterly peculiar philosophy, which can be best described as a "screw the customer" approach. Worse yet, they have packaged it with dishonesty, disrespect and lack of integrity. They reduced or took away elite benefits, hugely devalued their miles, drastically restricted award space, introduced expiration dates for miles and slapped on various fees for the privilege of using our own miles – and they tried to spin all those significant losses for customers as "enhancements."

I don't know what marketing and public relations rules they were following, but they grossly underestimated their loyal customers. Instead of having the courage and decency to be honest and respectful and to call a spade a spade, they became the laughing stock of millions of frequent travelers and lost much of their trust.

My explanation of this approach is that airline executives had a misguided idea about what the loyalty business was about. I'm using past tense, because some of those executives have recently seen the light and things are starting to improve. Still, many of them are stuck in the old way of thinking. Judging by their deeds, they find an inherent conflict between an airline's business interests and the desires of its loyal customers – despite of what they might say in public.

You might ask what's wrong with this philosophy, given that most frequent-flier programs have been profitable even when the airlines that own them weren't. Let's see how they made most of the money. First, as indicated above, by implementing dishonest and customer-unfriendly policies. Second and more important, by selling billions of miles to credit card companies. The next logical question is: How did they spend all that money? Instead of using it for the benefit of the loyalty programs, they poured it into other parts of the airlines that were losing money.

"Frequent-flier programs are major businesses, but unfortunately, in most cases, they haven't been run as businesses," said Jay Sorensen, president of IdeaWorks, an airline consulting firm. "There is fiscal recklessness, and the outcome for the consumer is not attractive." Sorensen, whom I met at an airline loyalty conference where I spoke in 2009, also said the airlines "have had a windfall of cash that has landed in their laps" from credit card deals. "With that comes a tremendous amount of responsibility, and that's what the carriers have forgotten."

So the answer appeared to be in running the programs as stand-alone businesses as much as possible. Some airlines have taken the jump, and the results so far have been positive for both the companies and their customers. The leaders in this trend have been mostly in North America, beginning with Air Canada, which decided to spin off its Aeroplan program and eventually sold it to another company in 2008. Impressed with Aeroplan's success, United seriously contemplated spinning off Mileage Plus – it certainly could have used the cash – but later dropped the idea.

In the process, however, something pivotal happened. United appointed Graham Atkinson president of Mileage Plus in the fall of 2008. This was the second reason why that year represents a turning point in the airline loyalty business.

I met Atkinson in Chicago, about a year before his appointment, when he was United's chief customer officer. It was immediately clear to me that he understood the essence of customer loyalty. In addition, he was a very pleasant and polite person with a grasp of the airline's various parts, which is not that common among senior executives. During our conversation, and especially in e-mail correspondence after he moved to Mileage Plus, I often advocated changing many of the program's rules and policies. My argument was not simply that those policies weren't good for customers, but that they were created for a different era, and adapting them would actually make business sense for the company.

What did I have in mind? At the time, Mileage Plus had many artificial rules that significantly limited what members could do with their miles. For example, you couldn't book a one-way award for half the required miles – it cost the same as a round trip. You couldn't mix and match awards, either, so if you booked Business Class one way, but only coach was available in the opposite direction, you still had to redeem the miles needed for a Business Class round trip. Changes to award tickets were not allowed once travel began.

In my column, I argued that eliminating those restrictions would go a long way to rewarding customer loyalty and winning their trust and good will – but more importantly, it would be good for Mileage Plus financially. Here is why.

According to the old way of thinking, having more restrictive policies made financial sense, because it forced customers to spend more miles. If you booked a round trip, you took up a seat on both your outbound and inbound flights – and if any of those flights were operated by partner-carriers, United had to pay them. However, if you only occupied seats on the outbound journey, United took the same number of miles but incurred only half the costs. That's why management thought it was better for the company. What it didn't realize was that very few customers were willing to play United's game and book tickets at such a disadvantage.

I argued the opposite: That more miles would be spent if Mileage Plus members had more freedom to use them. Offloading miles from the books would also be beneficial for the company, because unredeemed miles are considered a liability for accounting purposes – and thanks to the huge amount United had sold to Chase, its credit card partner, there were tons of miles on the books.

It didn't take Atkinson too long to start seeing things the way I did, although I take no credit for that whatsoever. I'm sure he reached the same conclusions on his own after analyzing Mileage Plus' financial situation. It took him some time to change the old policies, mainly because doing so required a significant investment in technology, but he proved that what's good for customers doesn't have to be bad for business. Even though he was president for only two years and left United when it merged with Continental, he knocked down many artificial barriers erected by his predecessors across the airline industry in the previous decades.

Some of the changes he made weren't fully implemented until after his departure, but none of the restrictions I mentioned above exists any longer. You can now book one-way awards for half the required mileage, you can mix and match different award levels and classes of service, and you change an award ticket after travel has begun. In addition, in the summer of 2009, Atkinson eliminated the so-called "close-in" fees of up to $100 for booking award tickets less than 21 days before departure. Only Delta has since followed suit, in April 2010. Unfortunately, after the Continental management took over as a result of the merger, it decided to reinstate those fees, though elite fliers pay less depending on their status, and top-tier members are still exempt.

American and Alaska have also tried to be innovative in the last few years, and both of them introduced one-way awards before United. Those awards existed in some foreign programs even earlier. But Atkinson's biggest achievement was changing the mentality among major airline executives. He also recognized that long-term customer loyalty is more beneficial than making a quick buck by imposing new fees or tighter restrictions.

The power of customer feedback

Despite Atkinson's efforts, the old approach to customer loyalty is still alive and well in many airline companies. One thing that seems to be changing across the industry is executives' willingness to listen – or at least give the impression of listening – to customer feedback. Almost every carrier in the world uses social media to reach out to its customers.

Very few executives, however, change their mind and reverse major policies because of what their customers want. Atkinson did it repeatedly, though not always. The most significant case was a 2009 decision to stop issuing so-called confirmed regional upgrade certificates – a rare benefit in the industry that allows top elite members (100,000-mile fliers, also known as 1K members) to secure a seat in a higher class of service on flights in North and Central America months in advance, if available, without spending miles. The reason cited for the change was a new system, under which all elite members would be eligible for free upgrades without having to use certificates, but only a couple of days before travel.

The announcement caused an uproar among top fliers, who let United know how they felt in direct correspondence, even before Facebook and Twitter became prominent channels for such feedback. Atkinson and his team listened, and a month later, they agreed to keep the regional upgrades in place.

This wasn't the first time United acted under pressure from its customers. In 2008, it had to abandon plans to charge for food in coach on flights from Washington to Europe – an effort in which Atkinson was involved in his previous position.

Other airlines, including US Airways and Continental, have also backtracked on unpopular changes they made to their frequent-flier programs, such as reducing bonus flight miles for elites, after loud and persistent complaints from customers.

United has continued to listen to its most loyal customers since Atkinson left the company. In late 2010, the airline announced that it would reduce the number of regional upgrades 1K members get from eight to just four a year. Instead of earning two upgrade certificates for flying 10,000 miles in each quarter, top elites would get two certificates after flying 75,000 miles, and another two when they hit 100,000 miles. Another uproar followed, and United agreed to postpone the change for a year, until 2012.

American's introduction of one-way awards in May 2009 pushed United in that direction, too, and although it took United more than nine months to catch up, it beat American to the punch in another respect. When American came out with its one-way awards, it eliminated stopovers on international round-trip awards – if you want to visit two cities, you now need to book three one-way segments, and that will cost you more miles. Naturally, United customers wondered if they would lose that benefit, too. It would have been easy for United to copy American's move, but it didn't. It still allows stopovers, and that makes Mileage Plus more valuable than the AAdvantage program.

One policy that has kept Mileage Plus from being the best program in the world is its blocking of award seats on Star Alliance partners, which I mentioned briefly at the beginning of this chapter and will devote more attention to in Chapter 14. That practice became known as StarNet blocking – manipulating the alliance's award "middleware," which provides access to any Star carrier's inventory on a first-come-first-served basis, to avoid paying other carriers for seats booked on their flights. Those filters were put in place long before Atkinson took over, and even if he wanted to remove them, he wasn't able to do so. Blocking was still being reported after he left, but its magnitude seemed much more limited as of February 2011.

There are plenty of examples of carriers listening more to their best customers in the last couple of years and adapting their policies to that feedback. Even Delta, whose SkyMiles program has been one of the least progressive, reluctantly had its hand forced by customers in 2009. The airline caused a furor when it announced the end of free changes to award tickets for top elites. After hundreds of complaints, Delta gave up some ground, agreeing to waive the fee for two reservations a year, with a $50 charge for each subsequent change. Later, however, it gave in all the way, restoring the old policy, which is the stand-ard in the U.S. industry.

While many complaints about the airlines are not serious, if you ever have constructive criticism or specific suggestions regarding a current or new policy, letting the airline know may very well make a difference.

I'm often asked why frequent-flier programs are so different from one another. Why do they all have such different rules and policies? It's really confusing for customers. I've directed those questions at airline executives at conferences, including from the stage while speaking on panels. I have yet to receive a good answer. Some say they want their program to be unique, but there are ways to do that without making travelers dizzy. A more logical explanation is that, when those programs were created and their rules written, executives didn't much care about what customers would think. It's time for a change.

Chapter 10 Lessons Learned

1. Each traveler should choose a frequent-flier program that best serves his or her specific needs and travel patterns – individual priorities should be determined before deciding where to place one's loyalty.
2. It makes sense for U.S. residents to sign up with a foreign airline program, even if they never fly on that airline, but as a second or third membership.
3. A high priority should be securing top elite status in one's main program before spreading oneself across several other programs.
4. Websites like AwardWallet.com, UsingMiles.com and MileageManager. com can monitor and manage multiple frequent-flier accounts.
5. When it comes to earning miles, U.S. carriers are typically more generous to coach fliers than their foreign peers – foreign carriers reserve their generosity for paying Business and First Class passengers.
6. The strategies for maximizing earned mileage include:
    *   Finding creative routings to receive more miles for no extra money.
    *   Securing a good price-per-mile ratio (PPM) when shopping for airfare.
    *   Using discount vouchers to lower spending.
    *   Converting discounted booking classes into full-fare codes, which often bring bonus miles that count toward elite status.
    *   Paying money for domestic tickets and using miles for international trips.
7. The easiest way to earn miles without flying is through co-branded airline credit cards, most of which offer sign-up bonuses of tens of thousands of miles.
8. Although most frequent-flier programs are mileage-based – what counts are the miles you fly, not the money you pay – there are a few schemes that reward customers according to the money they spend.
9. The main reason frequent-flier programs exist is not to make travelers happy, but to make money – and most of them do.
10. Airline executives have become more willing to listen to customer feedback, so using social media to let a carrier know what it's dong wrong can make a difference.

Chapter 11

Global Airline Alliances

A global airline alliance is one of the most fascinating concepts in the history of commercial aviation – at least for me – combining my two passions and areas of expertise, international affairs and air travel. In fact, what alliance executive teams do every day is nothing short of diplomacy. International negotiations and dispute resolution are two of their specialties, and a big part of their duties is selecting new members, not unlike NATO and the European Union.

When the pioneering Star Alliance was formed in 1997, the idea was not only to represent its members' best interests – that's primarily the job of trade associations – but to boost business by feeding passengers from one carrier to another in the smoothest possible way. Soon, airline diplomacy began in earnest – first among alliance members, which after all are rivals in a fiercely competitive industry, and then with airports, transportation authorities and governments around the world. As I've said before, the other two global alliances are Oneworld and SkyTeam.

"Much of what we do is diplomacy," Jaan Albrecht, Star's CEO, told me when I first met him in the alliance's Frankfurt office in 2008. "We try to educate airports, publics and governments about the benefits that come from a network like ours."

Why alliances are good for travelers

Global alliances are another example of the airline industry's creative thinking aimed at increasing revenues. However, unlike some of the questionable practices I described in Chapter 6, this one has dramatically improved the customer experience. Of course, in order to get the best of that experience, we need to have some knowledge about the alliance system and the benefits it offers – but by now you've read enough about my mantra that an educated traveler is a better traveler.

The benefits that come with an alliance membership are both tangible and intangible. The first category includes interline ticketing and check-in, harmonized schedules to provide seamless connections, worldwide lounge access, mileage-earning and redemption opportunities, as well as elite-status recognition across the alliance, and round-the-world and other special-fare products.

I may be one of few travelers who also appreciate the intangible benefits. The most important to me is that the experience on an alliance's various carriers is so similar and yet so different. I like the predictability created by consistent and aligned policies – knowing how things work and what to expect gives me comfort at the airport and in the air. At the same time, I love the individual touches that each airline adds to the travel experience, based on its national, cultural and even corporate uniqueness.

For example, Scandinavian Airlines and Thai Airways are both members of the Star Alliance, and technically there is no difference which one you are booked on – you will earn miles, check-in all the way through to your final destination and access their lounges anywhere in the world. But when you enter a lounge or board a plane, you will never confuse Scandinavian with Thai.

	Star Alliance	Oneworld	SkyTeam
Current Members	Adria Airways Aegean Airlines Air Canada Air China Air New Zealand All Nippon Airways Asiana Airlines Austrian Airlines Blue 1 British Midland Brussels Airlines Continental Airlines Croatia Airlines EgyptAir LOT Polish Airlines Lufthansa Scandinavian Airlines Singapore Airlines South African Airways Spanair Swiss TAM TAP Portugal Thai Airways Turkish Airlines United Airlines US Airways	American Airlines British Airways Cathay Pacific Finnair Iberia Japan Airlines LAN Malev Mexicana Qantas Royal Jordanian S7 Airlines	Aeroflot Aeromexico Air Europa Air France Alitalia China Southern Czech Airlines Delta Airlines Kenya Airways KLM Korean Air Tarom Vietnam Airlines
Future Members	Air India Avianca Copa Airlines Ethiopian Airlines Olympic Airlines TACA	Air Berlin Kingfisher Airlines	Aerolíneas Argentinas China Airlines China Eastern Airlines Garuda Indonesia Middle East Airlines Saudi Arabian Airlines

Figure 15: Current and invited – but not yet accepted – members of the three global alliances.

Critics of the alliance concept usually argue that consumers suffer, because closer cooperation among airlines leads to higher fares. They refer to special arrangements, known as anti-trust immunity exceptions, which are granted to some carriers so they can coordinate fares, schedules and inventory on certain routes. The largest members of the three alliances have received such waivers on intercontinental routes. Some have gone a step further, securing approval to operate certain routes as a joint venture. Price-fixing is illegal, so these carriers needed the exceptions to publish identical fares – and if you compare their tariffs, you will see they are indeed identical. When granting the immunity, the Department of Transportation is careful to exclude routes on which the only existing service is provided by the carriers seeking the waiver – those exclusions are known as "carve-outs."

So the government is supposed to protect consumers, and it seems it's doing its job. Overall, there is no question in my mind that airline alliances have had a positive impact on customers.

Star Alliance

As the first and largest global alliance, Star has been a trend-setter in most policies and practices fliers are used to today. Founded by United, Lufthansa, Air Canada, Scandinavian (SAS) and Thai Airways on May 14, 1997, it has grown to 27 members from 25 countries. According to the alliance's web-site, those carriers have more than 4,000 aircraft in their fleets, and they fly over 600 million passengers a year on 21,000 daily flights to 1,160 airports in 181 countries.

In addition to the founders, Star's current members include such world-class airlines as Swiss, Singapore, All Nippon, Air New Zealand, Asiana and South African. Four more carriers have been invited to join: TACA, Copa, Air India and Ethiopian Airlines.

In recent years, the alliance has surprised many travelers and industry watchers by admitting carriers with less than a stellar reputation like EgyptAir and Air India, but Albrecht, the CEO, assured me that every candidate that receives an invitation meets certain criteria. "We have 53 membership requirements, and an invitation is an incentive for a candidate to work hard to improve," he said. Interestingly, that same reasoning has been used by the EU and NATO when inviting poorer countries in Eastern Europe to join.

One of Star's most formidable challenges has been its "under one roof" project, which aims to group all members in the same terminal at airports around the world, as well as to provide passengers access to one large lounge instead of several small ones. Here, Albrecht's diplomatic skills have been essential, he said. "It's not easy to get an airport like London Heathrow to restructure its terminals in order to accommodate the Star Alliance." The co-habitation of all Star carriers at Tokyo Narita (NRT) has cut connection times from two hours to 45 minutes, he added. One airport where the project has no future, because of infrastructure issues, is Washington Dulles. "That's a bad one," he said. "It's a big problem." Several Star lounges have already opened, including those in Zurich (ZRH), London (LHR), Paris (CDG) and Los Angeles (LAX).

Star recognizes only two elite levels – Silver and Gold – and offers no extra benefits to customers who fly more than 50,000 a year. Silver status doesn't get you much beyond the occasional priority check-in and wait-listing, but Gold gives you lounge access around the world. The only caveat is that, if you are a member of a U.S. frequent-flier program, you don't have access to domestic U.S. lounges, unless you are flying in international First or Business Class. If you want to use those lounges, you need to buy a membership. However, if you have a Gold card from a foreign-based Star program, the lounge doors are open for you at no charge.

The alliance has a series of incredibly useful and money-saving special fares – both global and regional. We'll talk in detail about round-the-world fares later in this chapter, but there are more "circle fares," such as Circle Pacific, Circle Asia and Circle North Asia. They allow travelers to visit several countries in the respective region, and their pricing is based on flat rates depending on flown distance, class of service and country of origin. There are also air passes for North America, Europe, Africa, the Middle East and several large countries, priced per flight segment and offered just in coach, and only to non-residents of the respective region, in conjunction with a intercontinental ticket.

Each Star airline allows earning miles that count toward elite status, as well as redeeming miles, on every other alliance member. However, just because they all belong to the same alliance doesn't mean that their frequent-flier programs are similar. In fact, there are more differences between United Mileage Plus and Lufthansa's Miles&More than between Mileage Plus and American's AAdvantage (American is in Oneworld). They also have different award redemption charts.

They do have some common features. As I said in Chapter 10, mileage-earning on Star carriers is based on the airline operating the flight, regardless of how the flight is marketed. Even if a flight is booked as a code-share number, that number converts into the true number of the operating carrier when it posts to a frequent-flier account. So if your ticket shows you are on flight UA9093 from Munich (MUC) to Warsaw (WAW), what you will see on your account statement is flight LH1612.

Of all the intriguing relationships in the alliance, the most peculiar and strained one has been between United and Singapore. The two carriers never seem to say anything good about each other. Although it has been a Star member since 2000, Singapore has refused to code-share flights with United. That's not a requirement for membership, of course, but most foreign alliance members that fly to the United States do code-share domestic United flights. For years, I thought that Singapore considered United's standards too low compared to its own, but after US Airways joined in 2004, Singapore began code-sharing with it – and United's standards are by no means lower than those of US Airways.

In fact, what I call Singapore's maddening perfection has become an issue for many Star carriers, who feel that Singapore views itself as better than anyone else. That causes problems when alliance-wide decisions are made.

Flying on Singapore, which regularly tops various airline rankings, is an experience I wish any traveler could have at least once in a lifetime. It has long been the world's leading carrier in hard-product innovation and luxury, often years ahead of its competitors. The trouble with perfection is that it's impossible 100 percent of the time, and most of Singapore's policies are written for a perfect world, which is also impossible in the airline industry. Employees of every airline must follow certain rules, but Singapore's staff has almost no flexibility in making exceptions or bending the rules to respond to a specific case or situation.

While Singapore is among the least generous Star members when it comes to award availability, overall Star offers excellent redemption opportunities to more destinations than either of the other two alliances. It also has an upgrade program with 20 participating airlines, which allows customers to use miles from one frequent-flier program to upgrade flights on other carriers. That usually requires full-fare tickets.

Oneworld

Although less than half the Star Alliance's size, Oneworld has emerged as a strong Star competitor. It was founded on February 1, 1999, by American Airlines, British Airways, Cathay Pacific, Qantas and Canadian Airlines, which later withdrew following its merger with Air Canada. Its current 12 members include LAN, Finnair and Japan Airlines, among others. According to its website, Oneworld carries about 335 million passengers a year on more than 9,300 daily flights to 900 destinations in 145 countries. Two more carriers, AirBerlin and India's Kingfisher Airlines, have been invited to join.

Most of Oneworld's products and challenges are similar to those of Star, including a broad effort to relocate members to the same terminal at various airports around the world. It also offers such benefits as interline ticketing and check-in, harmonized schedules, special fares and access to 550 lounges. It plans to move its office from Vancouver to New York in 2011.

There are several important features that distinguish Oneworld from Star. Instead of being more aggressive in recruiting new members, it has focused on making some of its products more competitive. Unlike Star, it recognizes a third elite level (Emerald), which allows top fliers access to First Class check-in and First Class lounges. Star Gold members have no such privileges. Oneworld's lowest (Ruby) and middle tier (Sapphire) both provide access to Business Class check-in, which is the case only with Star Gold but not Star Silver.

Oneworld offers more special-fare products than Star, beginning with two round-the-world fares – one based on distance flown, and one on the number of countries visited. In addition to the circle fares offered by Star, Oneworld has Circle Atlantic and halfway round-the-world excluding the Americas (you can fly Australia-Asia-Middle East-Europe-Africa-Australia), and its Circle Asia product also includes the southwest Pacific.

Both circle fares and regional air passes on Oneworld are less restrictive than Star's. For example, any U.S. and Canadian city is eligible for inclusion in a Circle Pacific ticket, while Star only allows Los Angeles, San Francisco, Seattle, Honolulu and Vancouver. Star limits regional air passes to between three and 10 flight coupons; Oneworld requires at least two but allows as many as you want. Each coupon costs a fixed amount based on the flown distance. These tickets cannot be purchased online and are usually issued by the airline from which you buy your intercontinental ticket. The booking classes for those flights are determined by the operating carrier.

How does an air pass work? Let's say you are about to fly to Europe from the United States, and your ticket has you arriving in London and departing from Paris. During your trip, you'd also like to visit Austria, Hungary, Italy and Spain, but buying one-way tickets from point to point is too expensive. The "Visit Europe" air pass lets you put all flights you want on the same ticket: London-Vienna (€115), Vienna-Budapest (€55),

Budapest-Rome (€115), Rome-Madrid (€115) and Madrid-Paris (€115). That's a total base fare of €515 plus taxes and surcharges. True, sometimes you may be able to get lower fares on Ryanair or EasyJet, especially if you only need two or three flights, but think about the sacrifices you will likely have to make on those carriers – plus, you'd be earning miles if you stick to your alliance.

One area where Oneworld still lags behind Star and SkyTeam is an alliance-wide upgrade program, which is not "on the immediate horizon," alliance spokesman Michael Blunt told me.

In terms of earning miles, Oneworld's policy is different from Star's. As I mentioned in Chapter 10, the flight number on your ticket determines the mileage you will receive, regardless of the operating carrier. If you book a British Airways-coded flight operated by Cathay Pacific, it will be treated as a BA flight for mileage-accrual purposes.

When it comes to its membership, Oneworld has had its own intrigues. Its most serious recent problems have been with Mexicana, which suspended operations in August 2010. The way the Mexican carrier handled that episode was quite embarrassing for the alliance.

On the day Mexicana filed for insolvency proceedings in Mexico and bankruptcy protection in the United States, Blunt issued a press release, assuring travelers that Mexicana's position in the alliance was "unaffected" by the developments. "Mexicana has stressed that it will continue to operate normally, in line with Mexican legislation covering such restructuring. Its schedule is being maintained – though with some network and frequency changes – and it continues to take bookings and offer its full range of services. So the airline continues to offer full Oneworld services and benefits, and tickets for flights on Mexicana and its frequent-flier arrangements are unaffected," Blunt said.

Mexicana stopped selling tickets the very next day. In another press release, Oneworld called it a "temporary suspension," adding that, "during this time, Mexicana will continue to operate most of its previously scheduled international flights as normal, but further bookings will not be accepted." About three weeks later, the airline stopped flying. I asked Blunt in an e-mail message at the time whether the alliance was deliberately misled by Mexicana, but he declined to comment.

SkyTeam

The youngest of the three alliances, Sky Team was officially founded on May 22, 2000, by Delta, Air France, AeroMexico and Korean Air. Its 13 current members fly 384 million passengers annually on 13,000 daily flights to 898 destinations in 169 countries. They have 447 airport lounges.

Critics often mock SkyTeam for taking in carriers with lower standards that have been left out of Star or Oneworld, citing Russia's Aeroflot, Romania's Tarom and even Alitalia. The fact is that most world-class airlines were already aligned with one of the other alliances by the time SkyTeam came about, and alliances often prefer to have some coverage in a certain geographic region than to have none at all.

That said, Korean Air is no doubt a world-class carrier. Plus, several current and incoming SkyTeam members, such as Vietnam Airlines and Garuda Indonesia, have improved dramatically in recent years. Garuda, in particular, has staged a remarkable turnaround only three years after being banned from landing in Europe. In addition to Garuda, SkyTeam has invited China Eastern, Taiwan's China Airlines, Aerolíneas Argentinas and Saudi Arabian to join.

Mileage accrual on SkyTeam is similar to Oneworld's in that what counts is which carrier's code a flight carries, not who operates it. SkyTeam's elite tiers, however, resemble those of the Star Alliance – there are only two (Elite and Elite Plus). Also like Star, SkyTeam has an upgrade program with eight participating carriers. Four of them allow upgrades only on flights booked in full-fare Y class. Most Star airlines require either Y or B class. Award availability on SkyTeam tends to be worse than on the other two alliances, but we will talk more about that in Chapter 14.

SkyTeam has a more limited special-fare offering than Star and Oneworld. Round-the-world is its only circle product, and its air passes are fewer than those of either of its competitors.

A major issue with SkyTeam for U.S.-based frequent travelers has been Delta's SkyMiles program, which is considered one of the less competitive and customer-friendly programs in the U.S. airline industry today. Its upgrade and award policies are among the most restrictive and inflexible. It has further devalued its long-cheapened miles by introducing a third award redemption level to mask its poor availability at the lowest award level. Delta also charges some fees that are hard to justify, such as $50 for booking an award originating outside the United States. For more than a year, Delta didn't even publish an award chart, except out of the U.S. When it finally did in February 2011, mileage rates on many routes were increased.

Despite its flaws, SkyMiles has a couple of unique features. It has an official fourth elite tier (Diamond) in addition to Silver, Gold and Platinum, and it allows members at the top three status levels to benefit from complimentary domestic upgrade on award tickets – something not permitted by other airlines. Diamond elites also get free access to Delta's airport lounges, which no other carrier offers to its best customers at U.S. airports.

Round-the-world fares

Despite significant increases in the last couple of years, round-the-world fares remain a very attractive travel option, and one of the global airline alliances' best products. Not only are they cheaper than separate one-way fares between two cities, but in some cases, they may be even lower than a round trip. For example, a round-trip Business Class ticket from the United

States to Australia is often more expensive than a round-the-world ticket. Booking such tickets has become easier with online tools offered by Star and Oneworld, but they can be booked with any member-carrier of the respective alliance.

Several airlines, including United, Emirates and Singapore, have round-the-world products independent of alliances, typically in partnership with one or two more carriers. Those fares tend to me cheaper than alliance prices, but they have more restrictive rules and offer a limited number of destinations.

Let's first compare the three alliances' round-the-world offerings, starting with their similarities. They usually give you between 10 days and a year to complete your trip. You have to cross both the Atlantic and Pacific oceans, but you can do so only once, and to travel in the same general direction – either eastward or westward – though backtracking in permitted on the same continent. You need to have confirmed flights for your first international sector and those leading up to it, but the rest of your itinerary can be open-dated, as long as you select your stops.

All alliances base their pricing on the flown distance (Oneworld has a second round-the-world product that is not distance-based). The first level allows you to fly as many as 26,000 miles and lets you make up to five stopovers, but it's only available in coach and may not be offered out of every country. The second level is 29,000 miles, the third 34,000 miles and the last one is 39,000 miles. They all permit up to 15 stopovers. Typically, only one stopover is allowed in each city. As for the minimum stopovers, they are two on Oneworld and three on Star and SkyTeam. Changing dates, times and carriers is usually free, though routing changes incur a penalty of up to $125.

Now let's look at the differences among the alliances. Oneworld publishes Business and First Class fares only at the 34,000-mile level, with only coach available at 29,000 miles and 39,000 miles. Star and SkyTeam have no such restrictions. In terms of defining continents, SkyTeam considers the Middle

East a separate continent, while Star groups it with Africa, and Oneworld with Europe.

Although all alliances require each trip to begin and end in the same country – though not necessarily in the same city – Oneworld and SkyTeam have some rather liberal country definitions. They both consider the United States and Canada one country, as they do the more logical China and Hong Kong. SkyTeam counts all of Scandinavia and all of the South Pacific as one country. Oneworld does the same with Singapore and Malaysia, as well as the entire Middle East and all of Africa.

Another difference is in the cancellation penalties. Both Star and SkyTeam charge a flat $150 fee, but Oneworld comes down really hard on travelers who change their plans. Canceling a ticket will cost you 10 percent of the fare you paid in Economy and 5 percent in Business and First Class – that's at least several hundred dollars.

SkyTeam has its own peculiarity, which is screamingly unfair. In Chapter 8, I explained my problem with the name of U.S. domestic First Class. When it comes to round-the-world fares, you can see why that practice is undeniably harmful to customers. According to SkyTeam's rules, if you buy a Business Class round-the-world ticket, you will be "accommodated" in First Class on U.S. domestic flights for a $100 surcharge per segment in addition to your fare. There is no reason for this, given that Business Class doesn't exist, and both Star and Oneworld charge no extra fees for seats in the premium cabin.

As I mentioned above, Oneworld has a second round-the-world product called "Oneworld Explorer." It's priced not based on mileage but on the number of visited continents and is available in all classes of service. Flights segments within each continent are limited to four (six for North America), with only two in the continent of origin. Two additional segments in each continent can be purchased at extra cost.

If we compare base fares by alliance, out of the United States SkyTeam has lower coach prices than Star and Oneworld. In

Business and First Class, Oneworld and SkyTeam are similar and cheaper than Star.

What about the actual prices? It depends on the country where the trip begins. Some of the differences are as much as several thousand dollars. Let's pick just one level – 29,000 miles in Business Class on Star, with fare basis CRWSTAR1 – and compare countries on different continents. As of April 1, 2011, the base fare out of the United States was $11,849; from Argentina, it was $9,256; from Britain $9,056; from Japan $7,253; and from South Africa $6,885. It's worth noting that geographic regions have nothing to do with prices – they are determined by market conditions and currency exchange rates. For example, the Star fare for the level just referenced was $9,976 out of China, but only $7,382 from neighboring South Korea.

If you live in the United States but can't afford $11,849 plus taxes and surcharges of up to $1,000, what can you do to save money? You could start your trip in Japan – that would save you almost $4,600. You could buy a separate round-trip ticket from the U.S. to Japan, which you should be able to find for about $1,000. That would still save you $3,600 – plus, you would get many more frequent-flier miles this way. You could also use the miles you already have for an award ticket to Japan and back, instead of paying money for it.

The savings are not the only benefit of this strategy. One of the things preventing many people from booking a round-the-world trip is that they can't come home in the middle of it and pick it up again later on. That's not a problem when you start your trip in another country. You could take the first half of your trip in the spring, return home for a few months, and complete it in the fall.

In addition to the base fares and the taxes, there may be other surcharges on certain flights. Understandably, airlines impose extra fees for access to their premium coach cabins by Economy-paying customers. In the Star Alliance, three carriers also charge additional fees in Business Class, because they think their seats are much better than those on other airlines.

Air Canada charges $300 extra for many long-haul flights, while Asiana has a $620 surcharge only on flights between Seoul and San Francisco. Not surprisingly, Singapore Airline is the biggest abuser of additional fees – it has slapped them on most of its flights, including all routes in Europe and the Americas, except one, charging as much as $900 per segment.

Round-the-world fares are based on quotes provided by alliance members through "blind voting," Star's Albrecht told me. "Every airline sends blind information into a 'safe haven' whenever it wants. There is nothing we do – there are no meetings to discuss fares," he said.

Christian Klick, Star's vice president for corporate affairs, said the alliance does that "to be fully compliant with competition law requirements." Star "facilitates the process, receives the fares from individual members, calculates the global fare, applies the current rates of exchange in order to come to local market fares for every region of the world and publishes these fares on all distribution systems," he added.

The alliance has divided the world into 11 geographic regions or "points of origin," and the fares are calculated based on a "standard formula" for every zone, and then published in each country's currency, Klick explained. Although airlines can send quotes at any time, "there are two regular dates in the year" when fares are updated: in "mid-February to be effective as of April 1, and mid-August to be effective as of Oct. 1, which coincides with the worldwide change of airline timetables," he said. "Still, the process is dynamic as it foresees so-called foreign exchange amendments at carriers' request, and members can call for extraordinary amendments at any time if the competitive situation requires it."

Chapter 11 Lessons Learned

1. The three global airline alliances – the Star Alliance, Oneworld and SkyTeam – have dramatically improved the international travel experience.

2. Alliance-wide benefits include interline ticketing and check-in, harmonized schedules to provide seamless connections, worldwide lounge access, mileage-earning and redemption opportunities, elite-status recognition and round-the-world and other special-fare products.

3. The Star Alliance has 27 members from 25 countries, which have more than 4,000 aircraft in their fleets and fly over 600 million passengers a year on 21,000 daily flights to 1,160 airports in 181 countries.

4. Oneworld has 12 members from 12 countries, which carry about 335 million passengers a year on more than 9,300 daily flights to 900 destinations in 145 countries.

5. SkyTeam has 13 members from 13 countries, which fly about 384 million passengers annually on 13,000 daily flights to 898 destinations in 169 countries.

6. Star and SkyTeam have alliance-wide upgrade programs, though not all member-carriers participate yet.

7. Despite significant increases, round-the-world fares remain a very attractive travel option – not only are they cheaper than separate one-way fares between two cities, but in some cases, they may be even lower than a round trip.

8. Round-the-world fares are different out of each country – some of the differences may be as much as several thousand dollars.

Chapter 12

Elite Airline Status

"Flying is such a miserable experience, and elite status is about all there is to take the edge off the pain," Delaware business traveler Walt Frank told me while I was researching a 2009 column on whether airline status is worth the trouble to achieve it. At the same time, he warned, "status is the crack cocaine of frequent fliers." There is a good reason for that, and the airlines know it well: Once you've been a top elite flier, going back is very painful, indeed.

Not everyone, of course, would agree with this statement. Many travelers complain about erosion of benefits and the growing numbers of fellow elite fliers. It's no doubt disappointing to compete for an upgrade with dozens of people – and end up in coach – when you thought you were special. It's also frustrating when you finally reach a higher status level, and your airline decides to take away the very perks for which you went through the trouble of qualifying.

I find that the large majority of travelers who don't value their elite status are not educated enough and have unrealistic expectations. It's unreasonable to declare your status worthless just because you missed an upgrade or were unable to use your miles for an award seat on a particular flight. The people who get the most out of their status are those best educated about everything that status carries before they even achieve it. Having solid knowledge about all aspects of the air travel system covered in this book helps as well – as I explained in Chapter 9, blindly relying on airline agents to take care of you is not a good idea for a sophisticated flier.

I'm often asked whether one can earn elite-qualifying miles without flying. The most common way to do that is through credit cards. Many airlines offer a limited number of elite miles for signing up for certain cards, and additional miles for spending a certain amount each year. From time to time, some carriers also run promotions offering elite miles, but they tend to be rare.

There are actually airlines that will sell you elite status – all the way up to the highest tier – but more on that later in the chapter.

Is airline promiscuity cheaper than loyalty?

Most travelers don't bother to qualify for elite status for two reasons: They think that it's too complicated and confusing, and that they would spend less money if they went to whichever airline they perceive as having the lowest fare every time they fly. I can't argue with the first reason – and hopefully this book will make the process less complicated and confusing. I do, however, take issue with the second argument.

I'm not suggesting that you stay loyal to one airline if you fly once or twice a year. But I know people who fly tens of thousands of miles annually and still spread themselves across several airlines, resulting in elite status on none of them. Then they complain about not having access to good seats on the plane and being "treated like dirt" by airline agents. I have the following advice for such travelers:

▶   First, it's not necessary to stick with a single airline to achieve elite status – all you need to do is **pick an alliance**, as miles earned on any alliance carrier count toward elite status. I realize there may not be a big difference between airline loyalty and alliance loyalty if most of your travel is on U.S. domestic flights and you choose Oneworld, since its only U.S. member is American. The same applies to Delta and SkyTeam. The Star Alliance, however, has three U.S members – United, Continental and US Airways. Although they will become two when the United-Continental merger is complete, two is better than one. Of course, if you fly internationally, alliance loyalty can make a big difference.

▶ Second, **don't trust web agencies** to tell you which airline has the lowest fare. Just because Expedia says that Alaska Airlines has the cheapest option doesn't mean that's true. Remember, Expedia uses an automated process to make the "sausage," and now that you know the Kralev Method, you can access raw data and make the "sausage" yourself, if saving money is important to you. I'm not saying that online booking engines are always wrong, but here is a likely scenario: Let's say I want a Star Alliance flight, but the cheapest flights those third-party sites are giving me are on non-Star carriers. I'd go to ExpertFlyer and check the master tariff on my route, which would show me which airline has published the lowest fare. If that airline is not a Star member, I'd find the lowest fare offered by a Star carrier. If the difference is minimal, I'd stay loyal, and if not, I'd consider other options. In most cases, I manage to get a fare that helps me to avoid defection.

▶ Third, even if a non-alliance carrier offers the best fare, **think about additional fees.** How much more would you have to pay for a seat assignment, luggage, day-of-travel flight changes or standby, which would be free if you were a top elite flier?

▶ Fourth, **do a cost-benefit analysis** to see how much, if anything, airline promiscuity has saved you, and if it would have made sense to spend that amount on earning elite status. If you don't believe in loyalty, keep flying on different airlines, but keep track of the fares you would have paid had you stayed with the same alliance. At the end of the year, add up all those fares and see what the price of loyalty would have been.

By the way, trying to achieve elite status with one frequent-flier program doesn't mean you can't be a member of other programs, or even build status on another airline. In fact, many regular travelers face the dilemma whether to have lower status on two airlines or go for the top tier on one. Only you can make that decision, and hopefully the next few pages will help you do that.

Lowest elite tier

Most airline loyalty programs have two or three elite levels. The lowest tier is most often called Silver, though some carriers use different names – Gold (American), Premier (United), Bronze (All Nippon), Crystal (Japan Airlines), Blue (Brazil's TAM), Prestige (Air Canada).

The most common mileage requirement to qualify for this level is between 20,000 and 35,000 miles a year, with 25,000 miles needed on the major U.S. carriers. Some airlines also require a certain minimum number of miles accrued on their own flights, as opposed to partner flights (10,000 miles on Air Canada, for example). Many business people who fly short distances qualify based on segments, not miles. The major U.S. airlines award the lowest tier after 30 segments.

If you fly less than 20,000 miles, don't be discouraged. You can still be an elite flier. Some smaller carriers have extremely lower qualification criteria. The best example is Greece's Aegean Airlines, the newest Star Alliance member, which requires only 4,000 miles a year for its Silver level. You can easily earn this mileage on one round trip between the U.S. East and West coasts. I recommended that option to occasional travelers when I was a guest on "The Diane Rehm Show" on NPR in the summer of 2010, and I was amused when one listener accused me of being unpatriotic.

What benefits does this status offer?

▶ First, it **waives luggage fees** across the respective alliance. That Aegean status will get you a Star Silver card, which is enough to secure at least one free checked bag on every Star carrier. Suppose your four-member family needs to travel within the United States on US Airways. The first checked bag would cost $25 and the second $35 – that's up to $240 for all of you. However, your Silver membership will waive all those fees for everyone on your itinerary.

▶ Second, some airlines grant all elite members **free access to priority seating**, including rows with more legroom (United Economy Plus) and exit rows. Usually, this benefit is restricted to a carrier's own customers, and doesn't apply to Silver card-holders from other alliance programs.

▶ Third, the lowest elite tier gives you **bonus flight miles** of 25 percent (American, Lufthansa, LAN, Singapore) to 50 percent (Japan Airlines, Air France/KLM).

▶ The fourth benefit is **priority check-in, boarding and wait-listing**, though obviously the higher the status, the higher the priority. At many airports, there are dedicated check-in lines for this elite tier, and in some cases you can even use the Business Class line. But with online check-in becoming more common, this perk is losing some of its value. The boarding priority can still be useful, especially if you need space for your carry-on in the overhead bins.

▶ Fifth, most major U.S. carriers offer **complimentary domestic upgrades** to all their elite members – but again, by the time the top elites get upgraded, there may not be a seat left for you. Your chances would be better on flights between smaller airports with lighter elite traffic, rather than between two hubs. If you use miles to upgrade, most U.S. carriers charge cash co-pays in addition to the miles – however, elite members at any level are exempt from those co-pays on domestic flights.

▶ Sixth, very few airlines, such as Lufthansa and its subsidiaries Swiss, BMI and Austrian, give their lowest-tier fliers **free airport lounge access**. That benefit is not extended to other Star Alliance Silver members. In contrast, as mentioned in Chapter 10, U.S. carriers don't offer such access domestically even to their top elites.

Middle elite tier

The middle elite level in most programs, which is usually awarded after flying 50,000 miles, is actually the top tier in some programs (Emirates, Aegean, BMI). Aegean again stands out with its very low mileage requirement of only 20,000 miles. This tier is best known as Gold, though many carriers use other names – Premier Executive (United), Platinum (American and All Nippon), Diamond (Asiana), Red (TAM).

The qualification criteria can get tricky on certain airlines, so read them carefully before you start crediting miles to those accounts. According to Singapore Airlines' website, for example, 50,000 miles are required to reach Gold status. However, if you continue reading, you will discover that you need that mileage once you secure Silver status, after flying 25,000 miles. So in effect, Gold status really costs 75,000 miles. Once you have it, of course, you need 50,000 miles to keep it.

In contrast, when Aegean says 20,000 miles, it does mean 20,000 – once you achieve the first tier for 4,000 miles, you need 16,000 to qualify for Gold. This is the more common practice. On United, you need 50,000 miles to make Premier Executive, and that includes the 25,000 miles necessary to gain Premier status.

The qualification period also differs by airline. For American, United and many others, that period is a calendar year. However, Singapore, BMI, Aegean and others give members one year from the date of achieving Silver status to earn the mileage requirement for Gold.

Naturally, this tier carries all benefits afforded to Silver members, plus the following:

▶ First, it offers **free alliance-wide lounge access** to the member and a guest, no matter in what class of service they are traveling. There are exceptions, of course. As I said in Chapter 10, that policy doesn't apply to U.S. domestic airport lounges on purely domestic itineraries, even if you are flying in Business or First Class. However, Star and Oneworld provide a way around that rule. Star Gold cards, as well as Oneworld Sapphire and

Emerald cards, from non-U.S. carriers will get you domestic lounge access. SkyTeam doesn't offer that benefit.

This is another place where knowing your rights will save you headaches, as many lounge agents don't know the admission rules. I've had several such cases, the most recent of which was at the United lounge in Phoenix (PHX). The agent there insisted that my BMI (Star Alliance) Gold card wasn't enough to let me in, and I needed a Business or First Class boarding pass for an international flight. She called a supervisor who agreed with her, so I asked to speak with him. When he came, he took one look at a piece of paper with the admission rules that was taped on the counter, right before the agent's eyes, and said I was right.

▶ Second, Gold status comes with **flight bonus miles of up to 100 percent**, though some airlines are much stingier. While the bonus usually applies only to redeemable miles, as pointed out earlier, there may be carriers that also offer elite-qualifying bonuses.

▶ Third, this elite tier entitles passengers to **waived baggage fees for up to three bags** – a savings of as much as $50 per bag. This benefit is usually offered alliance-wide. Most airlines allow at least one free checked bag on international flights.

▶ Fourth, Gold members are entitled to **priority baggage handling**. Your bags will be marked with a special sticker, which means that they are supposed to come out among the first at the carousel. As you can imagine, sometimes things don't work out quite as planned, so don't be surprised if your bag arrives with the last ones.

▶ Fifth, it's logical that Gold fliers should have **higher check-in, boarding and waitlist priority** than Silver members. Whatever waitlist you are on – standby, upgrade or award – your chances are much better with this status. In terms of check-in, some airlines allow their Gold members to use the First Class line.

▶ Sixth, many carriers have a **dedicated reservations phone line** for Gold members. In most cases, that means that your wait time would be shorter than that of a caller with lower status – it doesn't mean that there is a group of agents somewhere tasked with answering calls only from Gold members. That may be the case with higher elite levels.

▶ Seventh, most airlines offer **a guaranteed coach seat** to this elite level, even on sold-out flights, provided the reservation is made two or three days before departure. You'd have to pay full Y fare, and as I said earlier, there may be a lower Business Class fare, so check all your options before pulling the trigger.

Top elite tier

We've arrived where any sophisticated frequent traveler should aspire to be. This is the only decent way to fly and actually enjoy the experience. Most airlines require 100,000 miles to qualify for this tier, though the range may vary from 70,000 miles (Air France/KLM) to 150,000 miles (TAM). Some carriers, such as Air France and Lufthansa, punish the residents of their own countries by requiring much higher mileage. Although the most common name for this level is Platinum, many carriers call it differently – 1K (United), Executive Platinum (American), Diamond (All Nippon), Black (TAM).

In addition to the mid-tier benefits, this level offers the most meaningful perks in the airline industry.

▶ First, Platinum members are **exempt from most fees**, including those for ticketing, standby and same-day confirmed changes, award booking, as well as changing or canceling awards and re-depositing of miles. Those fees' value can be up to $150 each. Naturally, the fee waivers for luggage, seat assignments and upgrade co-pays granted to lower-tier elites apply to this level as well. Top fliers do have to pay change and cancellation fees on revenue tickets, according to the fare rules.

▶ Second, some carriers award their best customers **confirmed upgrade certificates** that can be applied as early as the time of ticketing – without having to use miles. We will discuss those upgrades, which can be domestic or international, in detail in Chapter 13.

▶ Third, many carriers allocate **additional coach award seats** that can be redeemed only with miles from a Platinum account. In most cases, you can see that availability as a separate booking class.

▶ Fourth, some airlines have **dedicated reservations teams** to service their top elites. Those agents tend to be more knowledgeable and experienced than the average agent, which can be a life-saver. In the case of carriers with outsourced off-shore call centers, such as United, the only guarantee that you will talk to a U.S.-based agent every time you call is to have access to that special elite line.

▶ Fifth, Platinum members have the **highest check-in, boarding and waitlist priority**. This actually makes a big difference – you can be added to a waiting list at the last minute and go right at the top. In terms of boarding, most major U.S. carriers have dedicated red-carpet lanes at their gates, where top elites, as well as First and Business Class passengers, can board at any time and cut in line, even if there are 200 people waiting for general boarding.

▶ Sixth, some of the best perks that come with the top elite tier are **non-published benefits**, which is why being in the know is extremely helpful. As I pointed out in Chapter 9, airline employees are often more empowered and willing to bend certain rules for their best customers. Some of that bending is actually allowed in written documents, but of course those texts are available only to employees. Remember the requirement to present a credit card at check-in, about which I wrote in Chapter 7? Some carriers waive that requirement for top elites. Another reminder from Chapter 9: Your status level often determines the amount of compensation or "good will" you can get when something goes wrong during a trip.

A few airlines have four elite tiers, including US Airways. As I noted in Chapter 11, Delta added a fourth (Diamond) level in 2009. It requires 75,000 miles to reach Platinum status, and

125,000 miles for Diamond). Lufthansa is an interesting case. Its second tier (Senator) requires 100,000 miles to achieve, and it offers very similar benefits to the top level on most carriers. Lufthansa's third tier (HON Circle) is very hard to reach – the requirement is 600,000 miles over two years. Its benefits include additional upgrade certificates, access to First Class check-in, First Class lounges and to the legendary First Class Terminal in Frankfurt, which I described in Chapter 9.

Revenue-based elite tiers

In recent years, some airlines have added elite levels to their existing tiers meant to reward big spenders, as opposed to people who fly lots of miles. I promised in Chapter 10 to explain how those revenue-based mechanisms work.

Let's first look at a tier whose requirements and benefits are published, such as Singapore's PPS Club (the abbreviation stands for Premium Passenger Service). Miles play no role here – the only requirement is S$25,000 (Singapore dollars) spent on First and Business Class airfare only on Singapore flights. There is also Solitaire PPS membership, which requires at least S$250,000 over five consecutive years.

American and United both have non-published revenue-based tiers – United calls it Global Services, and American Concierge Key, which was the status George Clooney's character had in the film "Up in the Air." There are no official qualification criteria, and membership is only by invitation. High-flying business executives who pay tens of thousands of dollars a year for First and Business Class are the most likely recipients of those invitations. Another category includes people who don't fly as much, but they are important public figures, such as former Cabinet secretaries or TV news anchors.

Although it's difficult to know exactly how much money it takes to secure an initial invitation, anecdotal evidence suggests that, to retain the status, United requires members to fly at least 50,000 miles a year in full-fare coach, Business or First Class.

United also rewards big spenders who are not quite big enough for Global Services with lower elite status, even if they don't meet the published requirements. In 2010, a student of mine was granted 1K status, although he had flown about 70,000 of the 100,000 miles required for that tier – because a big part of those miles was earned in either full-fare coach or Business Class.

Buying and matching elite status

In early 2011, US Airways made an unusual announcement: All of its elite tiers, including the very top one, were on sale. Anyone could buy the elite-qualifying miles needed to reach their desired level – whether from scratch or to top off an existing balance. If you never stepped foot on a US Airways plane, you could buy the lowest status for $1,299, and the highest for $3,999.

This wasn't the first time an airline was selling elite status, but the top tier had usually been off limits. In early 2011, United was also selling elite-qualifying miles, but they were limited to 15,000 per member, and 1K status was excluded.

A more common practice in the airline industry has been matching status. If you are an elite flier on one carrier, its competitors might want to steal you away, and as an incentive might give you the same status you have on your current preferred airline. Some carriers will just grant you the status, while others will offer you a challenge to earn it faster than usual, and yet others don't offer status-matches at all.

In late 2008, I wanted to gain free access to United's domestic airport lounges, for which I needed a non-U.S. Star Alliance Gold membership. It was easiest to match status with BMI, but the British carrier required status with a competing alliance. So I used my United 1K card to match to Platinum on Northwest, which then still existed before its merger with Delta. Now that I belonged to a top elite tier with SkyTeam, I was able to match to BMI Gold, which got me the non-U.S. Star Gold card I needed to enter domestic United lounges.

Other airlines known to offer status-matches include Alaska, Delta, Cathay Pacific, LAN, India's Jet Airways and Israel's El Al. Some of them only need to see a copy of a competitor's membership card, while others require your latest account statement. Many of them match only to their mid-tier. Carriers that don't match status include Lufthansa, Air France, All Nippon, British Airways, Singapore, Air Canada, Emirates and Japan Airlines, among others. Websites like FlyerTalk and Milepoint usually keep good track of any changes or additions to this list.

A few airline offer status-match challenges. United will match to Premier if you fly 10,000 miles or 15 segments within 90 days, and to Premier Executive if you accrue 17,500 miles or 22 segments, according to the Mileage Plus customer service center. You receive the status as soon as you register, which of course helps the flying experience. Only flights on United and Continental qualify, and not on any other Star Alliance carriers. Until 2011, no matches were offered to 1K, but that's history – now you can get it if you fly 35,000 miles or 40 segments in 90 days.

In early 2011, United also extended a similar challenge to former 1K fliers who hadn't re-qualified the previous year. They could regain their top status if they paid a $999 fee in addition to having to fly 35,000 miles or 40 segments in 90 days. Some travelers reported on FlyerTalk that they received the same offer for only $499. A Mileage Plus agent told me the fee depended on how many miles a member flew in 2010.

American doesn't officially grant status matches, but there were reports on FlyerTalk in early 2011 about United 1K and Global Services members being offered a similar challenge to United's. However, those customers could only get mid-tier (Platinum) status up front, and the top level (Executive Platinum) once they completed the challenge. The American offer only lasted a couple of months.

Million-mile status

Many airlines offer lifetime elite status to customers who have flown 1 million miles or more. As can be expected, qualification criteria and elite levels differ quite a bit, so it might be wise to check your preferred carrier's policy.

Let's first look at those carriers that count only the miles earned on their own flights, and not on partner flights. They include United, Air Canada, Alaska, Air China and EgyptAir, among others. They typically bestow their mid-tier status on their million-mile fliers for life. After 2 million miles, some airlines throw in another benefit – United adds a free lifetime lounge membership, and Air Canada lifetime mid-tier status to a spouse or partner. For 3 million miles, both airlines award their top-tier elite status for life.

Other carriers, such as Delta, do count partner flights, but their qualification requirements are higher. For 1 million miles, Delta only grants lifetime Silver status. Lifetime Gold takes 2 million miles, and lifetime Platinum 4 million miles. Delta's fourth tier, Diamond, cannot be had for life.

American is quite unique in that it counts all miles earned through both flight and non-flight activities, including hotels, car rentals and even credit cards. It gives million-mile fliers its lowest-tier status, and those who fly 2 million miles its mid-tier status.

There are also airlines that don't count the miles but the years in which a member has maintained elite status. Both Air France and BMI award their top tiers for life to fliers who have retained that elite level for 10 years.

Maximizing elite benefits

Just because someone has top elite status doesn't mean that they take full advantage of all benefits they are entitled to. For years, I'd heard and read about frequent travelers who didn't know they had valuable upgrades sitting in their accounts and let them expire, but I didn't know anyone personally until a United flight from Washington to San Francisco in early 2010.

I sat in Business Class, next to a lady who had Global Services status. I'd had my upgrade confirmed weeks earlier, but the only reason she was in that cabin was last-minute luck. The person who was supposed to be in that seat didn't show up. My new seat mate hadn't requested an upgrade until she checked in at the airport. At that time, she was waitlisted for Business Class and given a coach seat – that's right, she didn't have a seat assignment at all until then. The only thing available at that point was a middle seat in the very last row of the Boeing 777, even though she was entitled to free access to Economy Plus.

Naturally, I had several questions. First, why didn't she get a seat assignment as soon as she booked her ticket? Because she used a travel agency and didn't want to bother with details. Second, why didn't she request an upgrade as soon as her ticket was issued? Because she paid a very low fare and didn't think it was eligible for a free upgrade. Why didn't she use one of the regional (domestic) upgrade certificates banked in her account? Because she didn't know what those were and that she had any of them. Of course, she didn't know that the regional upgrades could be used on any published fare, either.

Since we had time before the aircraft door closed, she logged in to her United account, and I showed her where to find her upgrade balance. Not only did she have regional certificates sitting there, but two of them were about to expire in three days. As you probably guessed already, she had let many more of those upgrades expire unused in the past – and she could have gifted them to anyone else if she didn't need them.

So what good did her exclusive, by-invitation-only status do for her? Had my no-show seat mate been there, the Global Services flier would have been stuck in a middle coach seat for nearly six hours. Several weeks after our flight, I invited her to one of my seminars, and now she knows much more about the benefits she had no idea existed.

My philosophy is that elite fliers should squeeze the most out of every benefit they are entitled to. In order to do that, of course, they need to be very knowledgeable about those benefits and the ways to use them.

Chapter 12 Lessons Learned

1. The people who get the most out of their status are those best educated about everything that status carries before they even achieve it.
2. It's not necessary to stick with a single airline to achieve elite status – all one needs to do is pick an alliance, as miles earned on any alliance carrier count toward elite status.
3. A cost-benefit analysis helps to find out how much, if anything, airline promiscuity can save a flier.
4. Trying to achieve elite status with one frequent-flier program doesn't mean that one can't be a member of other programs, or even build status on another airline.
5. The lowest elite tier requires between 20,000 and 35,000 flown miles a year. Its benefits include waived luggage fees across the respective alliance, priority seating, check-in, boarding and wait-listing, bonus flight miles, and in the U.S., complimentary domestic upgrades.
6. The middle elite level is usually awarded after flying 50,000 miles. Its benefits include free alliance-wide lounge access, flight bonus miles of up to 100 percent, waived baggage fees for up to three bags, priority baggage handling and a dedicated reservations phone line.
7. The top elite tier requires up to 100,000 flight miles a year. Such fliers are exempt from most fees, receive confirmed upgrade certificates that can be applied as early as the time of ticketing, get access to additional coach award seats and have the highest check-in, boarding and waitlist priority.
8. In recent years, some airlines have added elite levels to their existing tiers meant to reward big spenders, as opposed to people who fly lots of miles.
9. Some carriers sell elite status outright, while others offer "status matches" if a customer has elite status on a competing airline.
10. Many airlines offer lifetime elite status to customers who have flown 1 million miles or more.

Chapter 13

Seat Upgrades

The first thing I try to remember about upgrades is that none of us is entitled to them. Airlines have the right to sell Business and First Class seats to people willing to pay for them, so don't be angry and bad-mouth your airline if you miss an upgrade. You may find it ironic that these words come from a flier with a 100-percent upgrade success rate since 2002. But I've never had a problem with carriers holding premium seats until almost the last moment before they release them for upgrades.

That said, airlines can do a better job managing their inventory. If a 40-seat Business Class cabin has 15 unsold seats two days before departure, it's unlikely all those seats will sell. So why not open up a couple of them for upgrades?

Friends and colleagues often come to me seeking help with upgrading a ticket. Sometimes they are too late – they are booked in a class ineligible for an upgrade. One of my recent cases was a former senior official in the Bush administration who had a ticket to Europe issued by a travel agent, but its booking class didn't allow an upgrade. He had to buy up to a higher fare and pay the standard $250 change fee out of his own pocket in order to qualify. He was utterly confused by all the rules and conditions – and he is one of the brightest lawyers I know.

As I said in Chapter 1, airline websites don't make it easy for customers to figure out what booking class they are buying. While some carriers show the booking code at the end of the booking process, others keep it hidden throughout the process. In April 2011, I tried to book a ticket on the British Airways site and wanted to make sure the booking class would be eligible for an upgrade, but no codes were anywhere in sight.

In this chapter, we will review and analyze the most common types of upgrades in today's air travel system, and then, knowing what's possible, we will discuss strategies that can help us secure the best upgrade in a particular situation.

U.S. domestic upgrades

In the U.S. domestic market, upgrades are more prevalent than anywhere else in the world. Although there are no official statistics, it's probably safe to assume that on an average flight most First Class passengers end up in the front cabin thanks to upgrades. As a result, U.S. carriers have taken both their hard and soft domestic First Class products to embarrassing lows, which we discussed in Chapter 8. Still, as I said then, sitting up front is generally better than being stuck in coach.

Most U.S. carriers have a policy of **complimentary upgrades**, which can be confirmed no earlier than a couple of days before departure, on a schedule based on elite status. Naturally, top elites have the best chance of sitting in First Class. Those upgrades are usually requested automatically when a ticket is issued, so you don't have to do anything. Some airlines like Delta allow upgrades to be confirmed as early as the time of ticketing on full Y fares, if there is upgrade availability. That's different from the UP fares we discussed in Chapter 2, which have coach fares bases but book immediately in First Class codes and don't require upgrade space. Delta also permits elite fliers to upgrade award flights, which is not allowed on most other carriers.

American has a mixed system of complimentary upgrades and 500-mile coupons that can be earned or purchased. Only top elites are eligible for free upgrades on any booking class, while Y or B class is required for lower-level elites, who can use 500-mile coupons on discounted fares. All of those upgrades on American have to be requested.

Some carriers, such as United and Alaska, offer **confirmed upgrade certificates** to their top elites in addition to complimentary upgrades, which can secure First Class seats at ticketing in any published booking class. We discussed United's regional upgrades, as they are called, in Chapter 10. Up to eight of them a year can be earned by 1K members, though that number will be cut in half in 2012. Alaska gives its Gold members four certificates a year.

By the way, complimentary and confirmed domestic upgrade rules typically apply to flights to Canada, Central America and the Caribbean as well.

Of course, most major airlines also offer **mileage upgrades**, which can be confirmed at ticketing time if there is availability. As I said in Chapter 12, many carriers charge cash co-pays in addition to the required miles, but they are usually waived for elites. Upgrades to Hawaii, Central America and the Caribbean have much higher co-pays than those in the continental United States and Canada.

International upgrades

If you are a globe-trotter who can only afford to pay for coach, your ability to upgrade long-haul flights is probably the most important criterion in selecting a frequent-flier program. I know I wouldn't sit in coach on an intercontinental flight, even if someone else paid for my ticket. Unfortunately, most airlines around the world don't offer viable options – they would rather resort to randomly giving away premium seats when Economy is oversold (operational upgrades) than have a structured and customer-friendly upgrade program.

True, many carriers offer some sort of **mileage upgrades**, but they usually require full-fare tickets, or at least booking classes in the middle of the fare spectrum. When discounted fares are eligible, as in the case with some U.S. airlines, there are also hefty cash co-pays – assuming, of course, that you have enough miles in your account. American, for example, charges 15,000 miles for an upgrade from North America to Europe, Asia and South America on Y and B fares. For most discounted coach fares, an upgrade costs 25,000 miles and $350 each way. United's co-pay prices are more complicated – depending on the specific booking class, they run from $250 to $600.

The rules are even more restrictive when it comes to **partner upgrades**, which are not very common in the industry and only work on full-fare tickets. We discussed Star Alliance and SkyTeam upgrade awards in Chapter 11, and although Oneworld doesn't have such a program, American offers mileage upgrades on British Airways (BA) and Iberia (IB). It's important to know that tickets must be issued by American, though flights can be booked either as American code-share numbers or with the true BA or IB number of the operating carrier.

In contrast, the Star Alliance doesn't regulate who issues the ticket, but it requires that flights be booked with their true number. For example, if you want to use United miles to upgrade Lufthansa Flight 401 from New York (JFK) to Frankfurt (FRA), it must appear on your ticket as LH401 – not the code-share number UA8840.

The most valuable international upgrades are the very rare in the industry **system-wide upgrade certificates**. They can be used on flights anywhere in the world, including domestically, and require no cash co-pays. American and United have probably the best such products, which are awarded only to top-tier elite fliers. With only one certificate necessary from origin to destination in each direction (up to three segments on American, but no limit on United), they can be redeemed by the member who has earned them or by any other designated passenger, even when not traveling with the member. They are valid for one year from the date of issue.

American's certificates are more meaningful than United's – they can be used on any published fare, while United requires at least W booking class, excluding S, T, L, K and G classes in coach and Z in Business. That often means that customers have to spend hundreds of dollars more than the lowest available fare just to be eligible for an upgrade – and if it doesn't clear, they end up in coach, having bought a much more expensive ticket than necessary. Another advantage on American is that top fliers get eight such certificates a year, while United issues only six, with the option to earn two more for every 50,000 miles flown beyond 100,000.

Like United's domestic (regional) upgrades, the system-wide certificates are electronic, though United can also issue printed ones for use on Lufthansa. Upgrade requests on Lufthansa can be made only on the day of travel at the airport, and coach tickets must be booked in V or higher class, and Business Class only in J, C or D (no Z). Even though one system-wide certificate can upgrade all connecting flights from origin to destination on United flights, it covers only one segment on Lufthansa.

Lufthansa's own certificates, known as eVouchers, are much less appealing than those from United or American. They are non-transferable, and they cover only one flight segment and not connecting flights. One voucher is required to upgrade a short-haul flight but two for a long haul – and two vouchers a year is all Senator-level elites get. HON Circle members receive six a year. At least Lufthansa imposes no fare restrictions on the certificates.

Delta, on the other hand, has very strict rules. Its system-wide upgrades work only on the three highest coach booking classes (Y, B and M) and can be used by other passengers only if they are traveling with the sponsoring member on the same reservation. On flights in North America and to Bermuda, Mexico and the Caribbean, Delta allows another three booking classes (H, Q and K), which still leaves out the three lowest classes. Platinum SkyMiles member get four certificates a year, and Diamond fliers receive six.

Delta's system-wide upgrades can also be used on any KLM flight if booked in the four highest classes (X, S, B and M) and on transatlantic Air France flights. To be eligible for an upgrade from coach to Premium Economy (Premium Voyageur), tickets have to be booked in Y, B or K class, and from Premium Voyageur to Business in S, A or W class.

Air Canada implemented a somewhat complicated eUpgrade system in early 2011. Any elite member can earn eUpgrade credits, but only mid-tier and top-tier fliers can use them on any booking class. Bottom-level elites must be booked in Y, B or M class. The number of credits required for each upgrade depends on distance and booking class. The certificates can be gifted to other passengers, but if they have no elite status, they have to be booked in Y or B class. ·

Operational upgrades

If your head is spinning from all those rules and requirements, this section should provide some relief. Airlines resort to operational upgrades – known as "op ups" for short – when the coach cabin is oversold but there are still open seats in Business or First Class. Then they bump passengers to the front cabin to vacate space in the back.

How do airline agents decide who to upgrade for free? Many carriers have no rules and leave it entirely to gate agents to make the call. As a result, fliers who don't have seat assignments in coach are often the ones getting the good kind of bump.

A few years ago, I met a traveler who bragged about sitting in Business Class on All Nippon from Tokyo (NRT) to Washington (IAD), just because he arrived at the airport too late and all Economy seats were gone. I'm frequently asked at seminars whether it's a good idea not to get a seat in coach and hope for an upgrade. The trouble with such a strategy is that you may well end up in a middle seat in the very back of the plane. I have a better idea. Before you head to the airport, check the flight load to get a sense of how full it is. Remember, it may be oversold even if the inventory shows available seats, so call reservations for a better estimate if you have time. If it looks like they will need to upgrade some people, approach the gate agent when you get there and ask politely if you could be one of the lucky passengers. Using some of the airline jargon you learned from this book might help. It has certainly helped me a few times.

Charming gate agents rarely works on U.S. carriers – not because they are not susceptible to being charmed, but because those airlines have better ways of determining who should be rewarded with a operational upgrade. Logically, those are elite fliers. The major carriers typically use the same system designed to clear regular upgrade waitlists based on elite status and booking class. If a non-status passenger doesn't have a seat assignment, instead of putting him in Business Class, they will upgrade an elite customer and give his Economy seat to the first traveler. That said, some agents still end up choosing the short cut, even though they are supposed to follow the rules.

Cash upgrades

In the mid-2000s, some U.S. airlines came up with a creative way to make more cash – they began selling upgrades for cash at check-in.

For example, Business Class from Washington to Europe on United could be had for about $600 each way – even on fares that were ineligible for system-wide upgrades, and even on award tickets, which officially are not upgradeable. Once I was offered a First Class upgrade to Munich while checking in on the United website, with my ticket already upgraded from coach to Business with a system-wide certificate. Double upgrades aren't officially allowed, either, but United seemed happy to break its own rules for some extra cash.

Delta, which was a latecomer to this game, started experimenting with a similar idea in 2011, though with an important difference. United charges arbitrarily determined amounts, while Delta reportedly sells premium seats at published discounted First Class fares. For example, United may offer you an upgrade from coach to First Class from Washington to Las Vegas for $375, regardless of how much you paid for your ticket. Delta will determine the upsell amount differently: It will compare your price to the lowest published and available First Class fare on its tariff and collect the difference.

Emirates handles upsells differently from the above-mentioned carriers. In early 2011, it sent me an e-mail with an offer to upgrade a flight from Dubai to Kuwait for about $100 three days before departure. "This upgrade offer is exclusive to you and the passengers in your booking. It can only be purchased via the link in this email and is not available at the airport, via Emirates call centers or contact centers," said the message, which included a unique code needed to take advantage of the offer.

In 2010, United began selling cash upgrades at the time of ticketing. I was once offered a Business Class upsell from Washington to Kuwait for $999.

For years, United resorted to cash upsells only when a flight had upgrade space available in NF or NC booking classes, meaning that there were no elite members waiting for regular upgrades. In early 2011, however, reports surfaced on FlyerTalk about passengers getting upsell offers when there was no upgrade availability, and several elites lingered on a waitlist. In fact, some of them missed upgrades because those seats went to people who paid cash.

That has angered many top elite United fliers. As I said at the beginning of this chapter, I have no problem with airlines trying to sell premium seats at published fares. But this is very different – United gives its best customers system-wide certificates, but then it effectively tells them that those hard-earned rewards are not as good as a few hundred dollars to secure an upgrade.

Upgrade strategies

Most travelers' upgrade strategy consists of prayer. They buy a plane ticket, and only after it's issued do they start thinking about how to upgrade it – some wait until a few days before departure, or even until the travel day. Once they make their request, they hope and pray that their upgrade will clear.

As you can imagine, such a passive approach doesn't work for me. Avoiding the coach cabin on a long flight is just too important to surrender control of my upgrade chances to fate. That's not how one achieves 100-percent upgrade success rate. There is much more an experienced flier can do. As with the airfare techniques in Part I, figuring out the upgrade game may take time at the beginning, but once you get the hang of it, your efficiency will increase significantly – and the rewards are really worth it.

▶ First, **think about upgrades during the booking process**. Depending on your flight, you might make different decisions. If the flight is short, you probably won't mind sitting in coach. If it's a U.S. domestic flight and you have elite status in a U.S.-based frequent-flier program, you might rely on a last-minute complimentary upgrade. If, however, the flight is transcontinental and you don't want to risk spending up to six hours in the back of the plane, you might want to use miles or a confirmed upgrade certificate. Most people, of course, will try to upgrade an intercontinental flight.

▶ Second, **get access to upgrade inventory data**, so you know if there is an available seat to confirm at the time of ticketing. You can use the sources described in Chapter 1 – ExpertFlyer shows actual seat availability, while the KVS tool only indicates whether there is upgrade space or not. Their data is limited to certain airlines, and if yours is not among them, you have to call and ask a reservations agent if there are any seats open for an upgrade. Agents at some airlines, such as Lufthansa, don't know if there is upgrade availability in advance – a very peculiar practice for such a major carrier. They have to request an upgrade to see if it clears. Most U.S. carriers use unique booking classes for upgrades, as shown on Figure 16 on Page 238, while their foreign competitors use the same codes for both upgrade and award seats.

▶ Third, **check upgrade availability on all possible flights** to your destination on your chosen date and book one that has open space. If none of them has it, and if you are somewhat flexible with your travel dates, check if there is upgrade availability a day earlier or later. If you are not flexible with your date, see if a connection might provide an immediate upgrade opportunity. Most travelers would probably choose a nonstop from New York to Los Angeles in coach instead of upgraded connecting flights, and that's fine domestically. But if they are flying to Tokyo, they most likely wouldn't mind transferring in Chicago if that would guarantee them an upgrade.

▶ Fourth, if there is no available upgrade space on any of your flight options, you will be waitlisted. But don't think there is nothing you can do to improve your chances. **Make an estimate about which flight is most likely to clear.** Several factors can help you do that. Check the aircraft types. If there are two flights to your destination that day, and one is operated on an Airbus 320 with 12 seats in First Class and the other one on a Boeing 767 with 30 seats, your chances will be better in the bigger cabin. If the two planes are the same, see how many seats have been sold on each one so far – that can be misleading if there are weeks left before departure, but it will give you some sense about the loads. Also keep in mind the time of day – morning and evening flights tend to be most popular with business travelers.

Now you are ready to book your ticket. If you are waitlisted, check your upgrade status from time to time, and when it clears, get a seat in your new cabin. Some airlines have automated systems to notify passengers when upgrades clear, but as with schedule changes, that method is not very reliable.

▶ Fifth, if you are still waitlisted a couple of days before departure and you see that there are plenty of seats open in the premium cabin, **try to bring your flight to the attention of inventory management**. You can't do that directly, but you can call reservations and ask for a supervisor. Most of the time they will tell you that they don't interfere in the inventory management department's work, and don't even communicate with those people. However, if you are a top elite flier, some supervisors may be willing to send a message.

Remember, you shouldn't ask that a seat be opened up for you. All you want is to suggest to inventory management that they simply take a look at your flight. There are millions of flights in an airline system at any given time. Most of the inventory on those flights is left to computers to manage. As I've said before, airline computer models may be very sophisticated, but they are not perfect. Sometimes, just a brush of human intervention helps. We'll talk more about what one airline executive calls "tweaking" the yield-management system in Chapter 14.

▶ Sixth, if you haven't cleared the waitlist hours before departure and things don't look good, **reevaluate your options**. If the upgrade is important to you, see if another flight to your destination might have an upgrade seat open or might offer better chances than your original flight. If your flight is domestic, you can make a same-day confirmed change, which will be free if you have top elite status – and if you are not, perhaps you will be willing to pay the $75 fee to sit in First Class. Changing an international flight, of course, is more expensive on discounted fares, but it maybe worthwhile to you.

Preserving upgrades in case of rebooking

What happens if your ticket is affected by a schedule change, which we discussed in Chapter 7, and you are rebooked on a different flight? Could you lose your confirmed upgrade?

If the airline computer system rebooks you automatically, it should put you in the upgraded class. But if you don't like the new flight the system has chosen for you and you found a better one, it may not have upgrade space open. In that case, most agents would probably waitlist you for the upgrade. However, according to the rules of some airlines, such as United, once passengers have been confirmed in a premium cabin, they are entitled to seats in that cabin, even if there is no available upgrade inventory – as long as there is revenue space.

I have dozens of United schedule changes every year, but no agent has ever preserved my upgrade if there was no availability in the NF or NC fare bucket. They have always waitlisted me, and I didn't know better until late 2010, when I got a hold of the so-called Rule 260 – it governs schedule changes and has apparently been folded into Rule 240, which I mentioned in Chapter 9.

I was surprised to read the following under "Protection guidelines": "Upgraded [passengers] affected by a schedule change should be protected in the upgraded class if available. If NF/NC is not available, protect customer in F/C if available and contact SD for conversion." SD refers to service director, the first supervisory level in reservations call centers. This means that a seat should be opened up for you, provided you had a confirmed upgrade on your original flight that was affected by the schedule change. When I saw this rule, I called United to clear a waitlist I'd been put on after a schedule change a week earlier. The agent sounded unaware of the rule, but he found it on his computer, booked an F seat and called a service director to convert it to NF, as instructed in Rule 260.

Is it possible that no agent knew about this? Could it be that their training doesn't cover this particular detail? If it does, are they told not to offer such protection to customers proactively? When I asked those questions, I was told that agents should know the rule – and that a message was sent to the service director who had waitlisted me the week before to make sure she knows the correct procedure.

The same policy doesn't cover rebooking as a result of irregular operations (IRROPS) on the travel day, which we discussed in Chapter 9. In that case, agents don't have to preserve upgrades, but many are inclined to make exceptions for top elite fliers.

Chapter 13 Lessons Learned

1. Most U.S. carriers have a policy of complimentary upgrades on domestic flights, which can be confirmed no earlier than a couple of days before departure, on a schedule based on elite status.
2. Some carriers offer confirmed upgrade certificates to their top elites in addition to complimentary upgrades, which can secure premium seats at ticketing in any published booking class.
3. Most major airlines also offer mileage upgrades, which usually require full-fare tickets. When discounted fares are eligible, as in the case with some U.S. airlines, there are also hefty cash co-pays.
4. The rules are even more restrictive when it comes to partner upgrades, which are not very common in the industry and only work on full-fare tickets.
5. The most valuable international upgrades are the very rare system-wide upgrade certificates, which can be used on flights anywhere in the world and require no cash co-pays.
6. Airlines resort to operational upgrades – known as "op ups" – when the coach cabin is oversold but there are still open seats in Business or First Class.
7. Some airlines sell upgrades for cash at check-in or even as early as the time of ticketing.
8. Effective strategies to secure an upgrade include:
   - Thinking about upgrades from the very beginning of the booking process.
   - Accessing upgrade inventory data to find out if there is an available seat to confirm at the time of ticketing.
   - Checking upgrade availability on all possible flights to a destination and booking one that has open space.
   - If an upgrade is to be waitlisted, finding the flight most likely to clear.
   - If the waitlist hasn't cleared a couple of days before departure and there are plenty of seats open in the premium cabin, bringing the flight to the attention of inventory management.
9. In case of advance airline schedule changes, many carriers are supposed to protect customers in the upgraded cabin, though most agents won't do it unless asked.

Chapter 14

Airline Award Tickets

As addicted as many travelers have become to accumulating frequent-flier miles, airlines have acquired an addiction of their own. In an effort to make quick cash, they have given away so many miles that their value has diminished significantly. While this is an industry-wide problem, US Airways in particular has become known as a mile-printing carrier. It owes that reputation to a series of extremely generous promotions in recent years, including a 100-percent bonus when Dividend Miles members purchased miles.

With so many miles on their books and so many customers trying to use them, airlines began erecting barriers to mileage redemption. They became stingier with award seats on their flights and repeatedly increased the number of miles required for an award ticket. Another factor that contributed to the bigger competition for award seats were all the partnerships that airlines formed, which require that they provide award space to members of the partner-carriers' loyalty programs.

So successfully redeeming miles for flights, and especially for reasonable itineraries, is now a frustrating and time-consuming effort – and for many less experienced travelers, it's often impossible.

In this last chapter, we will review the most common mistakes customers make when searching for award seats, discuss specific strategies and tactics for finding the best possible flights, compare award availability and resources among the three global alliances, and learn how to maximize the benefits that come with an award ticket.

How much clout do your miles have?

We've talked about the many differences among frequent-flier programs enough to know that airline miles are not created equal. What do I mean by "clout"? Certainly not what United means when it claims in an advertisement that its miles have the clout to secure any seat on any flight. That's the case with many airlines – it's a reference to the so-called "standard awards," which can be booked using that carrier's miles as long as there are revenue seats available, usually for twice as many miles as the number required for "saver awards." Although those two terms are the most common in the industry, some carriers use different labels, such as "anytime awards," instead of "standard," on American.

When I say "clout," I mean the actual value of the miles. For example, do they cover any of the taxes and surcharges on an award ticket, or do you have to pay for those separately with money? Just recall the hundreds of dollars in international taxes and fuel surcharges we discussed in Chapter 3. If you have to pay them, what kind of a "free" ticket would that be? I'm asked that very question all the time. Passengers are always responsible for airport and government taxes. Unfortunately, most non-U.S. carriers also charge money for fuel surcharges in addition to the necessary miles. While U.S. airlines don't, there are exceptions – American AAdvantage members have to pay for fuel surcharges when redeeming miles for flights on British Airways.

Another example of more clout is when your miles can get you more than a simple round-trip award ticket. Can you book one-way awards for half the miles needed for a round trip? Can you pay a combination of miles and money? Can you change an award ticket? Can you make one or more stopovers? Can you have an "open jaw" – arrive in one city and depart from another? Some airlines allow either a stopover or an open jaw, while others permit both. So check the rules of your frequent-flier program carefully before you start the booking process.

In North America, Air Canada, American, United, Alaska, Hawaiian and Southwest offer one-way awards. Among other airlines that permit them are British Airways, Air France/KLM, Virgin Atlantic, BMI, Qatar, Singapore, Qantas, VirginBlue and Cathay Pacific. For several years, Lufthansa charged 75 percent of round-trip mileage, but it joined the rest of the group cited above by lowering that to 50 percent in 2011. Lufthansa's Miles&More program also includes Swiss, Austrian, Brussels Airline, Poland's LOT, Luxair, Croatia Airlines and Slovenia's Adria Airways.

Accessing award inventory

Getting access to airline award availability online is often a challenge, but things have improved significantly in recent years, as more carriers make it possible to search for award seats and book tickets on their websites. As for third-party sites, they all carry limited data but are still very helpful. They include the KVS tool, ExpertFlyer, UsingMiles and MileageManager, as well as the specialized AwardNexus.com.

The biggest problem with most online resources is the very scarce partner award inventory they carry. Why is that important? Let's say you want to use your US Airways miles for a Lufthansa flight. The US Airways website only shows availability on its own flights. So do you go to the Lufthansa site to look for seats? No, because the seats you will find there are available only to fliers using their Lufthansa miles, and the award inventory Lufthansa provides to its own customers is not necessarily

Airline Award Tickets   237

the same as what it gives to its Star Alliance partners. So you need to find a third Star carrier whose website shows partner award availability, such as All Nippon (NH). Generally, if a Lufthansa flight is available to All Nippon, it should be available to US Airways or any other Star member as well.

Of course, you can call US Airways to check availability on Lufthansa, but as with most things discussed in this book, I wouldn't completely trust airline agents. Even if you find award space online, you still have to call US Airways to book a ticket, but it's always best to do your homework before picking up the phone.

As I mentioned, in many cases, an airline has award seats allocated for its own members, and another, usually more limited, set of seats it provides to its alliance and non-alliance partners. That said, I've found that different sets of inventory apply to the Star Alliance, but not necessarily to Oneworld and SkyTeam. The members of the last two groups tend to offer the same seats to their own customers and those of partner-carriers.

I should note that most airlines also have non-alliance partners, such as Emirates for United, Air Tahiti Nui for American and V Australia for Delta. The miles required for redemption on those carriers are often different from the award charts that apply to alliance partners. In most cases, the only way to check availability on those other partners is to call the airline whose miles you are using. Emirates is a rare breed in that it publishes partner award inventory separately from its own availability, and you can search for coach award seats Emirates provides to its partners on ExpertFlyer.

So let's look at partner award availability by alliance. Keep in mind that, in order to search for award seats on most airline websites, you need to have an account with the respective frequent-flier program, and some may even require some miles in that account.

▶ In the **Star Alliance**, All Nippon's site has the most comprehensive partner data. It comes from StarNet, the alliance's "middleware" I mentioned in Chapter 10, which provides access to any Star carrier's partner inventory on a first-come-first-served basis. The Air Canada and Continental sites also show partner availability, but for fewer Star members than All Nippon's. The United site only has US Airways, Continental and Lufthansa data. Lufthansa naturally has the inventory for the airlines participating in its Miles&More program.

Airline	Upgrade Codes		Award Codes		
	Business	First	Economy	Business	First
American	C, R	A, X	T	U	Z
United	NC	NF	XY, NY	XC	XF
Delta	Z, X	G, V	N	O	R .
Lufthansa	I	O	X	I	O
Air France	O	F	X, L, A, S	O	F
Qantas	U	P	X, Z	U	P

Figure 16: Upgrade and award booking classes for six major global airlines.

Figure 16 shows the upgrade and award booking codes used by two of the largest members of the three alliances. Some carriers use more than one booking class in the same category – one of the codes usually signifies special inventory reserved exclusively for top-tier elite fliers.

Star is the most consistent of the three alliances in the booking codes it uses for awards – X for coach, I for Business and O for First Class. Some airlines may have different codes in their own inventory, but for StarNet purposes, they revert to the alliance-wide codes. For example, although United uses XY, XC and XF in its internal availability, what other carriers see in StarNet is X, I and O. Most of Star's non-U.S. members use the same codes for both upgrade and award space. We will devote more attention to United's StarNet blocking, which I mentioned in Chapter 10, a bit later in this chapter.

There are several great airlines on which to redeem Star Alliance miles – Singapore, Thai, All Nippon, Lufthansa, Swiss and Air New Zealand. Lufthansa is among the most generous when it comes to award space, while Singapore is among the stingiest. Unlike Continental, US Airways has good domestic First Class availability, but it's extremely hard to find a seat on flights to Europe. United's domestic and international coach availability is pretty good, but First and Business Class present bigger challenges.

Not surprisingly, Singapore is a special case. It has imposed a very controversial ban on booking Business and First Class award seats on almost all of its long-haul flights with miles from other Star frequent-flier programs. It implemented the ban when it started rolling out its new premium product – the Business seat is the most spacious in the industry – but those seats have been "new" since 2006. For several years, customers had a choice, as only some of its European and North American flights were operated on new aircraft, and seats were available on the old planes. Now, however, the only such route left is Singapore-Frankfurt-New York, which is flown on Singapore's few remaining Boeing 747 aircraft.

▶ In **Oneworld**, the Qantas and British Airways sites have the best partner award data, though neither of them shows all alliance members. The KVS tool can be very helpful here, too. Several Oneworld carriers share some award booking codes, but there is no consistency. For coach, eight airlines use X and four use T. For Business, 10 use U, one uses I and one R. For First Class, five use Z, one uses A and one P (the rest have only two cabins). Cathay Pacific, British Airways and Qantas are considered the most attractive options for redeeming Oneworld miles. Qantas is also one of the carriers with the worst award availability, while British Airways is quite generous – certainly more so than American – and Cathay Pacific isn't bad, either.

▶ In **SkyTeam**, the site of Flying Blue, Air France/KLM's frequent-flier program, is the only one showing availability for most alliance members. Inventory of some carriers, such as Korean Air, cannot be found online, so a phone call is the only option. At the same time, Korean Air has probably the highest-quality product, offering the most valuable redemption that SkyTeam miles can buy. The booking classes here are all over the place – there are seven coach award codes (X, O, W, N, U, A, E) and six Business Class codes (Z, J, D, I, C, O) among 13 airlines. Even Air France and KLM, which are owned by the same company, use different codes. Delta is among the SkyTeam carriers with the worst award availability, and Air France and KLM are probably your best bet from the United States to Europe.

Award-booking strategies

U.S. carriers claim that the most popular awards for which their customers redeem miles are domestic round-trip tickets at 25,000 miles each. However, you can get the best value for your miles if you use them for international Business or First Class tickets. As I said in Chapter 10, when you buy revenue tickets, if you want to minimize spending and maximize earned mileage, it's best to spend money on domestic travel and use miles for international, even in coach.

Why are First and Business Class awards most valuable? Because they usually cost only between two and three times as much as Economy awards, as opposed to several times more if you paid money for them. You have some idea about how high premium fares can get from Chapter 3. That said, I know many travelers who prefer to spend 50,000 miles on two coach tickets to Europe than 100,000 miles on one Business Class ticket. That's particularly true of families who may not have enough miles for several premium tickets.

Still, I wish everyone would have a chance to experience international First Class on one of the world's best airlines at least once.

While most carriers base their award redemption charts on fixed rates by geographic region, some like All Nippon, Qantas and Air New Zealand, have distance-based mileage requirements. For example, most programs charge the same miles from the U.S. East coast to Europe as they do from the West coast to Europe. In a distance-based model, you will pay fewer miles if you fly from the East coast. Yet other airlines' (JetBlue) mileage rates are directly related to actual fares on a particular route and can vary a lot.

Now let's move to my strategies for booking the best possible award ticket, some of which will be familiar to you. These strategies apply to saver awards, since standard awards are always available, as long as there are revenue seats on a flight – and they are a huge waste of miles.

▶ First, **do your homework before calling the airline**. As I said earlier, if that call is the first thing you do as part of your award search, you won't go very far. You will spend a long time on the phone, and the average agent is unlikely to build the best possible itinerary. Before there was online access to award inventory, I used to spend hours trying to find availability on the phone. But now, for the most part, there is no excuse – except for airlines whose award data is impossible to find online, such as Korean Air.

▶ Second, **don't rely on airline agents** to get you the best award. As I said several times in Part I and II, most agents wait for their computers to tell them what to do. They type in your origin and destination cities, and whatever appears on their screens, that's what they tell you is available. I can't even count the times when I was told incorrectly that there were no award seats on a certain route for months. There were seats, but you had to think and apply some creativity to find them. So after you've done your homework and found award space, give the agent that flight number and get booked on it.

Be extra careful when looking for international First Class seats. Many airlines offer only two-cabin service, and some agents assume you mean Business even when you say First Class, so they only search for Business Class seats.

You may encounter another problem if you try to redeem miles from a non-U.S. program. When searching for United and US Airways domestic First Class award seats, partner-airline agents see O booking class in the inventory. United and US Airways charge such as award at Business Class rates when there are only two cabins on the plane. However, foreign Star carriers charge First Class rates, as if the plane has three cabins. Continental, on the other hand, uses I class for those seats, so they are booked in Business Class and that problem doesn't arise. This is another reason why U.S. carriers should call the only premium cabin on two-cabin aircraft Business Class instead of First Class.

▶ Third, try to **book awards months or just days before a trip** – that's when you are likely to find most availability. It's more difficult in the interim period, because most people look for seats several weeks in advance. Many airlines release award space as soon as they begin selling a flight – about 330 days out, as I said in Chapter 1 – though they don't do that on every flight. After that initial release, they may open up none or very few seats, until closer to departure when they realize they won't sell the entire cabin for money and make some seats available for awards.

▶ Fourth, **look for seats on partner-carriers**. One of the most common mistakes travelers make is to search only for award space on the airline whose miles they are redeeming – and when don't find any, they pay double miles for standard awards. You are more likely to get a seat on a partner, simply because of their number. Remember, the Star Alliance has 27 members, as of March 1, 2011, with more carriers expected to join soon. So make sure you know who they all are.

You are unlikely to find a Business Class seat to Europe on US Airways if you are using its miles, but you have many more options with Lufthansa, Austrian, Swiss, Scandinavian, TAP Portugal, LOT, and even United and Continental. Be careful how you search for seats – a reminder that you shouldn't check the Lufthansa website for Lufthansa award availability, but the All Nippon or Continental sites. Otherwise, you may be disappointed when the US Airways agent doesn't see any seats.

▶ Fifth, **try all possible routing options** to your destination and don't rely on the computer. In addition to being familiar with all alliance members, it helps tremendously to know where their airport hubs are and what cities in your country they serve. Hubs are not difficult to figure out – they are usually either in capitals (Paris for Air France, Seoul for Asiana and Korean Air, Amman for Royal Jordanian) or major cities (Auckland for Air New Zealand, Toronto for Air Canada, Sao Paolo for TAM). In the United States, some of the hubs are not that obvious or well-known (Salt Lake City for Delta), especially if you live in another country and don't often fly on U.S. carriers. As for the routes various airlines fly, you have to check their websites.

Why is it important to know all this? Suppose you live in Denver (DEN) and need to go to Copenhagen (CPH) on the Star Alliance. You don't have nonstop options, but several single-connection options are possible: Lufthansa via Frankfurt (FRA), Continental via Newark (EWR), Air Canada via Toronto (YYZ) and United/SAS via Washington (IAD) and Chicago (ORD). Would you have thought about all these possibilities? These are actually the most obvious ones, because they involve transfers at Star Alliance hubs. But what if you can't find award seats on any of the above options and have to resort to a double connection? Then the possibilities are many more, and some are not that obvious.

Most airline agents and computers are likely to do the obvious and offer you connections from DEN to CPH in two hubs – for example, IAD and FRA or ORD and Zurich (ZRH). As one might expect, the most obvious flights are also the most popular, so it may be easier to find award space or a less predictable routing. You could have IAD as your first connecting airport, but for your second, instead of FRA, you could fly to Rome (FCO) or Amsterdam (AMS) on United, and then on to CPH on SAS. You could also first go to Detroit (DTW) or Dallas (DFW) on United, and take Lufthansa to FRA and CPH. All those transfer airports – FCO, AMS, DTW and DFW – are hubs for other alliances but not for Star, and that's what makes a big difference.

▶ Sixth, **search for seats segment by segment**. Looking all the way from origin to destination is another very common mistake – it causes people, including airline agents, to miss available flights, especially if you need an international ticket. There is no harm, of course, in searching for DEN-CPH all the way through, and if you find any seats, more power to you. But in most cases, that won't be the case. The best thing to do is identify all possible international (or intercontinental) gateways – the cities from which you would leave your country or continent, and secure your long-haul flight first. Then you can worry about your domestic or other short-haul connection.

In our Denver case, finding a transatlantic flight should be our first priority. It would be great if we could get a seat on the Lufthansa flight to FRA. But if not, we'd have to look for flights to Europe from every U.S. gateway until we find one at the most convenient time. Then we'd try to find the best connection to or from the long haul. Piecing together an itinerary can be time-consuming and frustrating. You will often find availability on one segment but not on the connecting leg, or the other way around. You may often have more trouble getting a seat on a domestic than an international flight, but keep working on it. Sometimes that's the only way to build a reasonable itinerary.

▶ Seventh, **take advantage of the 24-hour international connection rule**. As I said in Chapter 3, a layover of up to 24 hours is considered a connection, not a stopover, and it may be cheaper sometimes to overnight in your connecting city and continue to your destination the next day. The same logic applies to awards – it may not be possible to get seats all the way through on the same day, but there may be availability on your first segment on one day and on the second segment the following day. For example, you may find a seat from IAD to CPH on a Wednesday, but DEN-IAD may not be open that day. Don't give up – check if you can fly DEN-IAD the day before. You can either spend a nice day in Washington, or if you don't have time for that and prefer to arrive there in the evening, there are some really cheap hotels by Dulles Airport.

▶ Eighth, **take advantage of free stopovers** and visit more than one country on international trips. Most airlines allow at least one stopover on a round-tip award, and that's a great way to add more countries to your list at no additional cost – it also increases your flexibility while searching for seats.

▶ Ninth, **check your airline's routing and other award rules.** You don't want to spend hours looking for seats only to be told that your dates are blacked out or your routing is not allowed. Many carriers have "maximum permitted mileage" (MPM) between origin and destination, though not all agents enforce it. For example, Delta's MPM on the Vancouver-Singapore route is 9,556 miles each way. However, Delta's rules also say that "ticketed point deduction of 1,250 miles applies when travel is via LAX," which means that you can add 1,250 to the 9,556 for a total of 10,806 miles. Some airlines also allow the MPM to be exceeded by a certain percentage.

There are other, more specific routing restrictions imposed by individual carriers. For example, on itineraries between North America and Asia, some airlines (Air Canada) will let you cross the Atlantic in one direction and the Pacific in another, while most will consider that a round-the-world trip.

▶ Tenth, **book a ticket even if you don't find seats on your ideal days.** Many carriers permit free changes to flight dates and times, so keep checking for better availability. There are penalties for rerouting, but they are waived for top elite fliers, who can also cancel awards and redeposit their miles for free. Also, if you can't find a Business Class seat on one of your segments, book it in coach if available and keep checking if a premium seat might have opened up. But remember that if nothing has changed by the time you check in, you will most likely have to fly in coach. Many travelers complain that an airline didn't let them "upgrade" their flight, even though they were on a Business or First Class award and there were empty seats in the premium cabin. An airport agent only cares about in which class of service you are booked on that specific flight, and if your ticket says coach, that's where they want you. Things might be different if you were waitlisted for a seat up front, but many carriers don't allow that.

"Tweaking" flight inventory

As I said in Chapter 13, airline yield-management systems are not perfect and sometimes fail to predict correctly how many seats will be sold on a particular flight. Still, I was surprised when a top airline executive encouraged fliers in 2010 to alert reservations agents when the system fails, so it can be "tweaked."

"Occasionally, we see flights that, for whatever reason, the system says will be sold, but the booking pattern shows that there is no way we'll sell 40 seats in business class in the last seven days," Wally R. Mariani, Qantas' senior executive vice president for the Americas, told me during a visit to Washington. "So then you intervene manually. What we've found is that by tweaking the system a bit – by having more people reviewing what the status of the flight is – we can do the job better." Deciding whether to open seats for upgrades and "award" bookings is a balance between "satisfying more of our customers and protecting the integrity of our yield," he said. But he acknowledged that "there is also a benefit for an airline for customers to be able to burn miles, which are considered a liability."

There are various reasons why the yield-management system may not work in some cases. After all, it tries to predict human behavior. Some of it is easily predictable – people tend to travel during spring break, summer vacation and family holidays. Flights to and from Washington are certainly popular on the days before and after a presidential inauguration or other major national events. Other travel patterns, however, are hard to predict. For example, one of the factors in estimating how a flight would sell is that flight's historical performance on the same date in previous years. Selling First and Business Class seats in 2009 and 2010 was much more difficult than in 2008 because of the global recession.

There is one other part of this game worth keeping in mind. Because of overbooking practices – some airlines oversell coach by dozens of seats on three-cabin wide-body aircraft – they sometimes prefer to give an Economy passenger an operational upgrade rather than release Business Class seats for mileage redemption. In other words, they have decided that it makes better financial sense for them to take the coach flier's money – even though it could be thousands of dollars less than the cost of a premium seat on international flights – than to offload 100,000 or more miles from another customer's account. Of course, if you paid full Business Class fare, you probably wouldn't be happy that someone whose ticket cost 10 times less than yours ended up in the same cabin.

Airline award fees

I used to refer to airline awards as "free tickets," but I have since modified my vocabulary. First, because I feel like I work for my miles, and second because of the fees associated with an award. It's true that most of those fees are waived for top-tier elite fliers, but not all of us have that status in every program where we have an account. As I said in Chapter 12, it helps enormously to be a top elite in at least one program. It's also worth noting that Southwest is the only U.S. carrier with no award fees of any kind.

Let's begin with the fees for simply having the privilege to use your miles. They are not too common, and among North American carriers only US Airways charges them (up to $50). That's in addition to the fees for booking an award ticket on the phone, which are almost universal – and the highest at US Airways (up to $40), though the airline waives them for partner awards, as they can't be booked online. US Airways actually deserves credit for this gesture, which most other carriers don't make. But they don't charge a separate "award processing fee," either.

Next are the so-called "close-in fees" imposed on award bookings made 21 days or less before departure – I mentioned them in Chapter 10 when discussing United's decision to eliminate them in 2009 and reinstate them less than two years later.

Delta got rid of them of them, but American charges up to $100 and US Airways $75.

Almost all carriers worldwide impose penalties for changing and canceling award tickets. The major U.S. airlines charge $150, and the smaller ones between $50 and $100 – at least changes are often free as long as you don't alter the routing, as I said earlier in this chapter. Hawaiian Airlines has an unusual change policy – it charges between $30 and $50 per segment, rather than one fee for the entire ticket, regardless of how many segments are being changed. Some carriers also allow customers to pay those penalties with miles, instead of money. Cathay Pacific, for example, will change your routing either for $100 or 10,000 mileage credits.

Finally, there are some less common award fees, such as those for booking partner awards (Alaska) and Delta's fee for awards originating outside the United States, which I mentioned in Chapter 11.

United StarNet blocking

I briefly explained United's practice of blocking award seats otherwise made available by its Star Alliance partners in Chapter 10, but it deserves more attention because of its apparent uniqueness – and because I was the journalist who first exposed it publicly and forced United to admit to it in my "On the Fly" column.

I don't remember when exactly I detected something rotten in United's management of partner award inventory, but it must have been in 2005 or 2006. Once I was looking for Lufthansa seats within Europe, and there were none. I tried several routes with no success. Then I asked the agent to check Frankfurt to Munich – they are both Lufthansa hubs and had about a dozen flights between them in each direction at the time, so I figured there must be some award space. But still no luck. As suspicious as that was, there was no way to know for a fact which airline was responsible for it, so I swallowed it and moved on.

That pattern continued over the next couple of years, but something else changed – thanks to All Nippon, I now had online access to StarNet award inventory. So I'd first check on the All Nippon site whether a Lufthansa flight was available and then call United. After the first few discrepancies, I still gave United the benefit of the doubt – perhaps the two systems weren't talking to each other instantly, I thought, or maybe another passenger snatched the last seat while I was dialing United's phone number. But it soon became obvious that there was a serious effort to prevent United customers from using their miles on flights operated by Lufthansa, Air New Zealand, Thai, Asiana, Singapore Airlines and other Star carriers.

In September 2008, I asked the United press office in Chicago whether the airline blocked available partner award seats. It refused to comment, citing "competitive reasons." Then I asked if the award inventory each Star member provides to partners was the same for all partners. Although I thought it was, United reservations agents insisted that every carrier had its own quota. The press office didn't answer that question, either, and referred me to the Star Alliance.

Christian Klick, Star's vice president for corporate affairs, and Lufthansa spokesman Martin Riecken both confirmed that every Star partner makes the same inventory available on StarNet for any alliance member to use "on a first-come-first-served basis." Riecken added, "We offer each seat to every frequent-flier program and have no preference" who uses it.

Armed with those quotes, I went back to United. Finally, the press office admitted that the airline was indeed blocking award seats, because it didn't have a sufficient budget to compensate its partners for all the seats its customer would have booked using their United miles, had there been no blocking. "We manage award availability on our Star Alliance partners just as we do with United's own saver awards," said then-spokesman Jeff Kovick.

I have covered some of the most important events around the world since the end of the Cold War, traveled with four U.S. secretaries of state and interviewed foreign leaders, as well as some of Hollywood's biggest celebrities. Yet I've never written a story that has had more impact than my columns on United's StarNet blocking.

The response to the initial column was overwhelming. Hundreds of United customers complained about instances of blocking to me, the airline or in a dedicated thread on FlyerTalk. As of March 2011, that thread had been viewed about 140,000 times and had almost 2,300 posts. United was apparently worried enough about the exposure to lift some of the filters about two weeks after my first column ran, but the filters were soon back in place.

Some customers took action beyond complaining. London-based traveler Steve Kelly said he persuaded his company to cancel an almost $1 million contract with United. "This is such a shame as it is a corporate decision made by United that is cutting out valued revenue for the hard-working flight and cabin crew, check-in staff, etcetera, all of whom have been more than sterling in their customer-service performance," Kelly said. "Other carriers have been thrilled with the huge jump in revenue that they are gleaning, to the detriment of United."

Matt Holdrege, a telecommunications executive who divides his time between Los Angeles and France, said he had flown more than 1 million miles on United in the past decade, but because of the blocking, the Star Alliance became his third choice for air travel behind Oneworld and SkyTeam

Chicago traveler Bob Smiejek said he stopped using his United Chase Visa card in favor of a Citibank American Airlines card for most of his purchases. His preference was to earn miles on a Star Alliance carrier, but he doesn't see a point in piling miles he can't use for tickets. "I believe the only salvation to this blocking is to follow the money, and right now it's Chase Bank," he said.

One of the worst parts of this story is that United never told its reservations agents about the blocking, and they unknowingly continued to lie to customers by blaming other carriers for the lack of award availability.

Graham Atkinson, whose achievements as Mileage Plus president from 2008 to 2010 I described in Chapter 10, tried to limit the blocking and had significant success. The practice was detected even less frequently in early 2011, as the United-Continental merger progressed – a sign it may be ended for good.

In late 2010, many travelers encountered apparent partner award blocking by US Airways, judging by availability on the All Nippon website. The patterns resembled those on United, with the most filtering applied to Business and First Class cabins, though some fliers stumbled on coach seats as well. The most affected availability appeared to be on Lufthansa, but also on Swiss, United and others. However, US Airways denied those suspicions when I asked about them. "We don't block award inventory on other airlines," said spokeswoman Valerie Wunder, whom I previously quoted regarding flight schedule changes in Chapter 7.

Schedule changes on award tickets

Some of the most difficult schedule changes to deal with are those on award tickets, mainly because seats you can book using your miles are very hard to come by. On a paid ticket, even if your original booking class is not available on the alternate flight you want, most agents will still give you a seat. That's not always the case with mileage tickets, especially when they involve partner carriers.

Many airlines have rules that govern such changes, as is the case with United's Rule 260, which we discussed in Chapter 13. If you lose a seat on a mileage ticket because of a schedule change, you have the right to be rebooked on a logical alternate flight even if there are no awards seats on it. Again, most agents won't offer you that option unless you insist. They are

not required to do that if a schedule change has affected a partner flight – only if the partner's change has caused you to mis-
connect to a flight operated by the ticketing carrier.
I know this can get complicated, so let me give you an example. Suppose you redeemed your United miles for an award
ticket from Phoenix (PHX) to Munich (MUC), issued of course by
United. On the outbound, you have two United-operated flights,
with a connection in Chicago (ORD). A month before your trip,
United takes your Phoenix-Chicago flight off the schedule and
automatically rebooks you on a flight three hours earlier. That
would still allow you to make your connection to Munich, arriving there as originally scheduled, but you'd have to leave home
very early in the morning, which you can't or don't want to do.

Now you take matters in your own hands and look for alternatives. You find a connection via Washington, leaving Phoenix
about the time of your original – and now non-existent – Phoenix-
Chicago flight, which would get you to Munich even earlier that
initially ticketed.

However, there are no award seats on those flights. You call
United and that's exactly what the agent tells you. What they
should do is book you on the flights you want in the lowest available revenue booking class and call a service director – the first
supervisory level – for conversion to the proper award code.
Most agents won't do that for you, so ask them to read Rule 260
on their computer or get a service director.

On your return from Munich, you are ticketed on Lufthansa
to Chicago and on United from there to Phoenix. Two weeks
before your trip, Lufthansa decides to move its flight half an hour
later, and you can no longer make your domestic connection.
The United system automatically puts you on the next flight from
Chicago to Phoenix, getting you home three hours later.

Again, you don't like that and take the driver's seat – and
again there is a better connection via Washington, all on
United and no Lufthansa, but with no award availability. You
call United and the agent says they can't open award space for
you, because the schedule change was caused by Lufthansa,

not United. Again, ask them to read the rules. They say that, if another carrier's schedule change causes a customer on a United mileage ticket "to mis-connect to a UA flight," they should rebook you in the lowest available revenue booking class and call a service director for conversion into the proper award code.

Keep in mind that this is United's policy. While many airlines have similar rules, others don't, so make sure you do your homework. It's impossible to cover all of them in this book, but my seminars and private training do focus on whatever carriers my students most frequently fly on.

Chapter 14 Lessons Learned

1. With so many miles on their books and so many customers trying to use them, airlines have become stingier with award seats and have repeatedly increased the number of miles required for an award ticket.
2. Most non-U.S. carriers charge hundreds of dollars in fuel surcharges on award tickets, in addition to miles and airport taxes.
3. The KVS tool, ExpertFlyer, UsingMiles and MileageManager, as well as the specialized AwardNexus.com, provide online access to award inventory.
4. The biggest problem with most online resources is the very scarce partner award inventory they carry.
5. In the Star Alliance, All Nippon's site has the most comprehensive partner data. The Air Canada, Continental and United sites show limited partner availability.
6. In Oneworld, the Qantas and British Airways sites have the best partner award data, though neither of them shows all alliance members.
7. In SkyTeam, the site of Flying Blue, Air France/KLM's frequent-flier program, is the only one showing availability for most alliance members. Inventory of some carriers, such as Korean Air, cannot be found online, so a phone call is the only option.
8. Effective award-booking strategies include:
   - Do homework before calling the airline.
   - Not relying on airline agents to find the best award.
   - Booking awards months or just days before a trip – that's when there is likely to be most availability.
   - Looking for seats on partner-carriers.
   - Trying all possible routing options to a destination and not relying on the computer.
   - Search for seats segment by segment.
   - Taking advantage of the 24-hour international connection rule.
   - Taking advantage of free stopovers and visiting more than one country on international trips.
   - Checking the airline's routing and other award rules.
   - Book a ticket even if the flights are not ideal, as many carriers permit free changes to flight dates and times.

Postscript

The Case for Travel Education

As you master various parts of the air travel system, you will have many reasons to be proud of yourself. Perhaps you will beat a fare offered by automated booking engines or come up with a brilliant upgrade strategy in the face of an almost certain sentence to coach. Some of my proudest moments have been when I discovered that while flying in Business Class, I had paid much less than many Economy passengers.

I don't mean to rub this in anyone's face, but only to make the point that you can do it, too. You may wonder what would happen if everyone tried to follow suit. I wouldn't lose any sleep over that prospect. By now, you know that learning the science of air travel requires a significant investment of time and energy. I will be very happy if this book becomes a bestseller and the Kralev Method receives widespread recognition. But let's face it, not many people will make that investment.

So if you decide to make it, you will be in an exclusive club of dedicated travelers who are capable of getting the best of both worlds – lower fares and more comfort.

Even though it's unrealistic to expect that millions will choose to become sophisticated travelers, there is a tremendous benefit in educating as many people as possible about the basics of commercial aviation. I realize that most people think they already know those basics, but the reality is very different.

There are many things one can't control when it comes to air travel – the weather, earthquakes, tsunamis, volcanoes, war, civil unrest, labor strikes, aircraft mechanical problems and many others. However, there are plenty of things a smart flier can do to make the system work better and more efficiently – from booking a ticket to avoiding hassle and stress to creating an enjoyable in-flight experience. While airline employees are often expected to take care of all this, relying on them for everything won't take you too far. Even the best employees sometimes can't assist every passenger in need of help.

We are all stakeholders in the air travel system – airlines, travelers and government authorities. A more effective and less frustrating system than the one we have today would benefit us all. So let each of us do his or her part.

Why do I care about this so much? Because I want more people to travel and see the world. I spent the last decade being around diplomats and writing about them almost every day as a newspaper correspondent. Although different countries' national interests are the main drivers of international relations, the underlying mission of diplomacy is to make the world a better place. One way to do that is to give more ordinary people – not just diplomats – the opportunity to travel to other countries, experience different cultures and try to understand points of view they may not agree with.

Most people cite two main reasons for not traveling abroad: It's too expensive and too much of a hassle. If only there were ways to eliminate those barriers. As it happens, there are such ways – that's what this book is all about.

Still, a book is hardly enough to achieve such an ambitious goal. A nonprofit organization may be an even better vehicle, so I'm planning to set up the See the World Foundation. Part of the proceeds from the book will go to that cause. While my travel consulting and training company, Kralev International LLC, works with businesses and other experienced travelers, the foundation will provide educational opportunities to people who have done no international travel or very little of it. If you are interested in helping or getting involved in the foundation, feel free to get in touch on NicholasKralev.com.

At the beginning of the book, I said that most of what I know about the air travel system I have learned from experience. Even so, I couldn't have done it without the many airline employees who answered my questions and took the time to explain numerous policies and practices.

I also gave credit in the foreword to FlyerTalk, and I have to thank its founder, Randy Petersen, who was the first person to start playing the frequent-flier game at an expert level many years ago and created Inside Flyer Magazine. In March 2011, he founded a new website, MilePoint.com.

For the extraordinary opportunities they gave me while traveling with them around the world, I owe special thanks to my secretaries of state, as I call them – Hillary Clinton, Condoleezza Rice, Colin Powell and Madeleine Albright. I'm also much indebted to the people who made it possible for me to accompany these secretaries – my Financial Times editors Julia Marozzi and John Ridding, and my editors at various points during my nine years at the Washington Times, David Jones, Barbara Slavin, John Solomon and Fran Coombs.

For their help in this book's preparation, I'm profoundly thankful to my editors Darrell Delamaide and Markus Nottelmann, consultant Gary Leff, photographer Mary Calvert, as well as my interns Harrison Feind, Natalie Omundson, Billel Hariche, Xiangnan Lin and Rachel Schaub. For the support they offered during the writing process, I also owe a debt of gratitude to David Bass and Doug Grane of Raptor Strategies in Washington, and of course to my family.

I hope this book kept you good company, and I look forward to the day we meet.

Nicholas Kralev
Washington, D.C.
April 2011

Glossary of Terms

as defined by the author

Advance-purchase requirement – part of a fare's rules indicating how long before departure a ticket must be issued.

Airline consolidator – a travel company that sells tickets on a certain airline at heavily discounted prices as a result of a direct arrangement with the carrier.

Airline data – a combination of airline fare tariffs and flight inventory used to determine the price of an airline ticket.

Airline fare tariff – a list of all published fares between any two cities served by the publishing carrier or its partners, including their fare bases, allowed routings and a series of rules, such as advance-purchase requirements, permitted days of the week, and blackout dates.

Airline Tariff Publishing Company (ATPCO) – described on the company's website as an "airfare data provider for more than 460 airlines worldwide, which together represent 97 percent of scheduled commercial air travel."

Base fare – a price published on an airline tariff, which along with taxes, fees and surcharges, forms the price of an airline ticket.

Booking class – a letter of the alphabet used to categorize an airfare based on its price and determined by a fare basis code. An airline typically uses more than a dozen booking classes. Booking class is different from class of service.

Circle fare – a fare product allowing a passenger to circle a geographic region and make multiple stops and stopovers before returning to the point of origin. Such products may be offered by individual carriers or airline alliances and include round-the-world fares, as well as circle-Pacific, circle-Atlantic, circle-Asia and other fares.

Class of service – an aircraft cabin, such as Economy, Business or First Class. Service class is different from booking class.

Close-in award fee – a service charge imposed on award tickets issued less than 21 days before departure.

Code-share flight – a flight marketed and sold by one airline as its own but operated by another carrier.

Confirmed regional upgrade – a United Airlines upgrade certificate used to confirm a seat in a higher class of service, if available, as early as the time of ticketing on flights in North America, Central America and the Caribbean.

Direct Connect – a carrier-owned and controlled computer system that hosts and distributes its data and generates bookings instead of a GDS.

Direct flight – a flight consisting of two or more segments that have the same number and are operated by the same aircraft. Unlike a nonstop, a direct flight has more than one takeoff and more than one landing. See *fake direct flight*.

Elite status match – granting elite airline status to a customer on the basis of his or her status with a competing carrier, waiving qualification requirements, in an attempt to win that customer's business.

Fake direct flight – a flight consisting of two or more segments operated by different aircraft that have nothing in common but their number. They are regular connecting flights, deliberately marketed by airlines as "direct" to trick customers into thinking they would be avoiding the hassle of transfers.

False fare advertising – a practice by some airlines meant to advertise an amount lower than a ticket's final price in order to attract customer attention. Most U.S. carriers advertise fares as "each way based on a required round-trip purchase, excluding taxes and fees."

Fare basis – a code consisting of letters and numbers that determines a base fare, which along with taxes, fees and surcharges, forms the price of an airline ticket.

Fare bucket – an informal term used to indicate the availability in each booking class on a flight. Fare buckets are displayed in a descending order, starting with the highest (full-fare) booking class.

Fare-filing feed – a set of airline data sent out by ATPCO three times a day on weekdays and once a day on weekends.

Fare war – a competition between two or more carriers for customers out of the other airline's hub cities. One airline "attacks" another's hub by offering very low fares.

Flight coupon – part of an airline ticket containing data for a specific flight segment and used by the airline system to issue a boarding pass for that flight. It's similar to a coupon in a paper ticket, but all data is stored electronically.

Flight inventory – passenger seats on a commercial flight displayed in fare buckets that correspond to booking classes. The inventory shows which booking classes are available for sale and how many seats can be purchased in each class.

Full fare – a fully refundable and changeable for free fare, which is usually booked in Y or B booking class in coach, C or J in Business and F in First Class.

Global airline alliance – a network of several carriers based on different continents that have broad and deep cooperation in all aspects of their business. The current three global alliances are the Star Alliance, Oneworld and SkyTeam.

Global Distribution System (GDS) – a computer system that hosts and displays airline and other travel-related data and processes transactions such as issuing, changing and canceling tickets, and making hotel reservations. The three main GDS companies are Sabre, Travelport and Amadeus.

Good-will gesture – a token of appreciation (compensation) an airline gives an inconvenienced passenger in the form of a discount voucher or bonus miles.

Intercontinental flight – a flight originating on one continent and terminating on another.

International Air Transport Association (IATA) – a Geneva-based trade organization representing about 230 airlines.

Involuntarily denied boarding (IDB) – offloading a passenger from a flight for which he or she has purchased a confirmed seat against the passenger's will. That is usually a result of an airline overselling the flight and failing to find volunteers to give up their seats.

Involuntary change – altering an airline ticket caused by events beyond the passenger's control, such as airline schedules, weather, mechanical problems and medical emergencies. No penalties apply.

Irregular operations (IRROPS) – changes to airline schedules caused by unplanned flight disruptions related to weather, mechanical problems, crew issues, medical emergencies and other unexpected events.

Kralev Method – a process of matching airline tariff and flight inventory data independently of automated booking systems to produce the ideal fare.

Legal connection – the minimum and maximum time during which a passenger may connect from one flight to another on the way to the final destination. Minimum times are determined by specific airports. The maximum time is four hours on U.S. domestic itineraries and 24 hours on international itineraries.

Legal routing – a published list of cities in a specific order through which a passenger may fly en route to the final destination.

Married flight segments – two or more connecting flights booked as linked segments, which may change the available inventory and affect the fare. Some airlines manage the inventory on such segments differently from that on single segments to maximize revenue.

Maximum permitted mileage (MPM) – the number of miles a passenger can fly from origin to destination in each direction, which is published for some fares instead of specific routing options.

Network carrier – a full-service airline with an extensive network of domestic and international routes.

Oneworld – a global alliance of 12 airlines from 12 countries, which carry about 335 million passengers a year on more than 9,300 daily flights to 900 destinations in 145 countries. It was founded on February 1, 1999, by American, British Airways, Cathay Pacific, Qantas and Canadian Airlines.

Online travel agency (OTA) – a company selling airline tickets, hotel rooms and other travel-related products and services mainly on its website, providing direct consumer access to booking systems.

Open jaw – flying into one city and flying out of another.

Operational upgrade – seating a passenger in a higher class of service because his or her seat in the lower class of service is needed to accommodate another passenger.

Personal name record (PNR) – a record of a passenger's itinerary in an airline reservation system.

Price per mile – a ratio used to determine how many cents it will cost to fly one mile, so a passenger can maximize the mileage flown on a particular fare.

Pricing record – part of an airline ticket receipt showing the price construction, which includes the base fare, taxes, fees and surcharges.

Raw airline data – fare tariff and flight inventory data as published by an airline, before it's processed by an automated booking engine.

Revenue-based loyalty program – a frequent-flier program that awards miles or points to passengers based not on the number of miles they fly but the money the pay.

Same-day confirmed change – rebooking a passenger on a different flight from the originally confirmed flight, with a guaranteed seat, as opposed to being on standby, which applies only to U.S. domestic itineraries and can cost up to $75.

Schedule change – an alteration of a flight's departure and/ or arrival time on a published airline schedule planned weeks or months before departure. Irregular operations (IRROPS) are not schedule changes, as they are unplanned.

SkyTeam – a global alliance of 13 members from 13 countries, which fly about 384 million passengers annually on 13,000 daily flights to 898 destinations in 169 countries. It was founded on May 22, 2000, by Delta, Air France, AeroMexico and Korean Air.

Split (broken) fare – a fare from origin to destination that "breaks" in a connecting city, resulting in one fare component from the first to the second city, and another component from the second to the third city.

SITA – described on the company's website as a "specialist in air transport communications and IT solutions," it is also a data provider for some airlines in Europe, Africa and Asia. The acronym comes from the company's original French name, Société Internationale de Télécommunications Aéronautiques.

Star Alliance – a global alliance of 27 airlines from 25 countries, which have more than 4,000 aircraft in their fleets and fly over 600 million passengers a year on 21,000 daily flights to 1,160 airports in 181 countries. It was founded on May 14, 1997, by United, Lufthansa, SAS, Air Canada and Thai Airways.

Stopover – a period between two flights that exceeds the maximum permitted connecting time.

System-wide upgrade (SWU) – an upgrade certificate used to confirm a seat in a higher class of service, if available, as early as the time of ticketing on flights anywhere in the world.

Ticket number – a 13-digit number attached to the receipt of an airline ticket and generated automatically as soon as the ticket is issued. On tickets issued by the same airline, the first three digits are always the same. Airline systems cannot issue a boarding pass without a ticket number.

Traffic conference – a geographic zone designated by IATA for the purposes of commercial aviation. Zone 1 includes the

Americas, Zone 2 Europe, Africa and the Middle East, and Zone 3 Asia, Australia and the Southwest Pacific.

Transcontinental flight – a U.S. domestic flight originating on one coast and terminating on the opposite coast.

Through fare – a fare from origin to destination, regardless of where a passenger is transferring en route, as opposed to a split fare.

Voluntarily denied boarding (VDB) – offloading a passenger from a flight for which he or she has purchased a confirmed seat, as a result of the passenger's volunteering to give up that seat in exchange for compensation in the form of a voucher that can be used for a future ticket.

Voluntary change – altering an airline ticket caused by the passenger that may incur a penalty.

UP fare – a U.S. domestic fare that has a coach fare basis but books straight in First or Business Class.

YQ surcharge – designation of a fuel surcharge in the breakdown of taxes, fees and surcharges in an airline ticket's pricing record. Sometimes YQ may indicate a different type surcharge.

Online Resources

DecodingAirTravel.com
KralevInternational.com
OntheFlySeminars.com
NicholasKralev.com
ExpertFlyer.com
KVStool.com
ITAsoftware.com
FareCompare.com
AirfareWatchdog.com
FlyerTalk.com
MilePoint.com
SmarterTravel.com
BingTravel.com
FlightMemory.com
AwardNexus.com
AwardWallet.com
UsingMiles.com
MileageManager.com
TravelZoo.com

Made in the USA
Lexington, KY
12 December 2011